Neighborhood Poverty and Segregation in the (Re-)Production of Disadvantage

Dolores Trevizo • Mary Lopez

Neighborhood Poverty and Segregation in the (Re-)Production of Disadvantage

Mexican Immigrant Entrepreneurs in Los Angeles

palgrave
macmillan

Dolores Trevizo
Sociology Department
Occidental College
Los Angeles, CA, USA

Mary Lopez
Economics Department
Occidental College
Los Angeles, CA, USA

ISBN 978-3-030-08841-5   ISBN 978-3-319-73715-7   (eBook)
https://doi.org/10.1007/978-3-319-73715-7

Cover Image © Dolores Trevizo

Printed on acid-free paper

This Palgrave Macmillan imprint is published by the registered company Springer International Publishing AG part of Springer Nature.
The registered company address is: Gewerbestrasse 11, 6330 Cham, Switzerland

We dedicate this book to our students.

PREFACE

Dolores Trevizo developed an interest in immigrant entrepreneurs by observing people in the Mexican immigrant community in which she was raised. Some people, like her father, worked in factories. Others in the neighborhood were bellhops, cooks, or gardeners. The small number of women who engaged in paid labor did so as domestics, though a few worked in the garment industry as piece-rate sewers. From direct observation of the lives of neighbors and relatives, it was clear that neither the self-employed cleaning ladies nor the gardeners who sold their labor on a per-job basis had the market position, the complete work autonomy, or the extensive administrative roles of small business owners. Having herself worked in a small, family-owned tire store, Dolores knew from direct experience the difference between freelance workers and small business owners. The owners of the tire store employed about 25 people and lived in the nicer and Whiter area of Los Angeles. At night, they could escape the gun battles and crime to return to a part of the city that happened to be called Los Feliz. (The original Rancho Los Felis was named after its owner, Corporal Felis. In Spanish, "feliz" means happy. So, one could read the area as the place of "the Happy"). It was clear from her comparisons of people's living conditions that being a small business owner was a different kind of occupational and social position than being self-employed as a domestic.

Dolores' father, an immigrant from Mexico, considered opening a small shop in the same crime-ridden neighborhood as the tire store in which she worked. Her father had worked alongside his own father who, in the Sierra Madre of Chihuahua, Mexico owned a small store (which sold "*ropa, calzado y novedades*"). The idea of his owning his own little shop seemed like a feasible and reasonable option. But, after many conversations, Dolores' parents opted for the security and benefits of factory work without knowing that within just a few years, Pacific Clay Products, one of the largest sewer pipe production plants in the US, would dramatically downsize (in 1980). In this period of unemployment, this time due to Los Angeles's economic restructuring, Dolores' father would again have to reconsider his work options. He again opted for the security of waged employment and health benefits, but this time in the service sector.

Despite his prudent choices, her father's entrepreneurial disposition always found creative avenues. Dolores, however, never developed an entrepreneurial disposition and, against her father's advice to major in business, she became a sociologist. He warned her that her first book on Mexico would find no market and jokingly offered to pedal her books from a pushcart. He suspects that this book on small shopkeepers will sell better. We hope so. Even if it does not, Dolores will still have taken great pleasure in thinking about immigrant entrepreneurs. Their "*ilusiones*" (Spanish meaning intended), their creative thinking, risk taking, and hard labor are simply inspiring.

Mary Lopez's interest in immigrant entrepreneurship stemmed from previous work on the labor market outcomes of immigrants. She also participated in a 2007 workshop on entrepreneurship sponsored by the Ewing Marion Kauffman Foundation at the University of North Carolina, Chapel Hill. In addition, along with Dolores Trevizo, Mary participated in the 2008 conference on Mexican American Entrepreneurship and Wealth Creation sponsored by the Ewing Marion Kauffman Foundation and the IC^2 Institute at the University of Texas, Austin.

Los Angeles, CA, USA   Dolores Trevizo
                                                       Mary Lopez

ACKNOWLEDGMENTS

We could not have undertaken our study without the generous support of the Haynes Foundation, whose funding made it possible for us to hire the small army of students that we deployed to various neighborhoods in Los Angeles. We had no idea in 2007—when we received the Haynes Foundation Faculty Research Fellowship—that it would take us ten years to complete our project. We published a short outline version of what eventually evolved into a book-length project in the journal *Sociological Perspectives* (2016). The editors and anonymous reviewers at *Sociological Perspectives* offered many substantive and methodological suggestions in three different rounds of editing. We are so grateful for their careful and generous reviews, as well as for the extensive feedback from the anonymous reviewer at Palgrave, whose suggestions led to the creation of a new chapter. We also wish to thank Silvia Pedraza, Joe Foweraker, and William Roy for looking at some chapters. Gladdys Uribe, Jerome Keating, Jessica Blickley, Jeremiah Axelrod, Bruce Western, and John Lang helped us work through specific issues. Of course, all errors in the manuscript are our own.

Having trained in the Sociology department at UCLA, Dolores is deeply indebted to Ivan Light, whose course on immigrant entrepreneurs inspired her scholarly interest in the subject. Christine Ehrick, Karen O'Neil, Benita Roth, and Ericka Verba continue to encourage Dolores's intellectual passions while always understanding her disappearing acts (that only happen when she is completing a project). Dolores thanks her parents, Oscar and Elisa Trevizo, whose immigration journeys and bicultural experiences inform her point of view. Her children, Elisa and Jacob Montag, tolerate (and perhaps sometimes even appreciate) her passions.

Warren Montag, her life partner, deserves special thanks. Warren supported Dolores through the process, from start to finish. Not a single chapter (not even the prospectus) escaped his scrutiny, and the value added cannot be overstated given that the English professor fixed many of the infelicities common to social science writing. We are both deeply grateful for his generosity and interest in our work.

CONTENTS

LIST OF FIGURES

LIST OF TABLES

Introduction: The Social Ecology of Disadvantage for Mexican Immigrant Entrepreneurs

The scholarship on immigrant entrepreneurship is rich with analyses of different groups of immigrants who "make it" in their host society through the hard work involved in owning and managing small businesses.[1] Many start out as bootstrap entrepreneurs who, with the support of co-ethnics and the use of family labor, achieve a small degree of social mobility by becoming small business proprietors. This book focuses on Mexican immigrant entrepreneurs, a group of people who have been underrepresented in the ranks of small shopkeepers in the US despite their long and sustained history of migration since at least the early twentieth century. Their historic underrepresentation among Los Angeles's small business owners is particularly counterintuitive because the area has been a destination point for various cohorts of migrants from Mexico since the city's founding as a Spanish *pueblo* in 1781.[2] So, while their presence as a prominent and long-standing racialized ethnic minority—one that continuously integrates newly arrived immigrants—spans many decades, only at the turn of the twenty-first century has the number of Mexican immigrants engaged in storefront proprietorship begun to increase. This book not only documents some of the reasons for this change, but we focus on explaining why some of these small storefronts are more successful than are others.

The research presented in this book speaks broadly to stratification theory the aim of which is to explain social inequalities—whether in levels of wealth, earnings, social prestige, or in vulnerability to poverty, to give just

© The Author(s) 2018   1
D. Trevizo, M. Lopez, *Neighborhood Poverty and Segregation
in the (Re-)Production of Disadvantage*,
https://doi.org/10.1007/978-3-319-73715-7_1

a few examples. If stratification theory addresses the general question, *who gets what and why?* this book focuses on some patterns in incremental, or short-distance, upward mobility, as well as in social immobility. We do so by focusing on Mexican immigrants who moved from waged employment to small business proprietorship. Even if the experiences of our survey respondents are not the norm among their co-ethnics, they are noteworthy considering that the vast majority of the immigrants in our sample had been undocumented for years, if not decades, before legalizing their status. After laboring in low-skill jobs in the US, they first legalized their immigration status and started small storefront businesses with the goal of earning more money.[3] Their plan was reasonable not only because of the low entry costs of small business ownership, but because theirs was a proven strategy that had worked for other disadvantaged immigrants (e.g., Italian immigrants) at different times. Our research shows that for Mexican immigrants, however, the entrepreneurial pathway of upward mobility is mostly blocked. Nevertheless, the proprietors we studied still, to varying degrees, enjoyed a small boost from entrepreneurship, and this book explains the conditions under which some of their small shops achieved a modicum of success. Even though the small shops in our study are unlikely to become large firms, the aggregation of viable storefronts along commercial corridors in ethnic neighborhoods contributes to community stability (Butler and Kozmetsky 2004: viii). In addition, small business ownership is not only a marker of personal success and self-determination; in some cases, it offers employment opportunities to others.

Our research focuses on the neighborhood conditions under which such small shops are more likely to create employment opportunities. We specifically examine how neighborhood poverty, relative to other stratification variables, including racial segregation and gender, affects the business performance of small shopkeepers, and thus their capacity to employ others. We demonstrate that less poor and more multiethnic neighborhoods offer Mexican immigrant shopkeepers better opportunities for their businesses than do the highly impoverished and racially segregated Mexican neighborhoods of Los Angeles. While our findings clearly contribute to the scholarship of concentrated disadvantage that emphasizes the long-term consequences of neighborhood deprivation (Wilson 1987; Massey and Brodmann 2014), our analysis also studies both the effects of microclass differences as well as those of legal capital (defined below). Our central thesis is that even poor Mexican immigrants whose class backgrounds in Mexico imparted an entrepreneurial disposition can achieve a modicum of business success in the right (US) neighborhood context, and the more quickly they build legal capital, the better their outcomes. Therefore, while we show that the local place characteristics of neighborhoods both reflect and reproduce class and racial inequalities, we also demonstrate that there exists a diversity of experiences among Mexican immigrants living within the spatial boundaries of these communities and that this diversity matters to their economic mobility or immobility.

Our research is relevant to contemporary political debates because Mexican immigrants, along with their US-born children and grandchildren, are among the largest, poorest, and most negatively racialized ethnic groups in the US. Whereas African Americans comprise about 13% of the total US population as of 2010, Latinos/as of Mexican ancestry alone are nearly 11% of that US total. Recent data from the Pew Research Center indicate that there are 34.6 million Hispanics of Mexican origin in the US, although the number may be greater if the undocumented are undercounted in the Census. What is clear is that as of 2015, there were at least 11.5 million Mexican immigrants, a figure not only greater than that of Cubans and Puerto Ricans combined, but one on par with the figure of 11.6 million immigrants from both South and East Asia.[4] So, if neighborhoods—"the linchpin" of stratification—are largely defined by the social demographic profiles of the resident groups living within their boundaries (Massey and Brodmann 2014: 62), all such groups have class specific and even gendered histories that also matter to stratification. To explain how intra-ethnic and place characteristics matter for stratification, we will review the literature on individuals, neighborhoods, and entrepreneurship.

INDIVIDUALS, NEIGHBORHOODS, AND ETHNIC ENTREPRENEURSHIP IN STRATIFICATION THEORY

The study of small-scale entrepreneurship has a long tradition in sociology. Among the classic thinkers, both Max Weber (1930: 39) and Georg Simmel (1971 [1908]) observed that entrepreneurship is an adaptation—and therefore a survival strategy—to a minority's (religious or ethnic) blocked mobility. While some contemporary scholars argue that blocked mobility also leads to entrepreneurship among unemployed White workers in the post-industrial, post-union, flexible "gig" economy,[5] petty proprietorship has historically been one of the few survival strategies available to ethnic and racialized groups. Scholars thus continue to show that many racialized ethnic groups survive systematic discrimination and oppression by creating entrepreneurial opportunities for themselves that take the form of small business ownership (Bonacich and Modell 1980; Waldinger et al. 1990; Butler 1991; Butler et al. 2009).

If Weber, Simmel, and others explain *why* entrepreneurship is a common survival strategy for people whose mobility is blocked by widespread discrimination, Pierre Bourdieu's theoretical framework offers details as to *how* certain cultural competencies might help them negotiate their social worlds, including through entrepreneurship. In the spirit of Max Weber,[6] Bourdieu emphasizes that while economic class and social status are mutually constitutive, cultural processes play a role in the social construction of both. Bourdieu, however, goes further by conceptualizing various species of capital and even subspecies of what he calls cultural capital (defined below). So, if Weber theorized that social and ethnic groups are socially endowed with different degrees of honor and prestige, Bourdieu specifies various mechanisms by which symbolic status differentiators may convert to economic capital. In this way, Bourdieu's analysis of social mobility stresses that people negotiate labor markets, or complex fields,[7] as social-cultural hierarchies that require specific forms of cultural knowledge about the game itself. We rely on his framework to understand how specific combinations of economic, social, and cultural capital influence people's class standing as well as their social trajectory over time. Following Bourdieu, we conceptualize social classes by their different levels (volume) and composition (or types) of capital, including social and cultural capital (see below).

To explain further, Bourdieu conceptualized various species of capital beyond financial capital that contribute to the production and reproduction of class differences over time. For example, he defined *social capital* as the durable networks of people, friends, and family who can mobilize economic resources, power, job, and other opportunities. To take the case of business, friends and families can offer cash gifts, low-interest loans, information, investment opportunities, or connections to customers or suppliers (see also Anderson and Miller 2003). Bourdieu also observed that distinct subtypes of *cultural capital,* or cultural competencies, are transferred inter-generationally, each with a specific market exchange value. Some forms of cultural capital are formally credentialed (e.g., college degrees), others are informally acquired, some are tacitly understood, and others are deposited in the body as mannerisms, facial expressions, postures, and the like. These cultural competencies are also status signifiers that, because they have conversion rates, contribute further to social stratification; they do so, however, in gendered ways.

Although the conversion rates of various types of cultural and social capital partly depend on the local field in which these resources are activated and contested, subsequent generations will tend, over time, to reproduce at least some of the privileges or disadvantages of their upbringing (Bourdieu 1984 [1979]). Therefore, while a full range of learning affects class standing over one's life span, what people learn in the course of their upbringing contributes significantly to their life chances.[8] Informal learning within the family during childhood creates cultural competencies, some of which transfer well to distinct fields, and some have a good conversion rate even across international borders.

Given the fact that many people displaced from Mexico's countryside and cities end up in US neighborhoods, their experiences illustrate some of Bourdieu's ideas. When arriving in the US, impoverished Mexican immigrants must suddenly navigate a new and hostile society, and do so with few resources. In many cases, they lack the legal documents necessary for upward mobility. Their low levels of formal education and lack of proficiency in English leaves most with the lowest quality, worst-paid, working-class jobs in the US (Bean et al. 2004). While much scholarship documents the various ways in which their disadvantaged starting points affect their life chances, as well as those of their second-generation children, we arrive at a more nuanced view of the standard analysis. By paying attention to how granular class differences among migrants play out in distinct Latina/o neighborhoods, and how these microclass differences vary with gender, we explain why some Mexican shopkeepers in Los Angeles are more likely than others are to experience incremental economic mobility.

Our analysis of certain microclass differences among Mexicans, as well as of the disadvantaged neighborhoods in which they live, adds new knowledge to the study of ethnic entrepreneurship, a field that has historically focused on the cultural patterns that purportedly distinguish ethnic groups. We do not compare cultural differences (the big "c") between distinct ethnic groups. Instead, we focus on small, yet important, class differences—indeed, microclass differences that express themselves as (small "c") cultural capital—between people of the same immigrant group. Our focus on intra-ethnic class differences is thus a contribution because even scholars who document the diversity of migrant streams from Mexico—for example, that they increasingly arrive from multiple geographic regions (beyond traditional sending states), have both rural and urban backgrounds, include more women and indigenous groups than previously—underemphasize microclass differences among Mexicans.[9] This neglect is partly due to the fact that Mexican immigrants have historically been, and continue to be, poor. However, since people are more or less poor, their distribution along a poverty continuum itself creates diverse survival strategies and, thus, competencies. Still another reason for the tendency to neglect microclass differences among relatively poor Mexican immigrants is that data are limited. Official US censuses tend not to inquire about the immigrants' upbringing in Mexico beyond formal levels of education, while other sources are limited to data on English ability, labor market skills, age, and number of years in the US. Such traditional human capital variables do not permit a nuanced analysis of the migrants' class backgrounds.[10] Recent work has begun to examine how skills acquired informally, while on the job prior to emigration, yield better wages in the US. (Hagan et al. 2011, 2014; Hernández-León 2004). Even so, such analyses maintain the focus on specifiable, indexable, human capital variables. Although such competencies are extremely important, they are different from the more general, more informal and fluid, microclass cultural dispositions that lend themselves simply to an intuitive "feel for the game" (Bourdieu 1984: 114).

Our work contributes to the scholarship by looking at how a subtype of cultural capital that takes the form of an entrepreneurial disposition—one acquired informally, pre-migration, and through the family—can be leveraged by small business owners in the right neighborhood context. In short, while it is true that the vast majority of immigrants from Mexico are disadvantaged, they are not equally disadvantaged, and we specify how small class differences among them matter to their business performance in various neighborhoods in Los Angeles.

If only by analogy, Bourdieu's framework also provides insight into how legal status might itself be leveraged as a form of capital by small business proprietors. Hernan Ramirez and Pierrette Hondagneu-Sotelo define "legal capital" as legal "work authorization and the range of particular job permits and credentials dependent on it" (Ramirez and Hondagneu-Sotelo 2009: 80). Their definition moves beyond the binary of whether or not one is a documented or an undocumented immigrant. Focusing exclusively on legal status only allows us to determine in binary terms whether or not migrants have the legal right to live and labor outside of their country of birth, either because they moved to another country with the proper authorization or because they legalized their residency. To be clear, legal status is an important stratification variable affecting wages, living conditions, and the kinds of interactions that immigrants have with employers, schools, police, and hospitals, to list just a few examples. The notion of legal capital as we use it is different from the common-sense conception of "legal status" insofar as it applies specifically to once undocumented business people. The concept signals that once legal status is achieved, the rights associated with it *can* lead to additional advantages to small business owners who capitalize on their legal status. We discuss how the timing of such capitalization affects business performance over time in Chap. 6, but offer a summary in the book plan section of this introduction.

This book emphasizes that in addition to whatever socio-legal, subcultural, and economic differences exist between individuals of the same immigrant group, broader forces at the neighborhood level significantly structure people's life chances. Neighborhoods are "spatially delimited segment[s] of the urban landscape whose character is defined by the people and infrastructure it contains" (Massey and Brodmann 2014: 58). Neighborhood institutions—for example, schools, religious organizations, parks, police, health clinics, retail shops, and more—create a social environment. The social ecology of neighborhoods shapes people's educational attainment, their physical wellbeing, and their daily interactions. Along with rates of poverty, crime, the percent foreign-born and undocumented, as well as the degree of racial segregation, neighborhoods affect people's access to jobs as well as their odds of ending up in prison or murdered (Wodtke et al. 2011; Feldmeyer 2010; Harding 2009; Schulz et al. 2005). At a meso-level, there are aggregate investment or divestment patterns, mortgage-lending practices, homeownership and foreclosure rates, and, thus, variation in community stability itself (Rugh et al. 2015). In short, because neighborhoods spatially concentrate either advantages or disadvantages, they contribute to the reproduction of social inequalities over time. Although the literature on neighborhood effects extensively documents how place concentration affects individuals and communities as forms of *structural disadvantage*, few neighborhood studies focus on the business performance of small shopkeepers. Even Hipp (2010) who argues that high crime drives out retail stores does not focus directly on business performance.

Similarly, the ethnic enclave scholarship does not quite intersect with the literature on neighborhood disadvantage, though both focus extensively on immigrants (but for Logan et al. 2002). Since ethnic enclaves and neighborhoods are not identical, scholars from these distinct traditions emphasize either the benefits or disadvantages of the spatial concentration of co-ethnics. To illustrate, the "ethnic enclaves" literature holds that the spatial concentration of co-ethnics benefits small businesses because it creates a market in specialized ethnic products (Portes 1981: 290–291). In addition, the spatial concentration of co-ethnics facilitates forms of exchange based on intra-ethnic solidarity, and these exchanges may include business opportunities as well as the mobilization of cheap or free credit (Braymen and Neymotin 2014; Zhou 2004; Portes and Zhou 1993; Light 1972; Gold 1994; Ndofor and Priem 2011; Light and Rosenstein 1995). In contrast, the literature on concentrated disadvantage argues that the segregation of poor and negatively racialized people into specific neighborhoods will tend to reproduce disadvantages (Wilson 1987; Massey and Brodmann 2014). Although this insight has not been tested on business outcomes as such, it is consistent with the research of Victor Nee and his colleagues (1994). These scholars found that small firms operating in a mixed economy have higher profits over the long term as compared to those that operate primarily in ethnic enclaves (see also Light and Gold 2000: 127; Bates 1994).

In addition to putting into dialog specific insights from Bourdieu's stratification theory, the neighborhood/concentrated disadvantage school of thought, as well as the scholarship on immigrant entrepreneurship, our case study has implications for what Georg Simmel once described as stranger relations. Recognizable in "a stranger to the country, the city, the race, and so on" (Simmel 1971 [1908]: 148), stranger-native relations are increasingly prevalent in the world, if in modern form. According to Simmel, strangers are people who are spatially near yet are culturally remote. Unlike wanderers (sojourners) who come and go, the stranger "comes today and *stays* tomorrow" (1971: 143; emphasis ours). By *staying*, strangers are spatially proximate and have a role in the division of labor (and not infrequently as a trader or merchant). Yet, their cultural distance gives them an ambivalent standing within the native community. Simmel describes this ambivalence as a "peculiar tension" arising from the synthesis or "the union of closeness and remoteness" (1971: 144). So, while strangers may be physically near and even stand quite visibly through their roles in the division of labor, they are not of and therefore do not fully belong to the community.[11] According to Simmel,

> The stranger is an element of the group itself, not unlike the poor and sundry "inner enemies" [or "internal enemies"—*inneren Feinde*]—an element

whose membership within the group involves both being outside it and confronting it. The following statements about the stranger are intended to suggest how factors of repulsion and distance work to create a form of being together, a form of union based on interaction (1971: 144 [original in German, 1908: 686]).

Simmel's writings stress that strangers remain vulnerable to intolerance because they are not, and will never be, full members of the community. Consequently, shifts in conjuncture could turn the strangers' ambivalent standing into pariah status or even one of internal enemy. In other words, at just the right historical moment, strangers could easily be scapegoated by being defined as parasitic or, worse, as a threat. If Simmel developed his "stranger" concept as a "pure type" example of the medieval city, the social tensions that he describes—including processes of social distancing—are clearly relevant in the twenty-first century. We emphasize throughout our analyses that Mexicans have been scapegoated repeatedly, if in changing ways, given their long history in the US, the size of their population, and the variety of legal statuses held by people within their communities. As noted, roughly 34.6 million people of Mexican ancestry live in all regions of the US even if they are concentrated in the Southwest, especially in California.[12] Despite their very high employment rates and visibility in the workforce, they experience greater social distancing than they did in the early 1970s. They are "close strangers" and sometimes "intimate strangers"—for example, the nannies and cleaning ladies who work in private homes—who are defined both legally and derisively as "illegal aliens." This book thus looks at a long-term, yet estranged, group whose ambivalent standing in Los Angeles is paradoxical given that the city was once a part of Mexico and is currently nearly half-Hispanic.

OUR SURVEY DESIGN

The ideal data for answering our research questions about immigrant social mobility via small business ownership would consist of a nationally representative sample of all immigrant groups, with detailed information on business proprietors. Such information would include the immigrants' class backgrounds and their legal status upon immigration. Because such data do not exist, we conducted our own survey of Mexican immigrant small proprietors. To do so, we collected a small random sample of small shopkeepers from 20 neighborhoods in Los Angeles County. Los Angeles is a strategic research site because a very large percentage of foreign-born Mexicans continue to settle in this city that has been a destination point from Mexico since the city's founding in 1781. As of 2010, Mexicans comprised 41% of Los Angeles' immigrant population.[13]

In the absence of a list (or sampling frame) of Mexican storefront owners in Los Angeles, we created a unique data set through a multistage cluster sampling technique. In the first stage, we identified 20 neighborhoods that were at least 40% Mexican or at least 40% Hispanic foreign-born Latina/o.[14] In the second stage, we located the main commercial corridors of each of the neighborhoods by searching for "*panaderías*" (bakeries) or "*pupeserías*" (Salvadoran fast-food restaurants) on Google maps. The street view feature of Google maps helped us identify the major intersections of the commercial corridors. In our final stage, we created a probability sample by going to every other shop on each of the commercial corridors of our 20 neighborhoods. In doing so, we created a known probability of 50% of being included in the sample. The map in Fig. 1.1 indicates the areas of Los Angeles in which the specific neighborhoods of our study are embedded.

Twelve Spanish-speaking undergraduates, most of them children of Latina/o immigrants, administered face-to-face surveys to the business owners at their shops. They visited the firms mostly on weekdays, when shopkeepers were less busy, and interviews lasted about 30–45 minutes (on average). We reduced bias by instructing teams of two students per neighborhood to approach storefronts by starting from the North/West corner of each commercial corridor every time they went to a new neighborhood. They were then to walk southward (on North-South streets) or eastward (on East-West streets). Except for a few questions about profits and receipts, which many shopkeepers refused to answer, respondents generally reacted positively to the survey. Although we did not pay the shopkeepers for their time, our student researchers reported that some shopkeepers seemed to appreciate the survey as a form of recognition of their accomplishments.

Our sampling design originally yielded slightly more than 180 responses from multiethnic Latino entrepreneurs, many from Central America, and several US-born Mexican Americans. We limit our analyses in this book to the 111 cases of entrepreneurs born in Mexico. Although our sample is small, the fact that it is random makes it a reasonable data set from which to suggest some of the mobility and immobility dynamics among Mexican immigrant entrepreneurs in Los Angeles. Larger data sets based on very

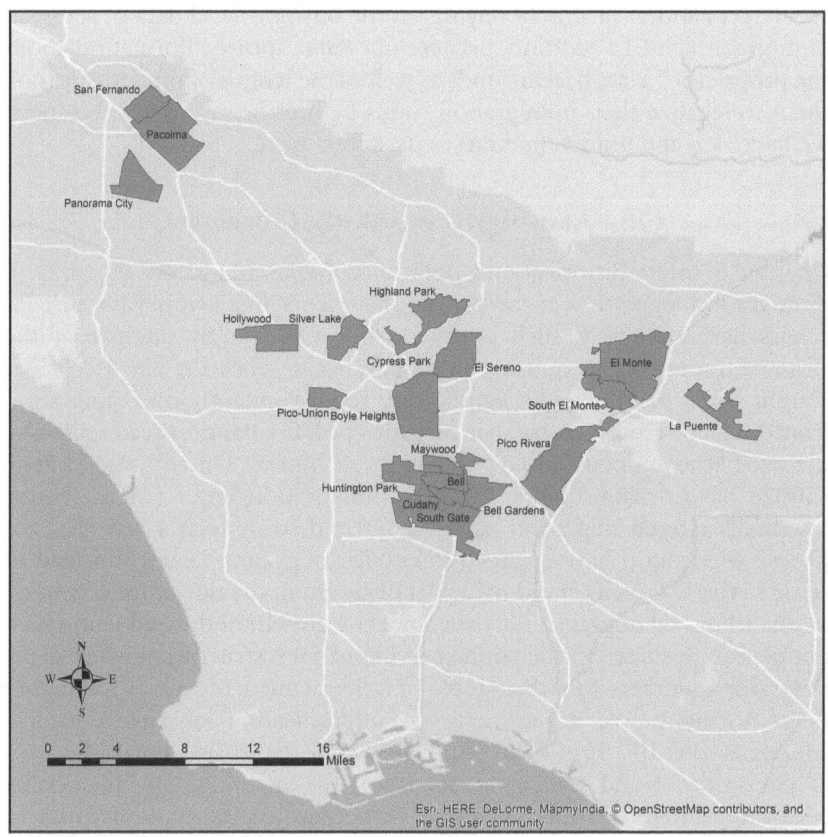

Fig. 1.1 Los Angeles neighborhoods surveyed. (Source: Data taken from the Los Angeles Times "Mapping LA" project found at http://maps.latimes.com/about/#the-data)

large PUMA census units (PUMAS are geographic units of a minimum of 100,000 people; Super-Pumas are at least 400,000 people) never offer more than an ecological analysis of the neighborhood level. Our data, in contrast, are of small storefronts anchored in local neighborhoods, the very communities to which they might potentially contribute by creating employment opportunities. Despite being small, our data set offers a contribution to the scholarship because we randomly sampled firms and their owners responded on site. As Robb and Fairlie (2009) observe, there are only a handful of studies relying on the business-level data of Mexican immigrant firms. In addition, because our data capture information about the proprietors' class backgrounds as well as the length of time that it took them to legalize their immigration status before they went into business, we have rich and unique findings as described next.

OUR ARGUMENT AND BOOK OVERVIEW

Chapter 2 offers historical and political context. It focuses on shifts in immigration legislation at the turn of the twenty-first century because, as others have observed, such policy became increasingly punitive at the close of the twentieth century. Immigration law since the late 1990s has sought to stop, or at least significantly reduce, unauthorized migration from Mexico. However, harsher penalties backfired and instead increased the size of the undocumented population. As Massey, Durand, and Malone (2002) have demonstrated, the new immigration enforcement regime essentially altered migration patterns and did so in such a way that the people who might have engaged in circular migration decided instead to settle in the US. Neither did the new policies stem the tide of fresh cohorts of unauthorized migrants. Further, since the growth of the undocumented population occurred in the context of industrial restructuring when many low-skilled workers lost their jobs, pundits blamed Mexicans for higher unemployment. We argue that the intensification of racism against Mexicans took the form of an ideological shift that first defined Mexicans as parasitic on, and then as a threat to, the nation. Many blue-collar Mexicans suffered in the labor market because of the intensification of racism, and they did so irrespective of their legal status or the human capital skills that they developed in the US. Their growing poverty led to their spatial marginalization in the poorest and most segregated neighborhoods of Los Angeles, one of the most expensive cities in the country. The primary evidence presented in this chapter shows that in the context of growing social distancing, greater scapegoating, and blocked economic mobility, more immigrants from Mexico turned to entrepreneurship. It is a known survivor's strategy, even if the returns to Mexican immigrants are lower than they have historically been for other disadvantaged groups.

Chapter 3 presents two key findings. First, we find that neighborhood poverty reduces people's buying power and thus undercuts the performance of the small shops clustered in the commercial corridors of Mexican communities. As this result proved important across all chapters, it illuminates one of the mechanisms by which neighborhoods are powerful stratifying forces. While this finding is clearly consistent with the theory of concentrated disadvantage, a second finding of the chapter is that some families informally endow their offspring with an entrepreneurial disposition and later, as adult emigrants, those so endowed capitalize on and capture returns from their entrepreneurial cultural capital. As such, this book also documents an intergenerational transmission of inequality by showing that the cultural capital that self-employed parents transmit informally to their children can pay dividends even in another society. Although casually learned in their youth in Mexico, the entrepreneurial disposition proves to be a subtype of cultural capital. This secondary finding contributes to the scholarship by observing how the intersection of pre- and post-migration class characteristics affect mobility. It suggests that small socio-economic differences structured by the pre-migration class experiences of migrants, even those with low levels of education, can yield returns in the right US neighborhood context.

Chapter 4 demonstrates that net of poverty, the extreme spatial segregation of Mexicans within neighborhoods, compromises their business performance. In other words, both poverty and racial segregation contribute to the social ecology of place, and each condition has an autonomous effect on business outcomes. Chapter 4 specifically demonstrates that racial segregation undermines small businesses because too much social homophily within neighborhoods contributes to the quick saturation of markets. Neighborhoods that are more multiethnic expand demand for products and responsive entrepreneurs can and do have better business outcomes. As such, both Chaps. 3 and 4 show how disadvantaged neighborhoods put downward pressure on the mobility trajectories of small business owners by spatially concentrating poor and racialized people. In doing so, disadvantaged neighborhoods also undermine the employment prospects of unemployed locals, further contributing to the reproduction of social class and inequality.

Chapter 5 engages an intersectional analysis aimed at understanding our results as gendered phenomena. With a sample of 50% women, we explain why Mexican female entrepreneurs tend to be more disadvantaged as compared to their male counterparts, all else equal. That said, their more conservative business strategy of purchasing existing shops, rather than starting firms from scratch, mitigates some of their vulnerabilities. Further, while the performance of firms owned by women appears to be more sensitive to the particular industry of their businesses, their odds of firm-level success improve with marriage, a result likely due to the increased financial and labor resources of a marital partner. Although our findings are generally consistent with the literature showing that self-employed women do not perform as well as their male counterparts do, we find that gender effects not only vary by marriage but that they are class specific. Mexican immigrant women entrepreneurs whose parents were business owners performed better in business than did their more working-class counterparts. However, like the men, their small firms hired more employees when they conducted business in less segregated and less impoverished neighborhoods. So, again, we find that neighborhoods significantly affect the life chances of those clustered within them, but that they do so in gendered- and class-specific ways.

The sixth empirical chapter lays bare the intricacies indicated by the concept of legal capital. This chapter interrogates the remarkable fact that three-quarters of our respondents reported that they were undocumented immigrants at one point during their history in the US. We find that immigrants who opened their businesses as soon as they legalized their immigration status cut their losses by withdrawing from an unrewarding labor market that would only cost them time and earnings capacity after they legalized their status. Put differently, those who abandoned the labor market earlier were more successful than the immigrants who postponed entrepreneurship after legalizing their status. This is true even after we control for the length of time in business or the number of years that they had lived in the US. Our evidence thus indicates that the timing of entrepreneurship after legalizing immigration status affects business outcomes. We suggest that net of business duration and time living in the US, operating firms in the formal economy develops business acumen and expands business networks in a way that accumulates small advantages to those entrepreneurs who capitalize earlier on their legal status. This chapter, in short, examines the impact of social-legal status through a Bourdieusian lens of various species of capital. We submit that like other subtypes of cultural capital, legal capital refers to the cultural knowledge about the formal economy that accumulates under the auspices of legal status. We demonstrate that this knowledge—and its attendant licenses—pays more dividends to businesspeople who deploy it earlier in the course of their working lives. That legal status affects stratification is not surprising, but that it does so in relation to the timing of entrepreneurship vis-à-vis the timing of legalization is a contribution to the scholarship. To put what happens negatively, those who continue to invest time in the labor market after their legalization continue to see wage penalties.

Chapter 7 summarizes our main findings. We argue that moving into the ranks of the petite bourgeoisie is much harder for people who must overcome more than racial and gender discrimination, undocumented status, or poverty. We demonstrate that while these factors are important, people live in communities that are nested in space and time. That, as we show, space and time affect the very viability of the entrepreneurship strategy suggests they also affect social mobility. Yet, precisely because disadvantaged neighborhoods create a harsh social ecology, this book offers a story of grit and survival. Some intra-ethnic differences among the immigrants in our study improved the odds of a modicum of success under these neighborhood conditions, and some intra-ethnic variation illuminates how temporality operates on their life chances. First, we found that those who acquired the cultural capital of their entrepreneurial parents had an advantage. This advantage was not only transmitted from one generation to another, but came to matter over time and across an international border. A second temporal dynamic that we observed was that the timing of entrepreneurship vis-à-vis the timing of legalization mattered for the business outcomes of the people in our sample. The second of these temporal dimensions has been undertheorized in the literature on immigrant integration (see Gonzales 2016). Finally, in addition to the spatial and temporal aspects affecting the business performance of our respondents, men and women were positioned differently within the neighborhoods in which their firms operated, and their distinct positions affected which of their firms would be slightly more competitive than others.

In sum, the theory of concentrated disadvantage, Bourdieu's theory of various species of capital, and the intersectional analytic strategy provided the frameworks illuminating how space, time, class, and gender positions affect stratification. Yet, ours is an empirical analysis of how some undocumented people came to live their version of the American Dream. While we do not argue that all or even most undocumented people are potential entrepreneurs who are simply trapped in low-skill work by their immigration status, we do suggest that the growing tendency to think of the undocumented as alien and potentially criminal is unfounded and unproductive. Our research, in fact, suggests that current immigration policy would do well to make the process of legalization easier for people who have lived and worked in the US. under the threat of deportation. Doing so would free immigrants to pursue better economic options given that current policy traps them in low-wage work. Easing the process by which people legalize their status would alleviate some poverty and thereby reduce at least some racial segregation. In addition to easing the process of legalization, our analysis suggests that the policy most helpful to immigrant entrepreneurs would be one that helps them to optimize the locations of their firms. Helping prospective and current entrepreneurs expand into multiethnic markets would yield better business outcomes and thus more employment opportunities for others. This type of policy would be a rational way of helping petty proprietors be a small but positive force in the impoverished communities in which they trade.

We conclude with two notes about our use of terminology. First, we refer to people who live in the US without legal authorization as undocumented or unauthorized, and we use these terms interchangeably. While immigration scholars refer to unauthorized migration to Europe as "irregular" migration, we use common American terminology. However, even though US immigration law makes use of the concept, we only refer to "illegal aliens" when quoting others or referencing public opinion. We avoid these terms despite their technical, or legal, meaning because the notion of "illegal alien" has dehumanizing connotations.[15] The second point of clarification about our language is that we refer to two types of blocked mobility. The second chapter focuses on the blocked mobility of individuals in the labor market. The remaining chapters of the book focus on the blocked mobility of small business owners given the harsh social ecology of the neighborhoods in which their firms are located. As we argue throughout, these ecological conditions put a downward pressure on the success of their tiny firms.

NOTES

1. Our focus on small business owners is consistent with Waldinger, Aldrich, and Ward's definition of entrepreneurs (1990: 17).
2. In the pre-Colonial era, California was home to a network of Native settlements. Founded as a *Spanish* pueblo (called *El Pueblo de Nuestra Señora de los Ángeles*) in 1781, Los Angeles became a part of Mexico after Mexican independence (in 1821). Many of the migrants to Los Angeles since 1781 have been from Mexico, a pattern that continues to date.
3. According to the Pew Research Center. See http://www.pewhispanic. org/2015/09/15/hispanics-of-mexican-origin-in-the-united-states-2013/
4. These data are from the Pew Research Center. See http://www. pewhispanic.org/2017/05/03/facts-on-u-s-immigrants-current-data/.

Alsosee http://www.pewhispanic.org/2015/09/15/hispanics-of-mexican-origin-in-the-united-states-2013/
5. For a recent argument about how deindustrialization has affected the UK, see Andrew G. Haldane (2017).
6. See Rogers Brubaker (1985).
7. See Neil Fligstein and Doug McAdam (2011) and Rodney Benson (1999) for a discussion of Bourdieu's theory of fields.
8. Weber's notion of life chances (or *lebenschancen*) is comparable to Bourdieu's idea of trajectory over time. Weber clearly emphasized that early access to material and educational resources structures people's long-term odds of landing in specific places within a stratification system.
9. For exceptions, see Hernández-León (2008) on skilled and semi-skilled workers. Also, see Hagan et al. (2011). On the "new migration" patterns comprising indigenous people moving from Mexico to the US, see Cornelius et al. (2007), Malpica (2005), and Rivera-Salgado (2016).
10. On these variables, see Borjas (1999), Doms et al. (2010), Mora and Davila (2014), Robb and Fairlie (2009).
11. Their ambivalent standing is determined both because they are "othered" by natives and because they themselves have mixed or uncertain feelings about their host society.
12. On the regional dispersion of Mexicans and Mexican Americans, see the Pew 2013 report on Mexican-Origin Hispanics in the United States. http://www.pewhispanic.org/2013/05/01/a-demographic-portrait-of-mexican-origin-hispanics-in-the-united-states/
13. The source for this statistic is: http://dornsife.usc.edu/assets/sites/731/docs/LOSANGELES_web.pdf
14. We used 40% as the cutoff since the percentage of Hispanics or Latinos in Los Angeles County was 44% in 2000, the most recent Census year available at the time we administered the survey (see Table 3.4 for the list of 20 neighborhoods).
15. For a full discussion, see Haynes et al. (2016).

References

Anderson, Alistair R., and Claire J. Miller. 2003. "Class Matters": Human and Social Capital in the Entrepreneurial Process. *Journal of Socio-Economics* 32: 17–36.

Bates, Timothy. 1994. Social Resources Generated by Group Support Networks May Not Be Beneficial to Asian Immigrant-Owned Small Business. *Social Forces* 72 (3): 671–689.

Bean, Frank D., Mark Leach, and B. Lindsay Lowell. 2004. Immigrant Job Quality and Mobility in the United States. *Work and Occupations* 31 (4): 499–518.

Benson, Rodney. 1999. Field Theory in Comparative Context: A New Paradigm for Media Studies. *Theory and Society* 28 (3): 463–498.

Bonacich, Edna, and John Modell. 1980. *The Economic Basis of Ethnic Solidarity: Small Business in the Japanese American Community.* Berkeley: University of California Press.

Borjas, George J. 1999. The Economic Analysis of Immigration. In *Handbook of Labor Economics*, ed. Orley Ashenfelter and David Card, vol. 3A, 1697–1760. Amsterdam: North-Holland.

Bourdieu, Pierre. 1984 (1979). *Distinction: A Social Critique of the Judgement of Taste.* Cambridge, MA: Harvard University Press.

Braymen, Charles B., and Florence Neymotin. 2014. Enclaves and Entrepreneurial Success. *Journal of Entrepreneurship and Public Policy* 3 (2): 197–221.

Brubaker, Rogers. 1985. Rethinking Classical Theory: The Sociological Vision of Pierre Bourdieu. *Theory and Society* 14 (6): 745–775.

Butler, John Sibley. 1991. *Entrepreneurship and Self-Help Among Black Americans: A Reconsideration of Race and Economics.* Albany: State University of New York Press.

Butler, John Sibley, and George Kozmetsky. 2004. *Immigrant and Minority Entrepreneurship: The Continuous Rebirth of American Communities.* Westport: Praeger Publishers.

Butler, John Sibley, Alfonso Morales, and David L. Torres. 2009. *An American Story: Mexican American Entrepreneurship & Wealth Creation.* West Lafayette: Purdue University Press.

Cornelius, Wayne A., David Scott FitzGerald, and Pedro Lewin Fischer. 2007. *Mayan Journeys: The New Migration from Yucatán to the United States.* Boulder: Lynne Rienner Publishers.

Doms, Mark, Ethan Lewis, and Alicia Robb. 2010. Local Labor Force Education, New Business Characteristics, and Firm Performance. *Journal of Urban Economics* 67: 61–77.

Feldmeyer, Ben. 2010. The Effects of Racial/Ethnic Segregation on Latino and Black Homicide. *The Sociological Quarterly* 51 (4): 600–623.

Fligstein, Neil, and Doug McAdam. 2011. Toward a General Theory of Strategic Action Fields. *Sociological Theory* 29 (1): 1–26.

Gold, Steve. 1994. Patterns of Economic Cooperation Among Israeli Immigrants in Los Angeles. *International Migration Review* 28: 114–135.

Gonzales, Robert G. 2016. *Lives in Limbo: Undocumented and Coming of Age in America.* Oakland: University of California Press.

Hagan, Jacqueline, Nichola Lowe, and Christian Quingla. 2011. Skills on the Move: Rethinking the Relationship Between Human Capital and Immigrant Economic Mobility. *Work and Occupations* 38 (2): 149–178.

Hagan, Jacqueline, Jean Luc Demonsant, and Sergio Chávez. 2014. Identifying and Measuring the Lifelong Human Capital of 'Unskilled' Migrants in the Mexico-US Migratory Circuit. *Journal of Migration and Human Security* 2 (2): 76–100.

Haldane, Andrew G. 2017. *Work, Wages and Monetary Policy.* Speech Given by Bank of England Chief Economist at the National Science and Media Museum, Bradford. https://www.bis.org/review/r170630f.pdf

Harding, David J. 2009. Collateral Consequences of Violence in Disadvantaged Neighborhoods. *Social Forces* 88: 757–784.

Haynes, Chris, Jennifer Merolla, and S. Karthick Ramakrishnan. 2016. *Framing Immigrants: News Coverage, Public Opinion, and Policy.* New York: Russell Sage Foundation.

Hernández-León, Rubén. 2004. Restructuring at the Source: High-Skilled Industrial Migration from Mexico to the United States. *Work and Occupations* 31 (4): 424–452.

———. 2008. *Metropolitan Migrants: The Migration of Urban Mexicans to the Unites States.* Berkeley: University of California Press.

Hipp, John R. 2010. A Dynamic View of Neighborhoods: The Reciprocal Relationship Between Crime and Neighborhood Structural Characteristics. *Social Problems* 57 (2): 205–230.

Light, Ivan. 1972. *Ethnic Enterprise in America: Business and Welfare Among Chinese, Japanese, and Blacks.* Berkeley: University of California Press.

Light, Ivan, and Steven J. Gold. 2000. *Ethnic Economies.* San Diego: Academic Press.

Light, Ivan, and Carolyn Rosenstein. 1995. *Race, Ethnicity, and Entrepreneurship in Urban America.* New York: Aldine De Gruyter.

Logan, John R., Wenquan Zhang, and Richard D. Alba. 2002. Immigrant Enclaves and Ethnic Communities in New York and Los Angeles. *American Sociological Review* 67: 299–322.

Malpica, Melero Daniel. 2005. Indigenous Mexican Migrants in a Modern Metropolis: The Reconstruction of Zapotec Communities in Los Angeles. In *Latino Los Angeles: Transformations, Communities, and Activism,* ed. Enrique C. Ochoa and Gilda L. Ochoa, 2005. Tucson: University of Arizona Press.

Massey, Douglas S., and Stefanie Brodmann. 2014. *Spheres of Influence: The Social Ecology of Racial and Class Inequality.* New York: Russell Sage Foundation.

Massey, Douglas S., Jorge Durand, and Nolan J. Malone. 2002. *Beyond Smoke and Mirrors: Mexican Immigration in an Era of Economic Integration.* New York: Russell Sage Foundation.

Mora, Marie T., and Alberto Davila. 2014. Gender and Business Outcomes of Black and Hispanic New Entrepreneurs in the United States. *American Economic Review* 104 (5): 245–249.

Ndofor, Hermann Achidi, and Richard L. Priem. 2011. Immigrant Entrepreneurs, the Ethnic Enclave Strategy, and Venture Performance. *Journal of Management* 37 (3): 790–818.

Nee, Victor, Jimmy M. Sanders, and Scott Sernau. 1994. Job Transitions in an Immigrant Metropolis: Ethnic Boundaries and the Mixed Economy. *American Sociological Review* 59: 849–872.

Portes, Alejandro. 1981. Modes of Structural Incorporation and Present Theories of Labor Immigration. In *Global Trends in Migration*, ed. Mary Kritz, Charles B. Keeley, and Silvano Tomasi, 279–297. New York: Center for Migration Studies.

Portes, Alejandro, and Min Zhou. 1993. The New Second Generation: Segmented Assimilation and Its Variants Among Post-1965 Immigrant Youth. *Annals of the American Academy of Political and Social Science* 530: 74–96.

Ramirez, Hernan, and Pierrette Hondagneu-Sotelo. 2009. Mexican Immigrant Gardeners: Entrepreneurs or Exploited Workers? *Social Problems* 56 (1): 70–88.

Rivera-Salgado, Gaspar. 2016. From Hometown Clubs to Transnational Social Movement: The Evolution of Oaxacan Migrant Associations in California. *Social Justice* 42 (3/4): 118–136.

Robb, Alicia, and Robert Fairlie. 2009. Determinants of Business Success: An Examination of Asian-Owneed Businesses in the USA. *Journal of Population Economics* 22: 827–858.

Rugh, Jacob S., Len Albright, and Douglas S. Massey. 2015. Race, Space, and Cumulative Disadvantage: A Case Study of the Subprime Lending Collapse. *Social Problems* 62: 186–218.

Schulz, Amy J., Srimathi Kannan, J. Timothy Dvonch, Barbara A. Israel, Alex Allen III, Sherman A. James, James S. House, and James Lepkowski. 2005. Social and Physical Environments and Disparities in Risk for Cardiovascular Disease: The Healthy Environments Partnership Conceptual Model. *Environmental Health Perspectives* 113: 1817–1825.

Simmel, Georg. 1971 [1908]. The Stranger. In *Georg Simmel: On Individuality and Social Forms,* ed. Donald Levine, 143–150. Chicago: University of Chicago Press. (The Title of the Original 1908 Version is *Soziologie. Untersuchungen über die Formen der Vergesellschaftung.* Berlin: Duncker & Humblot).

Waldinger, Roger, Howard Aldrich, and Robin Ward. 1990. *Ethnic Entrepreneurs: Immigrant Business in Industrial Societies.* Newbury Park: Sage.

Weber, Max. 1930. *The Protestant Ethic and the Spirit of Capitalism.* Trans. Talcott Parsons. London: Unwin Hyman Ltd.

Wilson, William Julius. 1987. *The Truly Disadvantaged: The Inner City, the Underclass, and Public Policy.* Chicago: University of Chicago Press.

Wodtke, Geoffrey T., David J. Harding, and Felix Elwert. 2011. Neighborhood Effects in Temporal Perspective: The Impact of Long-Term Exposure to Concentrated Disadvantage on High School Graduation. *American Sociological Review* 76 (5): 713–736.

Zhou, Min. 2004. The Role of the Enclave Economy in Immigrant Adaptation and Community Building: The Case of New York's Chinatown. In *Immigrant and Minority Entrepreneurship: The Continuous Rebirth of American Communities,* ed. J.S. Butler and G. Kozmetsky, 37–60. Westport: Praeger Publishers.

CHAPTER 2

Hardline Policies, Blocked Mobility, and Immigrant Entrepreneurs

INTRODUCTION

As compared to all other immigrants, Mexicans stand out by virtue of the size of their population, their place in the geo-political history of the US Southwest, and the complexity of the various legal statuses that people have within their communities, and even their families.[1] Their history in the Southwest and beyond (e.g., Chicago) helps to explain why at 11.5 million, Mexican immigrants outnumber all foreign-born immigrants from other countries, whether from Asia[2] or Latin America (in fact, all Latin American countries combined). Indeed, of the nearly 51 million Latino/as in the US today, nearly 32 million are of Mexican heritage, so they are roughly 63% of all Latino/as. Mexican immigrants also stand out because they constitute more than half (55%) of the 11 or 12 million unauthorized immigrants in the US today, according to Passel and Cohn (2009; see also Massey and Pren 2012: 14). As such, they loom large in the public's imagination. Indeed, (many) Americans increasingly view Mexicans as a threat to the nation in a way that recalls George Simmel's analysis of stranger-native relations.

This chapter traces the hostility toward Mexican immigrants that has grown in tandem with the ever more punitive immigration legislation of the twentieth and twenty-first centuries. Before addressing this book's central concern—the business performance of their small shops in Los Angeles—we offer a brief contemporary history of Mexican immigration

© The Author(s) 2018
D. Trevizo, M. Lopez, *Neighborhood Poverty and Segregation in the (Re-)Production of Disadvantage*,
https://doi.org/10.1007/978-3-319-73715-7_2

to the US as context for changing immigration policy. Following Douglas Massey and his colleagues, we argue that an increasingly hardline immigration policy altered long-established migration patterns, and did so in ways that undermine the social mobility of Mexican migrants in the US. Our evidence specifically shows that Mexican immigrants responded to the conditions that threatened their livelihoods with more entrepreneurial ventures. This chapter, in short, documents social and political shifts nationally and in Los Angeles to show that blocked mobility led to higher levels of entrepreneurship among Mexican immigrants in the early part of the twenty-first century than in earlier periods.

As markets alone do not determine business opportunity, this chapter first examines policy changes since 1986, along with their national and local labor market effects in Los Angeles. After establishing the changing climate of reception, we then describe the migrants and firms in our sample. We show that the blocked mobility of Mexicans in Los Angeles motivated their entrepreneurship. Our conclusions about their rationale for business ventures set up the cast of characters whose business performance we analyze as the main objective of the remainder of this book.

POLICY REFORMS AND RISING HOSTILITY AGAINST MEXICANS SINCE 1986

No historical sketch of Mexican migration, no matter how broad, would make sense without first recognizing that Mexico lost about one-third of its territory to the US in the US-Mexican war of 1846–1848.[3] Therefore, even if concrete economic and familial concerns have historically motivated migration, the massive loss of Mexican territory is a part of the geo-political and cultural backdrop to the eventual and sustained northern-bound movement of people. That flow, however, was initially small and regionally concentrated in the late nineteenth century despite the absence of physical borders separating the neighboring countries and despite labor recruitment efforts by some mining operations (Marcelli 2004: 208). Emigration from Mexico increased in response to US labor shortages in the first decade of the twentieth century, specifically during World War I and the "roaring twenties," although some migrants also fled across the border in response to the violence of the Mexican Revolution. However, by 1930, the number of Mexican immigrants had not passed 800,000

(Massey 2009), and these numbers were cut by nearly 50% when 458,000 people (including legal residents and their US-born children) were summarily deported in the wake of the Great Depression (Ibid).[4]

The emergence of mass Mexican migration of both authorized and unauthorized workers is, thus, a relatively recent phenomenon. It increased after the temporary guest worker program (1942–1964) with Mexico ended, and after the Immigration and Nationality Act of 1965 amended US immigration policy, above all visa rules. Initiated by the US government in 1942, the Bracero program sought to alleviate wartime labor shortages by recruiting temporary guest workers from Mexico as farm laborers. Since labor shortages continued in the post-war boom, the program expanded in the second half of the 1950s when temporary guest workers crossed the border at the rate of about 450,000 people per year (Massey and Pren 2012: 3). Legal migrants also obtained resident visas at an annual rate of about 50,000 per year during this period (Massey and Pren 2012: 3). So when the Bracero program ended in 1964, it closed a well-established legal pathway into the US from which hundreds of thousands of Mexicans had benefited for nearly a quarter of a century.[5] The Immigration and Nationality Act of 1965 that followed restricted other passageways by capping the legal annual entry of people from the Western Hemisphere for the first time to 120,000 per year.[6] Although the number of Latin American immigrants rose significantly after the Act, the new cap on legal annual entries radically reduced access to the US. As such, the Act challenged Mexicans who had grown accustomed to US wages during more than two decades of experience with the Bracero program (Galarza 1978 [1964]; Craig 1971; see also Massey and Pren 2012: 1–3). While Mexicans benefited from the family reunification provisions of the 1965 Act, other opportunities for legal entry into the US diminished when Congress further reduced the number of residence visas in 1976, this time to just 20,000 per country per year (Massey and Pren 2012: 1–2). In sum, the elimination of the temporary guest worker program and the new caps on permanent resident visas restricted the pathways for migrants from Mexico to enter the US legally to work for the employers who clamored to hire them.

This new reality dramatically increased unauthorized migration because the very success of the Bracero program had cultivated a demand for inexpensive Mexican labor among farm growers and a dependence on, or a desire for, American wages among prospective migrants. Some Mexicans had grown accustomed to solving their economic problems by working on a seasonal basis in the US. Moreover, given the existence of Mexican American communities already in the Southwest, restrictive immigration policies led to larger inflows of undocumented laborers who could rely on their established US networks for essential support (Massey et al. 2002; Marcelli 2004: 209). Until the mid-1980s, many unauthorized migrants remained in a circular migration pattern in which they worked seasonally in the US and returned to Mexico off-season (Massey 2009: 18). Still, public controversy over what many Americans perceived as a porous US-Mexico border grew with the size of the undocumented population.

Congress has sought to address the public's increasing concerns about unauthorized Mexican immigrants for several decades through the use of deportations—for example, Operation Wetback of 1953–1954 deported 3.8 million people[7]—and their efforts have grown increasingly punitive from 1986 forward (see Table 2.1, see also Massey 2009: 19). As indicated in Table 2.1, The Immigration Reform and Control Act (IRCA) of 1986, which followed a sharp rise in unauthorized migration, increased border enforcement and funding. It also threatened to penalize employers for knowingly hiring unauthorized migrants. IRCA also included an amnesty provision giving long-term residents a path toward legalizing their immigration status. Unauthorized migrants could legalize their status and thereby gain the rights to work and live in the US if they had entered the country before January of 1982. They also had to demonstrate a rudimentary understanding of the English language, US history, and government. Seasonal agricultural workers also qualified for amnesty but under a different set of rules (in which they were required to have worked in the US in 1984, 1985, and 1986 for a specific number of days). Over 3 million previously unauthorized migrants benefited from amnesty within three years of IRCA's passing in 1986 and the vast majority of the beneficiaries (about two-thirds of the total) were from Mexico (Bean et al. 1990; Orrenius 2001). IRCA, however, failed to curtail unauthorized immigration, as people found it easy to circumvent the documentation requirements and employer penalties were rarely enforced (Bansak et al. 2015).[8]

Ten years later, Congress passed three policies that made the social-political and economic context for unauthorized migrants more hostile. The 1996 Illegal Immigration Reform and Immigrant Responsibility Act (IIRIRA) stipulated that unauthorized migrants who committed crimes were subject to removal and expanded the definition of criminality so that re-entry into the US after removal became a felony punishable with time

Table 2.1 Select immigration reforms since the mid-1980s affecting Mexican immigrants

Year passed/ enacting body	Immigration law and regulatory action	Goal/strategy	Some key provisions and effects on Mexican immigrants
1986 Congress	Immigration Reform and Control Act (IRCA)	Deter unauthorized migrant flows by militarizing border.	1. Increased the number of Border Patrol agents (BPA). 2. Employer sanctions for knowingly hiring undocumented workers. 3. Amnesty for unauthorized migrants who could prove arrival before 1982 or who were farmworkers (Special Agricultural Workers [SAW]).
1996 Congress	The Illegal Immigration Reform and Immigrant Responsibility Act (IIRIRA)	Deter unauthorized migrant flows by militarizing border; Remove (deport) immigrants convicted of crime.	1. Dramatically increased the number of BPA. 2. Extended the border fence, employed surveillance equipment and sought interior enforcement. 3. Deputized some local police forces for immigration enforcement. 4. Removal (deportation) *at entry ports* without judicial review (expedited removal). 5. Expanded the definition of aggravated felony and authorized expedited removal of criminal migrants. The retroactive application of this law allowed. Removal orders not subject to appeal. 6. Mandatory detention in INS facilities for some (not all) people found inadmissible or removable (deportable) pending immigration proceedings. 7. Instituted 3–10 year bans for undocumented seeking to legalize status.
1996 Congress	Anti-Terrorism and Effective Death Penalty Act (AEDPA)	Remove/exclude foreign terrorists. Reform asylum procedures.	1. Mandatory detention of noncitizens convicted of aggravated felonies, even if long ago, who were now subject to immediate removal. Nearly doubled immigrants in detention facilities. 2. Expanded the definition of aggravated felonies to include misdemeanors under state law (s/a minor drug charges). 3. Circumscribed judicial review of removal orders.

(continued)

Table 2.1 (continued)

Year passed/ enacting body	Immigration law and regulatory action	Goal/strategy	Some key provisions and effects on Mexican immigrants
1996 Congress	Personal Responsibility and Work Opportunity Reconciliation Act (PRWORA)	Welfare reform.	1. Documented immigrants ineligible for federal welfare entitlements for the first 5 years upon US entry. Undocumented people ineligible for any entitlements.
2001 Congress	US PATRIOT Act	Obstruct terrorism.	1. Increased the power of executive authorities to remove (deport) without due process. 2. Created Department of Homeland Security (DHS). 3. More investigative power to US Attorney General and DHS. 4. Tripled Border Patrol, Customs, DHS (INS) agents. 5. Increased detentions and deportations of Mexican immigrants from the interior of the US (not just at the border).
2005/ Department of Homeland Security (DHS)	Secure Border Initiative (SBI)	Punish illegal migrants via criminalization and place in detention centers.	1. Increased number of BPA. 2. Increased number ICE investigators. 3. Expanded interior enforcement. 4. Removal of "illegals" within 100 miles of land and coastal borders with limited judicial review. 5. Criminal charges possible for those who re-enter illegally. 6. Migrants caught at border may be charged with immediate crime. 7. Repatriate Mexicans to locations far from the border.
2017/ Executive order	Border Security and Immigration Enforcement Improvements	Remove more unauthorized migrants from Mexico/deter asylum seekers.	1. Remove more unauthorized migrants even if they do not have criminal pasts. 2. Enlist police forces for interior immigration enforcement. 3. Create new immigration detention facilities. 4. Speed up removals (deportations).

Source: Authors' table. In immigration law, the technical term for deportation is "removal" after the passage of IIRIRA. For more information on INS operations, see Donato and Armenta (2011)

in prison. IIRIRA also made it more difficult for unauthorized immigrants to apply for legal permanent status by barring them from re-entry for many years. They were barred for three years if they had resided in the US in an unauthorized capacity for a short period of time (less than a year). The law barred unauthorized migrants for ten years if they had been in the US without permission for longer than one year. These re-entry bars prevent migrants from obtaining legal permanent resident status (LPR) even if family members are willing to sponsor them (Bansak et al. 2015). The IIRIRA Act also dramatically increased the number of the Border Patrol agents (it mandated a doubling of the Border Patrol by 2001), extended the fence along the US-Mexico border, and deputized some local police forces to enforce immigration laws in the interior of the country. Patrol practices at the border changed dramatically so that people caught crossing the border, or who were in proximity of the border without legal status, faced expedited removal. The immediate removal (i.e., deportation) of people caught in close proximity to the border was a dramatic shift from previous practices of "catching" and then "releasing" people with official notice of their eventual immigration hearing. The Anti-Terrorism and Effective Death Penalty Act (AEDPA) of 1996 further expanded the definition of criminal alien, this time to migrants who had long ago committed crimes. This law also narrowed the provisions for discretionary relief. Finally, the Personal Responsibility and Work Opportunity Reconciliation Act (PRWORA), or simply the Welfare Reform Act of 1996, barred post-enactment immigrants (those entering the US legally after August 22, 1996) from receiving means-tested programs (e.g., Temporary Assistance for Needy Families, Supplemental Security Income, Medicaid) for their first five years.[9]

The 1990s also witnessed a greater number of local and place-specific policies that aimed to make illegal entry more costly. Operation Hold-the-Line in El Paso (1993), Operation Gatekeeper in San Diego (1994), Operation Safeguard in Arizona (1994), and Operation Rio Grande in South Texas (1997) are just some examples of local policies aimed at diverting unauthorized migrants away from border cities. The goal was to channel migrants toward more remote areas in order for the Border Patrol to more easily spot and detain unauthorized entrants. During this period of time, the number of Border Patrol agents increased from 4200 in 1994 to 7700 by 1999 (Orrenius 2001).

While both national and local policies sought to curtail the flow of unauthorized migration and to reduce the fiscal impact of immigrants, they actually contributed to greater undocumented immigration from Mexico by complicating the mechanisms for legal entry into the US and by reducing the number of legal visas. To illustrate just how challenging it became to migrate legally, unskilled people from Mexico could work in the US only if they obtained either "green cards," which indicate legal permanent resident status, or temporary work visas (such as the H-2A or H-2B visas). However, to qualify for a green card, a close family member who is either a US citizen or has LPR status would have to sponsor the low-skill relative, and the process from application to approval could take as many as 13 years (Hanson 2009). Alternatively, prospective migrants might "obtain one of only 5,000 employment based visas available for low skilled workers, be a refugee, or win one of the few lottery visas" (Hanson 2009: 6). In addition, temporary H-2B visas awarded to seasonal non-agricultural low-skilled workers are capped at 66,000. While temporary H-2A visas for agricultural workers are not capped, they are subject to strict rules that limit their use by employers (Hanson 2009). Immigration policy has thus made unauthorized migration the only viable option for low-skill Mexican workers desperate for work, particularly since they are aware that US employers clamor to hire them. Further, increases in the number of Border Patrol agents and in apprehensions along the US-Mexico border have only resulted in migrants crossing through harsher terrain, exposing themselves to dangerous climates and even death in order to gain access to jobs (Ellingwood 2004).

Finally, these policy changes also began the process of depriving many unauthorized migrants of their liberty before deporting them, a radical change that some scholars refer to as the criminalization of immigration law (Stumpf 2006).[10] Recall that prior to these 1996 reforms, Border Patrol agents essentially treated unlawful entry as an administrative infraction by releasing unauthorized migrants apprehended at the border (a practice colloquially referred to as "catch and release"). After 1996, however, border enforcement toughened and many unauthorized migrants caught were detained in centers. If they had no criminal records, they could be released on their own recognizance. Those with criminal records could be detained for months before appearing before an immigration board. In addition, the number of deportations (called "removals" after IIRIRA) rose dramatically, so that by 2001 there were three times as many as there had been in 1996 (Gentsch and Massey 2011: 891).

Gentsch and Massey (2011) argue that the "new enforcement regime" grew harsher still after the terrorist attacks on US soil on September 11,

2001 (see Table 2.1).[11] When Congress passed the Patriot Act in response, it delegated more immigration authority to the executive branch. Among other powers, this Act gave Presidents the right to remove aliens, whether legal or unauthorized, without judicial review (Massey 2009: 20). The Patriot Act dissolved the Immigration and Naturalization Services (INS) and established Immigration and Customs Enforcement (ICE) under a newly formed Department of Homeland Security (DHS). The immediate task of ICE was to ensure national security and, as such, it became the largest law enforcement body within the DHS. Operation Streamline (2005) and Secure Communities were two programs initiated by the DHS that strengthened the power of ICE. Operation Streamline mandated the criminal prosecution and detention of all unauthorized immigrants. Secure Communities required participating local authorities to verify the identification of immigrants taken into custody with ICE records. Both programs gave ICE greater police powers and the capacity to incarcerate unauthorized immigrants (Kilgore 2015).

The total number of removals continued to rise rapidly so that by "2008, internal deportations had increased to seven times their 1996 level" (Gentsch and Massey 2011: 891).[12] Interior enforcement intensified even further with the rise in the number of programs that made it easier for state and local law enforcement agencies to collaborate with federal authorities to enforce immigration violations (Nguyen and Gill 2015; Wong 2012). For example, in the period between 2008 and 2013, every jurisdiction in the country adopted Secure Communities, the information-sharing program utilized to apprehend and remove unauthorized immigrants. In roughly the same period, several local states and even municipal governments passed an unprecedented number of local laws that also contributed to border and interior enforcement of immigration laws (Hopkins 2010; Martos 2010; Varsanyi 2008; Provine and Varsanyi 2012). To give just a couple of examples, Arizona adopted SB 1070 in 2010 that allowed local police to verify the immigration status of someone arrested or detained and that made being unauthorized a state criminal offense (but the criminal offense provision was struck down by the Supreme Court on June 25, 2012). Alabama, with HB 56, went so far as to require that school administrators verify the legal status of children enrolled in K-12. While federal courts struck down these laws in 2012, their passage attests to the hostility that some local states developed toward unauthorized migrants.

The evidence of hardening immigration policies at the national, state, and local levels is incontrovertible. Figure 2.1 graphs the total number of removals (deportations) over time, as well as the number of *non-criminal removals* that contributed to that total number. As the figure shows, hundreds of thousands of non-criminals were removed on a yearly basis since 2001, with that number surpassing 2.5 million by 2014. Therefore, if mass deportations happened periodically in the twentieth century (in the 1930s, during the Depression and then again in 1954 with Operation Wetback), removals became a massive and sustained practice at the turn of the twenty-first century.

The Social and Ideological Effects of the New Enforcement Regime

Some unintended consequences of these reforms include the actual growth and long-term residency of undocumented people in the US, along with

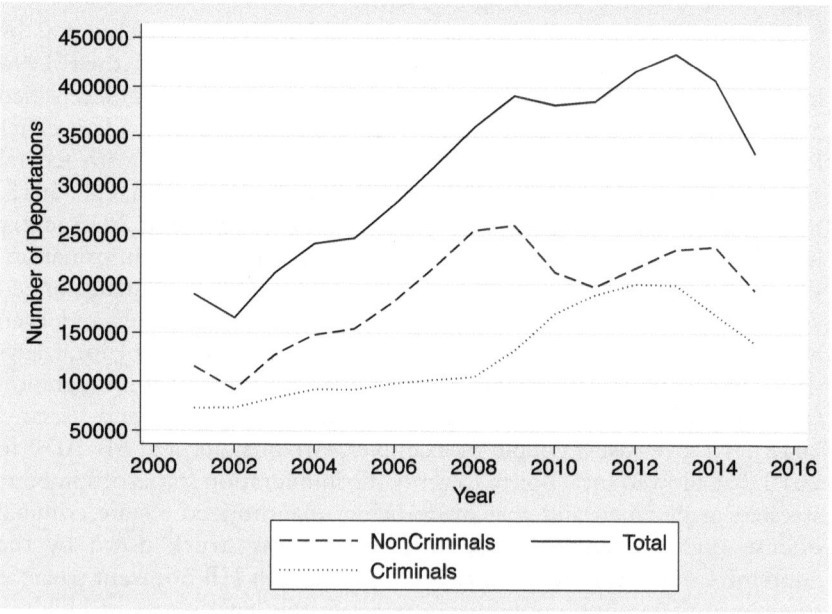

Fig. 2.1 Number of deportations, 2001–2015. (Source: United States. Department of Homeland Security. *Yearbook of Immigration Statistics: 2010 and 2015.* Washington, DC: US Department of Homeland Security, Office of Immigration Statistics, 2011 and 2016)

the elaboration and intensification of racist ideas about people of Mexican ancestry.[13] First, the increasing costs of migration—for example, the higher coyote fees, the increased odds of deportation and even death—associated with crossing the border illegally altered long-established circular migration patterns (Durand and Massey 2003; Massey 2009; Argueta 2016). People who typically engaged, or who might have engaged, in seasonal work before returning to Mexico opted instead to remain in the US after immigration enforcement became more stringent. They opted to settle in the US to avoid the costs of crossing the border and specifically to avoid detection at entry. For example, by 2014, 78% of unauthorized immigrants from Mexico had lived in the US for more than ten years (long-term residents) and only 7% were recent immigrants (those living in the US for less than five years). This compares to only 52% of unauthorized immigrants from countries other than Mexico who are long-term residents and 22% who are recent immigrants (Gonzalez-Barrera and Krogstad 2017). The growth of the undocumented population in the US, in turn, intensified the social hostility aimed at Mexican immigrants and their descendants, and did so especially in non-traditional immigrant-receiving states. Therefore, whereas two mass deportation campaigns in the twentieth century manifested animus toward Mexican migrants, the political rhetoric of the twenty-first century frames illegality as a predisposition toward violent criminality.

Nicholas De Genova argues that the notion of "illegality" in illegal alien "has long served as a constitutive dimension of the specific racialized inscription of 'Mexicans,' in general, in the United States" (De Genova 2005: 226). Similarly, Robin Dale Jacobson (2008) traces the development of various new racial meanings in the 1990s from the categories "Mexican" and "foreigner." Both scholars underscore that Mexican immigrants are regularly presumed to be unauthorized and, thus, guilty of other legal infractions.[14] Many people also leap to the conclusion that undocumented people are plausibly also violent criminals. According to Jacobson (2008), it was precisely this heightened sense of threat that motivated political action in California when its electorate voted for the "Save Our State" ballot initiative in 1994. Also known as Proposition 187, this initiative sought not only to penalize undocumented migrants who utilized false documents for employment, but also to exclude them and their children from public education as well as non-emergency health services. Harsher than the "English Only!" demands of other anti-immigrant movements in California, a federal court almost immediately ruled that

Proposition 187 was unconstitutional shortly after it passed.[15] Not coincidently, voters approved of Proposition 187 in 1994, when an extended economic recession had especially devastated jobs in southern California (Jacobson 2008). In Jacobson's view,

> The schema of criminality was embedded in the metaschema of racial realism and depicted racialized characteristics that threaten the safety and power of others. Notions of Mexican criminality have a long history in the United States in general and the Southwest in particular. However, it was as supporters created bridges between race-neutral notions of law enforcement and raced concerns about criminality that they were mobilized to act on the [Proposition 187] campaign. (p. 48)

The sense of heightened threat eventually scaled up to the national level, as evidenced by the fear of Mexicans expressed widely in Trump rallies held during the presidential race of 2016, where "build the wall!" became one of the mobilizing slogans. Though it is also the case, as Jacobson argues (2008), that Mexicans and other immigrant groups have historically been depicted as criminals, the trope of "Mexican as violent criminal" was foregrounded in the 2016 presidential elections as an immediate and dire threat. The evidence from election rallies in 2016 is that many people voted for an unlikely, unpopular, and inexperienced presidential candidate because he promised to build a wall to protect US citizens from their Mexican neighbors whose men he described as "bad *hombres*, criminals, and rapists." Since criminality implies concrete victims, this is clearly a more threatening image than one that frames unauthorized migrants merely as "unassimilable" (see Huntington 2004). Defined as a real threat, or, in Georg Simmel's conceptualization, as "inner enemies"—the intensification of racism against Mexicans since the 1970s has had consequences beyond political rhetoric and voting behavior. We argue that hardening attitudes contributed to blocking the mobility of all Mexicans, and analyze their specific labor market consequences next.

Blocked Mobility Nationally and in Los Angeles

Increasingly dehumanizing tropes about Mexicans have had labor market consequences affecting all workers who look Latin. They are more likely than others to be denied employment, and they earn less than non-Latina/o workers when they are hired.[16] Massey described some of the dynamics as follows: "Beginning in the 1970s...and accelerating in the 1980s and 1990s, Mexicans were increasingly subject to processes of racialization that have rendered them more exploitable and excludable than ever before" (2009: 12). Matthew Hall and his colleagues similarly contend that "nativism and hostility toward undocumented Mexican immigrants has increased in recent years, and as political efforts further marginalize these individuals, it is plausible that the wage penalties for not holding legal authorization may increase" (Hall et al. 2010: 509). Their research demonstrates that, indeed, as compared to other immigrants and natives in the US, both undocumented and legal Mexican immigrants receive the lowest wages (Hall et al. 2010; see also Gentsch and Massey 2011: 882). The unauthorized, however, are the most vulnerable to wage exploitation because they have so few labor rights and little bargaining capacity to fight for better wages (see Gentsch and Massey 2011: 875; see also Rivera-Batiz 1999). Research shows that many undocumented migrants who live in states with mandatory E-Verify laws are forced into the underground economy, precisely where labor laws cannot be enforced, while other unauthorized migrants relocate to states without this legislation (Amuedo-Dorantes and Bansak 2012, 2014; see also Bohn and Lofstrom 2013). Also contributing to their lower wages is the dramatic growth of the more permanent unauthorized immigrant population that resulted from the more stringent immigration policies.

Moreover, these labor market dynamics have occurred in the context of a sharp decline in heavy manufacturing, when employers cut costs by hiring fewer workers or by taking low-wage workers off their payroll. Industrial restructuring has led to so-called flexible employment practices by which employers hire inexpensive labor through subcontractors on an "as needed" basis. Earnings decline even further when this happens because middlemen take a portion of the wages that would otherwise go directly to workers (Massey 2007: 145; Massey 2009: 22). Subcontracting can lead to other super-exploitative practices in those industries—such as construction, which employs many Mexicans—when subcontractors underbid the actual costs of finishing a job, and then pay their workers on a "per job" basis. These "by the job" pricing and remuneration agreements can be comparable to "piece-rate" work in which some workers' earnings fall below the minimum hourly wage. In fact, recent news reports show that the exploitation of Mexican immigrants may be getting worse in the garment industry, a traditional piece-rate industry. Many garment workers earn wages that are below the legal minimum in this industry because clothing retailers are especially dependent on subcontractors, given the brutal competition they face from e-commerce (Kitroeff and Kim 2017).

Put differently, the growth of the undocumented population that resulted from hardline immigration policies combined with racism and economic restructuring to expose Mexican immigrants to the worst kind of wage exploitation. These trends, in turn, increased the supply of low-skill workers who competed for a smaller number of poorly paid jobs after 1986 and especially after 1996 (Gentsch and Massey 2011). Low-skill immigrants and even US-born Latina/os have seen their wages fall as a result. Nevertheless, as emphasized, the most vulnerable people under this heightened enforcement regime are the undocumented[17] who are roughly 60% of the entire Mexican immigrant population (Gentsch and Massey 2011: 877–881) and who number in the millions. These political, social, and labor market dynamics clearly constitute structural barriers that block the social mobility of Mexican immigrants as well as their second-generation children. According to Massey,

> the political economy facing Hispanics is now vastly harsher and more punitive than the one prevailing before 1986. Historically, Hispanics have occupied a middle position between blacks and whites in the American stratification system, but with the restructuring of the political economy of immigration in the late 1980s and early 1990s, the relative standing of Hispanics declined and they came to replace African Americans at the bottom of the class hierarchy. (Massey 2009: 22)

The blocked mobility of Mexicans and their descendants has been especially acute in Los Angeles, a city outranking all other US metropolitan areas both for its concentration of Hispanics—79% of whom are of Mexican ancestry—and unauthorized migrants (Krogstad 2016). When manufacturers in Los Angeles dramatically decreased the production of durable goods, light manufacturing—for example, the garment, plastics, and food production industries—as well as construction and service sector jobs absorbed low-skill immigrant workers (Waldinger 1999).[18] Today, fully 91% of Los Angeles' immigrants are actually employed, yet most are among the working poor because they are concentrated in the low-pay niche jobs of the light manufacturing or service sectors (Pastor et al. 2012). As compared to Mexican women who concentrate in domestic and personal services, Mexican immigrant men tend to work in landscaping services, grounds keeping, automotive repair and maintenance, construction, and truck transportation (Pastor and Ortiz 2009; Ortiz 1996). Making matters worse is the intense competition for jobs in highly segregated and low-skill occupational niches because this hyper-competition among Mexican immigrants drives their wages down even further. As such, nearly one-third of all immigrants in Los Angeles earn below 150% of the official poverty level (Pastor et al. 2012). Enrico A. Marcelli carefully documents the negative wage impact of unauthorized migration for all Mexico-born migrants in Los Angeles County at the start of the twenty-first century. In his words, there was a

> 34 percent unauthorized-authorized Mexican male wage gap and the likelihood that most (67 percent) of this gap emanates from social forces (such as employer discrimination, public attitudes toward unauthorized immigrants and the work they do, and migrant job networks) rather than unobserved individual characteristics (such as the quality of one's education or attitudinal constitution). (Marcelli 2004: 223)

Consequently, while the 1990s saw a decline in poverty in many US cities, Los Angeles saw rising indigence due to the arrival of poor immigrants (Jargowsky 2009). Jargowsky (2009) argues that the concentration of poverty among immigrants who arrived in Los Angeles between 1990 and 2000 was more than double what it was for immigrants who arrived before 1970. Estimates from the 2015 American Community Survey show that the City of Los Angeles's poverty rate is fully 22.7, and this is worse than either California's or the nation's average (California's poverty rate is 17.2% and the national poverty rate is 17.5%). By 2000, Los Angeles outranked all other major metropolitan areas (including New York, Chicago, and Houston) for concentrating poverty among the foreign-born in many neighborhoods. To be clear, 50% of people in poor neighborhoods were US born (Jargowsky 2009), though we suspect that many among the US born are children of immigrants.[19] Further, since more than half of the city's unauthorized migrants are denizens by virtue of having lived in Los Angeles more than ten years, many raise families in impoverished neighborhoods that are also racially segregated. Families have few housing options because Los Angeles is one of the most expensive cities in all of the US. As such, the city of Angels distinguishes itself as one of the country's most segregated residential cities for Latinos/as (see Wilkes and Iceland 2004; Tienda and Fuentes 2014; Rugh and Massey 2014). According to

Tienda and Fuentes, as of the 2000 census, Hispanics in Los Angeles (and New York) meet the hyper-segregated threshold for living in conditions of "maximum social exclusion" due to segregation along multiple dimensions (2014: 505). Finally, this extreme segregation has a feedback, or circular, effect on poverty because spatial isolation removes access to various kinds of job and social opportunities while also concentrating social problems—such as homicides, inadequate public services, unemployment, and the like—and, thus, long-term disadvantages.

In sum, the increasingly punitive immigration policies since the late 1980s and 1990s led to the growth of the undocumented population in the US and contributed to the intensification of racism against as well as the wage suppression of people of Mexican ancestry. Consequently, Mexican immigrants and especially those who are undocumented are worse off financially than are most working poor, and they have few prospects for upward mobility.[20] As we have described here, the labor and housing market conditions for Mexican immigrants in Los Angeles have been especially dire.

Immigrant Entrepreneurship in Los Angeles

The fact that a new political economy blocks the avenues for upward mobility for Mexican immigrants, legal or not, explains why many increasingly turned to self-employment (which is not identical to small business proprietorship, as we emphasize in a later chapter). Despite a long migration history dating back to the first half of the twentieth century, the trend toward self-employment among Mexican immigrants in Los Angeles is recent. It became noteworthy in the period between 1980 and 1990, when the number of unincorporated foreign-born, self-employed Hispanics increased from 18,480 to 54,768 (see Light and Roach 1996). Not coincidently, this nearly threefold increase in self-employment outpaced the number of jobs created in Los Angeles during this same period, which was, as noted, a period of economic restructuring (Light and Roach 1996: 198). Light and Roach further documented that self-employed Hispanics earned either roughly the same or slightly more than their wage/salary counterparts did by staying in the labor market in the period between 1970 and 1990. In a previous study, we similarly found that Mexican immigrant shopkeepers in Los Angeles earn more, on average, than they otherwise would if they had remained in the labor market at any point between 1990 and 2003 (Lopez and Trevizo 2009: 141). Our prior research, thus, concurs with and updates Light and Roach's study (1996) in demonstrating that there is, in fact, a "self-employed bonus" to Hispanic immigrants in Los Angeles. While this bonus is smaller for Hispanics than it is for other immigrants, it remains a real bonus just the same. As such, Light and Roach (1996) argued,

> Despite all the area's economic problems and the heavy immigration to the region, even Hispanic immigrants—generally the poorest and least prepared of any immigrants—could still settle in Greater Los Angeles and obtain upward economic mobility if they started their own businesses. (p. 209)

The self-employment trend among Hispanics in Los Angeles continues[21], and both male and female Mexican immigrants participate in the general pattern. A 2017 report from the New American Economy, the City of Los Angeles, and the Los Angeles Chamber of Commerce shows that Mexican immigrant entrepreneurs in Los Angeles are concentrated in construction (37.3%), general services (25.4%), and professional services (17.9%).[22] Further, US census data indicate that fewer than 20% of self-employed immigrants were engaged in "non-storefront" businesses at the start of the twenty-first century, according to Pearce (2005). Our book, therefore, is timely. It offers original information about Mexican immigrants' relatively recent engagement with storefront proprietorship in Los Angeles. While census data provides information on self-employed individuals, they do not distinguish between those entrepreneurs who have actual storefronts or retail space to conduct their businesses and self-employed freelance workers who exchange labor for a fixed price. Our survey offers rich information on storefront proprietors in 20 neighborhoods in Los Angeles.

In what follows, we first present some of the sample characteristics of the entrepreneurs in our study. As we noted in the introduction, our multistage cluster sampling method yielded a random sample of 111 cases of storefront proprietors whose characteristics we describe next. The findings in this chapter focus on *why* the particular shopkeepers in our study went into business and *how* they accumulated their start-up capital. We specifically hypothesize *that as the labor market yielded fewer rewards to immigrants after the implementation of the new enforcement regime (post 1996), some Mexican immigrants opted to go into business.*

Sample Characteristics of Mexican Immigrant Entrepreneurs and Their Shops

Table 2.2 presents the socio-demographic, migration, as well as firm characteristics of the proprietors and the businesses in our sample.[23] As shown in Table 2.2, women constitute a little more than half of our respondents, and while this is a considerably higher percentage than the percentage of Mexican female entrepreneurs reported in official data sources (See Appendix A), it is not entirely surprising. Relying on the 2000 census, Susan Pearce observed that women, especially women from Latin America, are "among the fastest growing groups of business owners in the United States." She further observed that much of the growth is, in fact, concentrated in the Los Angeles-Riverside-Orange County metropolitan area, which is, as she notes, home to "13 percent of all immigrant women entrepreneurs in the nation" (Pearce 2005: 1).

Most of our respondents—fully two-thirds of them—reported being married at the time of the survey. The immigrants in our study were young, just 19 years of age when they entered the country, and most did so without authorization. However, after an extended period of working in the US without legal status, the overwhelming majority of our respondents eventually obtained a green card (legal permanent residency status); some also became US citizens (See Table 6.1). As we shall see, the vast majority of our respondents had to legalize their status before they could open storefront businesses. Because doing so is a lengthy bureaucratic process that can take many years (see Chap. 6 in this book), the proprietors' median age when they started their businesses was 36. As indicated in Table 2.2, the storefronts they owned at the time of the survey were the first business ventures for 78% of them, and they had owned their businesses a median number of five years at the time of our study. As indicated in Table 2.2, they invested a small amount of start-up capital into their shops, most of them in wholesale and retail stores (63%) or in services (33%). These storefronts were so small that nearly half of them relied exclusively on the proprietor or his/her family for labor. Another half hired anywhere between one and four employees. Still, because most small retail businesses falter after four or five years (Waldinger et al. 1990), it is reasonable to conclude that most proprietors in our sample were established.[24] Further, since they were only in their mid-40s at the time of the survey, the business owners and their firms had clear potential for further development.

Table 2.2   Characteristics of Mexican immigrants and their Los Angeles businesses

	All entrepreneurs %	N[a]
Demographic characteristics		
Female	51	109
Married	66	110
Median age at time of survey	43	108
Median age when opened business	36	108
Migration characteristics		
Median age at entry	19	107
Median years in the US at time of survey	26	110
Currently undocumented	7	110
Business type and history		
Wholesale and retail stores	63	111
Services (restaurants, hair salons, dry cleaners, welder services)	33	111
Other professional service	4	111
First business opened in US	78	111
Duration of business (median years)	5	111
Median hours a week spent on business	60	111
Start-up capital		
Mean start-up capital	$25,640	106
Median start-up capital	$15,000	106
Start-up capital acquired through:		
Personal savings or assets	70	110
Loan from relative or friend	6	110
Cundina, tanda, cooperativa	6	110
Credit cards or financial institution	8	110
Other type of loan	10	110
Business outcome: paid workers		
Mean paid workers	1.5	109
Median paid workers	1	109
Paid workers quartiles		
No employees	47	109
1–2 employees	27	109
3–4 employees	20	109
More than 5 employees	6	109

Source: Authors' survey of Mexican immigrant business owners in Los Angeles, 2007

Notes: [a]Some of our respondents skipped or refused to answer some questions resulting in varied sample sizes

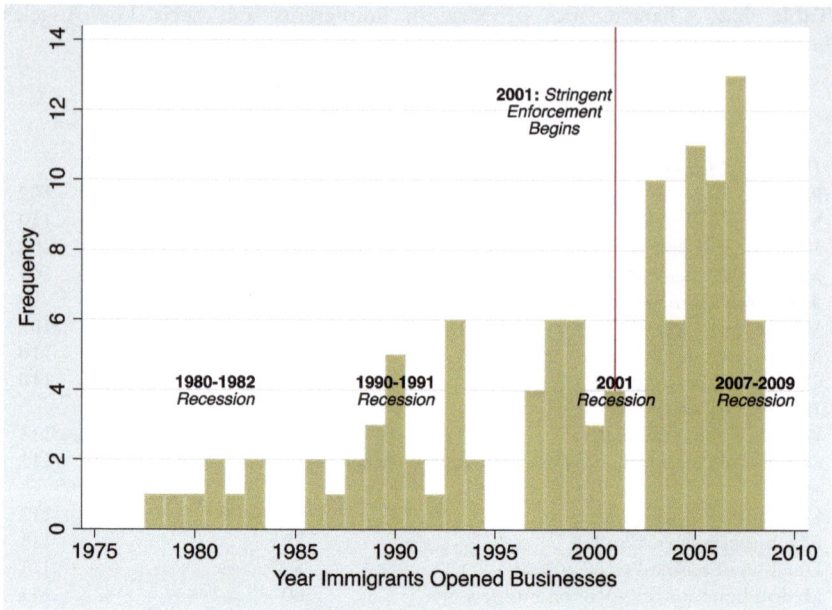

Fig. 2.2 Year immigrants opened businesses. (Source: Authors' tabulations of Mexican immigrant entrepreneurs in Los Angeles, 2007)

Figure 2.2 shows the year in which the immigrants in our sample opened their businesses. The first observation is that the timing of some of the small surges in the number of business start-ups loosely follows the significant national recessions that led to sustained job losses in Los Angeles County. Further, while the business start-ups in our sample follow the recessions of 1980–1982, 1990–1991, 2001,[25] and 2007–2009, they do so in variant ways. Specifically, whereas most businesses in our sample opened after the late 1980s, there is a sharp increase in business start-ups after 2001, the very period in which the immigration enforcement regime grew harshest. Independent research relying on the 2000 census points in the same direction as our observation about an increasing number of small businesses among immigrants at the turn of the twenty-first century (Pearce 2005: 1). Because the surges in business start-ups follow recessions and especially follow the implementation of the hardline immigration laws, we argue that our data are consistent with our blocked mobility hypothesis.

The skeptical reader might object that the increasing propensity for petty proprietorship at the start of the twenty-first century in Los Angeles is due to the greater availability of easy credit during that period. Our evidence shows that this is not the case, at least not among our survey respondents. Table 2.3 compares the ways in which the shopkeepers in our sample obtained their start-up capital by the decade in which they opened their businesses. As indicated in Table 2.3, the immigrants in our study overwhelmingly relied on their personal savings or assets to start their businesses and did so regardless of the decade in which they opened up their shops. Consequently, there are no (statistically significant) differences by decade in the way our respondents obtained their start-up capital. Although Table 2.3 does show a jump in the percentage of people using a credit card or turning to a financial institution for their start-up capital in the 2000s, 13% of 63 total possible cases for that decade refers to only eight people. To put this in perspective, the data in Table 2.3 show that when our respondents did borrow money for their start-up capital in the early 2000s, they were as likely to do so from friends and family as from

Table 2.3 Methods of obtaining start-up capital, by decade in which business opened, 110 entrepreneurs

Year	Personal savings or assets	Loan from a relative or friend	Cundina, tanda, cooperativa	Credit card or financial institution	Other type of loan	Total	N
1970s	100%	0%	0%	0%	0%	100%	2
1980s	69%	0%	8%	0%	23%	100%	13
1990s	78%	9%	3%	3%	6%	99%	32
2000s	65%	6%	6%	13%	10%	100%	63
Total count	77	7	6	9	11	100%	110
Pearson χ^2	9.51 (d.f. = 12)						

Source: Authors' survey of Mexican immigrant business owners in Los Angeles, 2007

Notes: $*p < 0.10$, $**p < 0.05$, $***p < 0.01$ (two-tailed tests), $^\wedge p < 0.10$ (one-tailed test). The total column may not add up to 100% due to rounding errors. In an analysis not presented here but easy to re-create with these data, we created a two by two contingency table. We did so to compare the acquisition of start-up capital during the three decades in the period 1970–1990 to the start-up capital acquisition methods of the 2000s. The columns only included the frequency counts of personal reliance on loans from credit cards or any other financial institution (so we excluded loans from friends, families, and *cundinas*). The results remained statistically insignificant because most people rely on their personal savings or assets for their start-up capital and do so irrespective of the decade

their credit card or a bank. This is because loans obtained through informal rotating credit associations—called *tandas* or *cundinas* in Mexico—are from people with whom borrowers have strong ties.[26] Thus, by adding the family and friends column to the *cundina/tandas* column (4 + 4 = 8 cases), we see that loans from people with whom the borrower has strong ties were as common (8/63) in the early 2000s as borrowing from credit cards and banks (8/63). The timing of easy credit, in short, is not an alternative explanation to our blocked mobility argument about why Mexican immigrants went into small business ownership in increasing numbers at the turn of the twenty-first century.

Another alternative explanation of our hypothesis might be that the surge in business ownership after 2001 (see Fig. 2.2) is nothing more than the reflection of the timing of our fieldwork. Recall that we surveyed proprietors of businesses in 2007 and 2008 (see Introduction.). The evidence in Table 2.4, however, makes it clear that the surge in small business ownership in the early 2000s is not a function of the timing of our survey. Table 2.4 specifically documents the migrants' subjective rationale for opening a business by the decade in which they did so. It shows that the most common rationale for going into small business ownership is usually to make more money. In and of itself, this response indicates clear aspirations for upward mobility. Nevertheless, other answers in the table suggest different levels of desperation and risk by decade. Importantly, the differences in motives by decade are statistically significant in Table 2.4. It is thus meaningful that the migrants in our study were roughly twice as likely to report feeling that they had no other option but to start a business in the 1980s and 2000s as compared to those who opened up storefronts in the 1990s. Perhaps more tellingly, far fewer migrants in our study reported either having experience in the specific trade or craft of their business or following a family tradition in the early 2000s, as compared to at any previous decade in our sample (excluding the 1970s, which only had two cases). Without prior direct experience with business or in the specific craft of their new trade, many migrants were essentially putting their start-up capital at great risk. We contend that they opted for this gamble because they felt unable to advance through the labor market.

Table 2.4, thus, strongly suggests that while the desire to make more money is usually one of the reasons that migrants open a small shop, the degree to which our respondents report having "no other option" or taking an occupational risk has varied historically, increasing in the 2000s as

Table 2.4 Reasons for starting business, by decade in which business opened, 111 entrepreneurs

Year	Make more money; better lifestyle; investment; retire early	Be own boss; spend time with family; better working conditions	Lost job; no other option; needed steady job; overcome obstacles	Had experience; all subject knows how to do	Family tradition	Give others job	Inspired by others	Total	N
1970s	100%	0%	0%	0%	0%	0%	0%	100%	2
1980s	0%	43%	21%	14%	14%	7%	0%	99%	14
1990s	47%	13%	9%	22%	6%	3%	0%	100%	32
2000s	43%	29%	19%	6%	0%	2%	2%	101%	63
Total count	44	28	18	13	4	3	1		111
Pearson χ^2	28.56** (d.f. = 18)								

Source: Authors' survey of 2007 Mexican immigrant business owners in Los Angeles

Notes: $*p < 0.10$, $**p < 0.05$, $***p < 0.01$ (two-tail tests), $^p < 0.10$ (one-tailed test). Total column may not add up to 100% due to rounding errors

compared to the 1990s. This is the very period that followed the implementation of the harsh immigration enforcement policies described earlier that made the lives of undocumented immigrants harder than at any previous point since the mid-1950s. To be sure, these punitive state policies trickled down even to the progressive city of Los Angeles, where local policies toward Mexican immigrants have been contradictory[27] and, at times, openly hostile.[28] In aggregate, therefore, our findings support the blocked mobility hypothesis according to which Mexican immigrants responded to labor market obstacles by going into storefront proprietorship.

Our observations in this chapter are comparable to Bohn and Lofstrom's (2013), who found that self-employment among less-skilled men doubled after the passage of the 2007 Legal Arizona Workers Act, a law that prohibited businesses from knowingly hiring unauthorized immigrants and required employers to use the E-verify system. We thus conclude that in response to their blocked labor market opportunities, Mexican immigrants self-employ.[29] As Kanas et al. put it about low skill immigrants in the Netherlands, "self-employment provides the second-best solution for immigrants who are at risk of unemployment and poverty" (2009: 203). Our respondents, however, went a step further than self-employment. After they legalized their immigration status (see Chap. 6) and raised sufficient start-up capital, they opened small storefront businesses in Latino neighborhoods. They did so not just to survive, but as a strategic effort to break out of poverty.

CONCLUSION

This chapter demonstrates that many Mexicans, like other immigrants arriving in different historical periods, now increasingly respond to their blocked mobility by opting for small business ownership. Our findings are noteworthy because historically Mexicans did not engage in storefront proprietorship in large numbers (in the US), despite their many decades of immigration (see Valdez 2011: 43; Logan et al. 2003; Bates 1997; Waldinger et al. 1990). Although a large number of Mexican immigrants have historically been self-employed as domestics, babysitters, gardeners, day laborers, and the like, only a small percentage had previously engaged in business ownership. If they tended to eschew shopkeeping in the past, they did so because so many were engaged in circular migration. Moreover, the more permanently settled low-skill immigrants preferred the stability of decently paid jobs, especially the union jobs in heavy industry that offered significant benefits, like health insurance. However, the new enforcement regime dramatically changed migration patterns and did so in the context of economic restructuring. Both sets of dynamics contributed to worsening experiences in the labor market because the caging effects of hardline immigration policies led to the growth in the ranks of the undocumented, as well as greater animus toward them. Intensified racist attitudes framing "illegals" as potentially violent "criminals" led to what George Simmel describes as social distancing. In the labor market, greater discrimination swelled the ranks of low-skilled immigrants looking for work. These combined changes resulted in lower wages and ever-greater social marginalization of all Mexican immigrants, whether legal or undocumented and irrespective of their educational level, work experience, and English-language ability.

Although we do not have granular historical evidence to indicate the exact magnitude of change in storefront ownership over time, here we simply report that many more Mexican immigrants now follow the pattern of poor immigrants from other countries who engaged entrepreneurship in response to their blocked mobility. As many of the immigrants in our sample stated, they went into business because they felt that they had no other option, though others put it positively by stating that they wanted to make more money. Our blocked mobility argument, therefore, is not just theoretical. Our respondents could not have been clearer about their rationale for going into business: their stated reasons point to blocked mobility. In what follows, we assess the conditions under which some of their small neighborhood shops perform better than others do.

Notes

1. According to Dreby, as of 2010, millions of people live in mixed-status families where one or more member is unauthorized. Consequently, millions of families live with the stress that someone in their family could be, or is already, deported (2015: 5).
2. As of 2015, the largest group of Asian immigrants is from China, and they comprise roughly 2.6 million immigrants. Immigrants from India comprise nearly 2.4 million people. See http://www.pewhispanic.org/2017/05/03/facts-on-u-s-immigrants-current-data/

3. The treaty of Guadalupe Hidalgo signed in 1848 ended the Mexican American War in which Mexico lost California, Arizona, New Mexico, Texas, as well as parts of Nevada, Utah, Wyoming, and Colorado.

4. According to Massey, though the population from Mexico had nearly quadrupled (to 739,000) in the period 1907–1930, it was still small, at less than 1 million people. Still, because Mexicans were regionally concentrated in the Southwest, they became a noticeable minority in the context of the Depression (Massey 2009).

5. Although the Bracero program ended in 1964, Braceros continued to enter the US until 1968.

6. The 1965 Act was progressive insofar as it abolished the rule about national origins quotas. However, Latin Americans did not benefit from the 1965 Act since the original national origins quotas never included countries from Western Hemisphere. Mexicans, in short, did not benefit from the elimination of national quotas.

7. See Jacobson (2008: xxii) and García (1980).

8. In fact, apprehensions along the US-Mexico border spiked in 1986 as migrants attempted to enter the US to apply for amnesty (Bansak et al. 2015).

9. Legal immigrant children, refugees, and asylees, as well as some groups of immigrants who had been trafficked or who had experienced domestic abuse, were exempted from the five-year bar. Congress also authorized states to extend means-tested benefits to some post-enactment immigrants who would otherwise have been barred from the benefits.

10. For a sense of the magnitude, consider that 350,000 migrants were in detention centers in 2009, and many of the detained appeared to be victims of excessive force (whether by local police or federal authorities), according to Donato and Armenta (2011: 534).

11. A report prepared for Congress concurs, though the author frames the rise of deportations (removals) as a "high consequence outcome." In her words, "Historically, immigration agents permitted most Mexicans apprehended at the border to voluntarily return to Mexico without any penalty. Since 2005, CBP [Customs and Border Patrol] has limited voluntary returns in favor of three types of 'high consequence' outcomes" (Argueta 2016: 7). The new penalties include but are not limited to the following: (1) formal removal; (2) criminal charges for those who cross the border without permission; and (3) remote repatriation.

12. Massey and Pren (2012) point out that Mexicans constituted the vast majority of the people removed (deported) since the Patriot Act as of 2009 even though no one from Mexico has ever been involved in an act of terrorism against the US (p. 8).

13. To be clear, we are not arguing that the racism that Mexicans and their descendants face is without historical precedent. The racism against the 50,000 or so people living in Mexico's lost territories was real, as was the prejudice directed against immigrants and their descendants in subsequent decades. For a sample of the scholarly literature tracing the history of anti-Mexican hostility, see Grebler et al. (1970), Mazon (1984), Bean and Tienda (1987), Zamora (1993), De Leon (1993), Sanchez (1995), Gutierrez (1995), Dunn (1996), Andreas (2000), Chavez (2001), and Molina (2014). What we do argue is that because racist ideas are constructs, they change. In the case of Mexicans, racist tropes about them have become more alarming since the late 1980s and 1990s.

14. See, De Genova (2005: 246–247 and Chap. 3), Jacobson (2008), Romero (2008), as well as Sáenz and Douglas (2015).

15. A legal injunction blocked its implementation before the federal court ruling.

16. See Lowell et al. (1995), Donato et al. (2008), Bansak and Raphael (2001), and Orrenius and Zavodny (2009).

17. See Hall et al. (2010) as well as Donato and Massey (1993).

18. Before Los Angeles restructured its economy, Mexican immigrants found blue-collar jobs in the city's robust manufacturing and construction sectors. Los Angeles manufactured such durable goods as steel, auto, and rubber production until auto plants and tire factories closed in the 1970s and 1980s; the aerospace industry shut down in the first half of the 1990s.

19. As noted, many families constitute mixed-status households. In many cases, this means that US-born children (who automatically obtain birthright citizenship) have one or more undocumented parents.

20. For the gendered way in which families fear and experience deportations, see Dreby (2015).

21. Their businesses generated $3.5 billion or 45.6% of all self-employed income in Los Angeles (self-employed Mexican immigrants created $801 million).   See   http://www.newamericaneconomy.org/wp-content/uploads/2017/02/LA_Brief_V8.pdf

22. See the joint study "New Americans in Los Angeles, A Snapshot of the Demographic and Economic Contributions of Immigrants in Los Angeles County and the City of Los Angeles," from the New American Economy, the City of Los Angeles, and the Los Angeles Chamber of Commerce at http://www.newamericaneconomy.org/wp-content/uploads/2017/03/LA.pdf. The category general services includes personal services (e.g. laundry services, barbershops, and repair and maintenance), religious organizations, social services, labor unions, etc.

23. The size of our sample (N) varies slightly from one variable to the next in Table 2.2 because some respondents did not answer a specific question or

the question was not applicable to their situation (e.g., questions regarding legal status).

24. About two-thirds of young businesses survive the first two years of their existence and about 50% fail within the first five years. This is true irrespective of business sector. See https://www.sba.gov/sites/default/files/Business-Survival.pdf

25. Mary Daly and Fred Furlong published an "FRBSF Economic Letter" for the Federal Reserve Bank of San Francisco, which argued that jobs did not systematically decline in Southern California until September of 2001.

26. Ivan Light has written extensively on the importance of rotating credit associations for Asian immigrant entrepreneurs (Light 1972; Light and Rosenstein 1995; Light and Gold 2000). Rotating credit associations are called "hui" in Chinese, "kye" in Korean, or "tanomoshi" in Japanese.

27. To illustrate the contradictions, although the Los Angeles Police Department has a tolerant stance toward all of the city's denizens, the Los Angeles Sheriff's Department follows some of the U.S.'s more punitive policy trends. In 2005, Los Angeles County became the first county in California to sign a Memorandum of Understanding with ICE to implement the 287(g) program (Alarcon et al. 2016). This agreement between county authorities and ICE allowed specially trained sheriff's deputies to verify the immigration status of people in county jails to determine whether such inmates are deportable. At the same time, however, the Los Angeles Police Department (LAPD) has long worked under a 1979 rule (Special Order 40) prohibiting the LAPD from initiating contact with people solely to investigate their immigration status (Alarcon et al. 2016: 192). Neither does the LAPD turn people over to federal agents if they have committed minor offenses (Mather and Chang, L.A. Times November 14, 2016). The LAPD's stance calms unauthorized immigrants' fears about deportation and has resulted in greater communication between police and immigrants (Alarcon et al. 2016). Also, despite a long history of intolerance toward street vendors, the Los Angeles City Council passed an ordinance in 2008 requiring that home improvement retailers ensure a safe and orderly space (shade, restrooms, garbage cans) for day laborers to gather when they open new stores (Alarcon et al. 2016).

28. On the hostility toward street vendors who are predominantly unauthorized immigrants from Mexico and Central America, see Alarcon et al. (2016).

29. On the self-employment of low-skill immigrants in the Netherlands whose mobility options are blocked, see Kanas et al. (2009).

REFERENCES

Alarcon, Rafael, Luis Escala, and Olga Odgers. 2016. *Making Los Angeles Home: The Integration of Mexican Immigrants in the United States*. Berkeley: University of California Press.

Amuedo-Dorantes, Catalina, and Cynthia Bansak. 2012. The Labor Market Impact of Mandated Employment. *American Economic Review: Papers & Proceedings* 102 (3): 543–548.

———. 2014. Employment Verification Mandates and the Labor Market of Likely Unauthorized and Native Workers. *Contemporary Economic Policy* 32 (3): 671–680.

Andreas, Peter. 2000. *Border Games: Policing the US–Mexico Divide*. Ithaca: Cornell University Press.

Argueta, Carla N. 2016. *Border Security: Immigration Enforcement Between Ports of Entry*. Congressional Research Service Report Prepared for Members and Committees of Congress 7-5700. www.crs.gov R42138.

Bansak, Cynthia, and Steven Raphael. 2001. Immigration Reform and the Earnings of Latino Worker: Do Employer Sanctions Cause Discrimination? *Industrial and Labor Relations Review* 54 (2): 275–295.

Bansak, Cynthia, Nicole Simpson, and Madeline Zavodny. 2015. *The Economics of Immigration*. New York: Routledge.

Bates, Timothy. 1997. *Race, Self-Employment and Upward Mobility: An Illusive American Dream*. Washington, DC: Woodrow Wilson Center Press.

Bean, Frank D., and Marta Tienda. 1987. *The Hispanic Population of the United States*. New York: Russell Sage Foundation.

Bean, Frank D., Barry Edmonston, and Jeffrey S. Passel, eds. 1990. *Undocumented Migration to the United States: IRCA and the Experience of the 1980s*. New York: Urban Institute Press.

Bohn, Sarah, and Magnus Lofstrom. 2013. Employment Effects of State Legislation. In *Immigration, Poverty, and Socioeconomic Inequality*, ed. David Card and Steven Raphael, 282–314. New York: Russell Sage.

Chavez, Leo R. 2001. *Covering Immigration: Population Images and the Politics of the Nation*. Berkeley: University of California Press.

Craig, Richard B. 1971. *The Bracero Program: Interest Groups and Foreign Policy*. Austin: University of Texas Press.

De Genova, Nicholas. 2005. *Working the Boundaries: Race, Space and "Illegality" in Mexican Chicago*. Durham/London: Duke University Press.

De Leon, Arnoldo. 1993. *Mexican Americans in Texas: A Brief History*. Wheeling: Harlan Davidson.

Donato, Katharine M., and Amada Armenta. 2011. What We Know About Unauthorized Migration. *Annual Review of Sociology* 37: 529–543.

Donato, Katharine M., and Douglas S. Massey. 1993. Effects of the Immigration Reform and Control Act on the Wages of Mexican Migrants. *Social Science Quarterly* 74 (3): 523–541.

Donato, Katharine M., Chizuko Wakabayashi, Shirin Hakimzadeh, and Amada Armenta. 2008. Shifts in the Employment Conditions of Mexican Migrant Men and Women: The Effect of U.S. Immigration Policy. *Work and Occupations* 35 (4): 462–495.

Dreby, Joanna. 2015. *Everyday Illegal: When Policies Undermine Immigrant Families*. Oakland: University of California Press.

Dunn, Timothy J. 1996. *The Militarization of the U.S.–Mexico Border, 1978–1992: Low-Intensity Conflict Doctrine Comes Home*. Austin: Center for Mexican American Studies, University of Texas at Austin.

Durand, Jorge, and Douglas S. Massey. 2003. The Costs of Contradiction: U.S. Border Policy 1986–2000. *Latino Studies* 1 (2): 233–252.

Ellingwood, Ken. 2004. *Hard Line: Life and Death on the U.S.-Mexico Border*. New York: Pantheon Books.

Galarza, Ernesto. 1978 (1964). *Merchants of Labor: The Mexican Bracero Story*. Santa Barbara: McNally and Loftin, West.

García, Juan Ramon. 1980. *Operation Wetback: The Mass Deportation of Mexican Undocumented Workers in 1954*. Westport: Greenwood Press.

Gentsch, Kerstin, and Douglas S. Massey. 2011. Labor Market Outcomes for Legal Mexican Immigrants Under the New Regime of Immigration Enforcement. *Social Science Quarterly* 92 (3): 875–893.

Gonzalez-Barrera, Ana, and Jens Manuel Krogstad. 2017. *What We Know About Illegal Immigration from Mexico*. Pew Hispanic Research Center. http://www.pewresearch.org/fact-tank/2017/03/02/what-we-know-about-illegal-immigration-from-mexico/

Grebler, Leo, Joan W. Moore, and Ralph C. Guzman. 1970. *The Mexican American People: The Nation's Second Largest Minority*. London: Free Press/Macmillan.

Gutierrez, David G. 1995. *Walls and Mirrors: Mexican Americans, Mexican Immigrants, and the Politics of Ethnicity*. Berkeley: University of California Press.

Hall, Matthew, Emily Greenman, and George Farkas. 2010. Legal Status and Wage Disparities for Mexican Immigrants. *Social Forces* 89 (2): 491–514.

Hanson, Gordon. 2009. *The Economics and Policy of Illegal Immigration in the United States*. Migration Policy Institute Report. http://www.migrationpolicy.org/research/economics-and-policy-illegal-immigration-united-states

Hopkins, Daniel J. 2010. Politicized Places: Explaining Where and When Immigrants Provoke Local Opposition. *American Political Science Review* 104: 40–60.

Huntington, Samuel P. 2004. *Who Are We? The Challenges to America's National Identity*. New York: Simon and Schuster.

Jacobson, Robin Dale. 2008. *The New Nativism: Proposition 187 and the Debate Over Immigration*. Minneapolis: University of Minessota Press.

Jargowsky, Paul A. 2009. Immigrants and Neighborhoods of Concentrated Poverty: Assimilation or Stagnation? *Journal of Ethnic and Migration Studies* 35: 1129–1151.

Kanas, Agnieszka, Frank van Tubergen, and Tanja van der Lippe. 2009. Immigrant Self-Employment: Testing Hypotheses About the Role of Origin- and Host-Country Human Capital and Bonding and Bridging Social Capital. *Work and Occupations* 36 (3): 181–208.

Kilgore, James. 2015. *Understanding Mass Incarceration: A People's Guide to the Key Civil Rights Struggle of Our Time*. New York: The New Press.

Kitroeff, Natalie, and Victoria Kim. 2017. Behind a $13 Shirt, a $6-an-Hour Worker: How Forever 21 and Other Retailers Avoid Liability for Factories that Underpay Workers to Sew Their Clothes. *Los Angeles Times*, August 31.

Krogstad, Jens Manuel. 2016. *10 Facts for National Hispanic Heritage Month*. Pew Hispanic Research Center. http://www.pewresearch.org/fact-tank/2016/09/15/facts-for-national-hispanic-heritage-month/

Light, Ivan. 1972. *Ethnic Enterprise in America: Business and Welfare Among Chinese, Japanese, and Blacks*. Berkeley: University of California Press.

Light, Ivan, and Steven J. Gold. 2000. *Ethnic Economies*. San Diego: Academic Press.

Light, Ivan, and Elizabeth Roach. 1996. Self-Employment: Mobility Ladder or Economic Lifeboat? In *Ethnic Los Angeles*, ed. Roger Waldinger and Mehdi Bozorgmehr, 193–214. New York: Russell Sage Foundation.

Light, Ivan, and Carolyn Rosenstein. 1995. *Race, Ethnicity, and Entrepreneurship in Urban America*. New York: Aldine De Gruyter.

Logan, John R., Richard D. Alba, and Brian J. Stults. 2003. Enclaves and Entrepreneurs: Assessing the Payoff for Immigrants and Minorities. *International Migration Review* 37 (2): 344–388.

Lopez, Mary, and Dolores Trevizo. 2009. Mexican Immigrant Entrepreneurship in Los Angeles: An Analysis of the Determinants of Entrepreneurial Outcomes. In *An American Story: Mexican American Entrepreneurship and Wealth Creation*, ed. John Sibley Butler, Alfonso Morales, and David L. Torres, 127–149. West Lafayette: Purdue University Press.

Lowell, B. Lindsay, Jay D. Teachman, and Zhongren Jing. 1995. Unintended Consequences of Immigration Reform: Discrimination and Hispanic Employment. *Demography* 32 (4): 617–628.

Marcelli, Enrico A. 2004. The Institution of Unauthorized Residency Status, Neighborhood Context, and Mexican Immigrant Earnings in Los Angeles

County. In *The Institutionalist Tradition in Labor Economics*, ed. Dell P. Champlin and Janet T. Knoedler. Armonk: M.E. Sharpe.

Martos, Sofia D. 2010. Coded Codes: Discriminatory Intent, Modern Political Mobilization, and Local Immigration Ordinances. *New York University Law Reivew* 85: 2099–2137.

Massey, Douglas S. 2007. *Categorically Unequal. The American Stratification System*. New York: Russell Sage Foundation.

———. 2009. Racial Formation in Theory and Practice: The Case of Mexicans in the United States. *Race Social Problems* 1: 12–26.

Massey, Douglas S., and Karen A. Pren. 2012. Unintended Consequences of U.S. Immigration Policy: Explaining the Post-1965 Surge from Latin America. *Population Development Review* 38 (1): 1–29.

Massey, Douglas S., Jorge Durand, and Nolan J. Malone. 2002. *Beyond Smoke and Mirrors: Mexican Immigration in an Era of Economic Integration*. New York: Russell Sage Foundation.

Mazon, Mauricio. 1984. *The Zoot-Suit Riots: The Psychology of Symbolic Annihilation*. Austin: Austin University Press.

Molina, Natalia. 2014. *How Race Is Made in America: Immigration, Citizenship, and the Historical Power of Racial Scripts*. Berkeley: University of California Press.

Nguyen, Mai, and Hannah Gill. 2015. Interior Immigration Enforcement: The Impacts of Expanding Local Law Enforcement Authority. *Urban Studies*: 1–22. https://doi.org/10.1177/0042098014563029.

Orrenius, Pia M. 2001. Illegal Immigration and Enforcement Along the U.S.-Mexico Border: An Overview. *Federal Reserve Bank of Dallas Economic and Financial Review*, Qtr. 1.

Orrenius, Pia M., and Madeline Zavodny. 2009. The Effects of Tougher Enforcement on the Job Prospects of Recent Latin American Immigrants. *Journal of Policy Analysis and Management* 28 (20): 239–257.

Ortiz, Vilma. 1996. The Mexican-Origin Population: Permanent Working Class or Emerging Middle Class? In *Ethnic Los Angeles*, ed. Roger Waldinger and Mehdi Bozorghmehr, 247–278. New York: Russell Sage Foundation.

Passel, Jeffrey S., and D'Vera Cohn. 2009. *A Portrait of Unauthorized Immigrants in the United States*. Washington, DC: Pew Hispanic Center, Research Report. http://assets.pewresearch.org/wp-content/uploads/sites/7/reports/107.pdf

Pastor, Manuel, and Rhonda Ortiz. 2009. *Immigrant Integration in Los Angeles: Strategic Directions for Funders*. Program for Environmental and Regional Equity, and Center for the Study of Immigrant Integration. Los Angeles: University of Southern California (USC). Report found at http://dornsife.usc.edu/assets/sites/731/docs/immigrant_integration.pdf

Pastor, Manuel, Rhonda Ortiz, Vanessa Carter, Justin Scoggins, and Anthony Perez. 2012. *California Immigrant Integration Scorecard*. Center for the Study of Immigrant Integration.

Pearce, Susan C. 2005. Today's Immigrant Woman Entrepreneur. *Immigration Policy In Focus* 4:1. Washington, DC: Immigration Policy Center.

Provine, Doris Marie, and Monica W. Varsanyi. 2012. Scaled Down: Perspectives on State and Local Creation and Enforcement of Immigration Law: Introduction to Special Issue of Law and Policy. *Law and Policy* 34 (2): 105–112.

Rivera-Batiz, Francisco L. 1999. Undocumented Workers in the Labor Market: An Analysis of the Earnings of Legal and Illegal Mexican Immigrants in the United States. *Journal of Population Economics* 12 (1): 91–116.

Romero, Mary. 2008. Crossing the Immigration and Race Border: A Critical Race Theory Approach to Immigration Studies. *Contemporary Justice Review* 11 (1): 23–37.

Rugh, Jacob S., and Douglas S. Massey. 2014. Segregation in Post-Civil Rights America: Stalled Integration or End of the Segregated Century. *DuBois Review: Social Science Research on Race* 11 (2): 205–232.

Sáenz, Rogelio, and Karen Manges Douglas. 2015. A Call for the Racialization of Immigration Studies: On the Transition of Ethnic Immigrants to Racialized Immigrants. *Sociology of Race and Ethnicity* 1 (1): 166–180.

Sanchez, George J. 1995. *Becoming Mexican American: Ethnicity, Culture, and Identity in Chicano Los Angeles, 1900–1945*. New York: Oxford University Press.

Stumpf, Juliet. 2006. The Crimmigration Crisis: Immigrants, Crime, and Sovereign Power. *American University Law Review* 56 (2): 367–419.

Tienda, Marta, and Norma Fuentes. 2014. Hispanics in Metropolitan American: New Realities and Old Debates. *Annual Review of Sociology* 40: 499–520.

Valdez, Zulema. 2011. *The New Entrepreneurs: How Race, Class, and Gender Shape American Enterprise*. Stanford: Stanford University Press.

Varsanyi, Monica W. 2008. Immigration Policing Through the Backdoor: City Ordinances, the 'Right to the City,' and the Exclusion of Undocumented Day Laborers. *Urban Geography* 29 (1): 29–52.

Waldinger, Roger. 1999. Not the Promised City: Los Angeles and Its Immigrants. *Pacific Historical Review* 68 (2): 253–272.

Waldinger, Roger, Howard Aldrich, and Robin Ward. 1990. *Ethnic Entrepreneurs: Immigrant Business in Industrial Societies*. Newbury Park: Sage.

Wilkes, Rima, and John Iceland. 2004. Hypersegregation in the Twenty-First Century: An Update and Analysis. *Demography* 4: 23–36.

Wong, Tom K. 2012. 287(g) and the Politics of Interior Immigration Control in the United States: Explaining Local Cooperation with Federal Immigration Authorities. *Journal of Ethnic and Migration Studies* 38 (5): 737–756.

Zamora, Emilio. 1993. *The World of the Mexican Worker in Texas*. College Station: Texas A&M University Press.

CHAPTER 3

Re-producing Economic Inequality Across the US-Mexican Border

Introduction

This chapter explores how neighborhood poverty in Los Angeles affects the business outcomes of Mexican immigrant entrepreneurs in our sample. We demonstrate that neighborhood poverty impinges on business performance, preventing small proprietors from advancing along one of the most established pathways of immigrant upward mobility. Our findings that the spatial concentration of poverty undermines the viability of small businesses is consistent with the burgeoning literature showing that neighborhoods are powerful meso-level mechanisms by which class inequalities are reproduced over time. Yet, while many of these studies find that the spatial concentration of disadvantage or, at the opposite extreme, privilege creates dynamics and conditions that reproduce inequality over time (Wilson 1987; Newman and Massengill 2006; Massey and Brodmann 2014), few studies have focused on how neighborhoods affect the business outcomes of small shopkeepers.

Our focus on neighborhoods does not ignore the differences between the individual shopkeepers in our study. A second finding of this chapter is that some families informally endow their children with what Jan O. Jonsson et al. (2009) call "occupation specific cultural capital," and they do so in ways that yield future benefits, even across international borders. This line of argumentation follows Pierre Bourdieu (1984) who argued that various kinds of cultural resources acquired early and informally

© The Author(s) 2018   55
D. Trevizo, M. Lopez, *Neighborhood Poverty and Segregation
in the (Re-)Production of Disadvantage*,
https://doi.org/10.1007/978-3-319-73715-7_3

from the family have specific exchange values that can, in the right context, convert to financial capital (and, for some, even power). As Bourdieu observes, informally acquired cultural resources are not only more general than human capital (i.e., formal educational attainment and work experience),[1] but cultural capital develops and operates as reflexes, or dispositions (See Bourdieu 1984). Our chapter builds on Bourdieu's theory by showing that as adult immigrants living in a host society, those endowed with the cultural capital of small-scale entrepreneurs by their parents perform better in business than shopkeepers whose parents were not entrepreneurs. That microclass differences in cultural capital as structured by *pre-migration experiences* in the family can be consequential across borders has implications for stratification theory. Specifically, as our analysis accounts for start-up capital and educational attainment, we demonstrate that class reproduction is not reducible to the volume of available financial resources. Nor are such forms of human capital as the level of formal educational attainment and work-related skills the only other types of class resources. Further, by virtue of studying immigrants who do not have easy access to their family's business networks in the sending country, our research highlights the role of cultural inheritance in the microclass reproduction of petty proprietors in another country.

This chapter, in short, documents two different types of class effects: those that result from pre-migration microclass cultural dispositions and those that result from the meso-level neighborhood dynamics of the migrant's host country. Both sets of factors affect the business performance of immigrant shopkeepers in distinct communities. To make our case about these two distinct types of class effects, we first describe a variety of self-employment situations among Mexico's poor. Next, we define microclass cultural capital, the conceptual cornerstone of our first hypothesis, before describing the concentrated disadvantage argument about impoverished neighborhoods. Our empirical section then addresses our central questions about whether variations in microclass cultural capital and whether variation at aggregate levels of neighborhood poverty within Los Angeles matter to the business performance of Mexican immigrant entrepreneurs.

SELF-EMPLOYMENT IN MEXICO

Although Mexico is now a middle-income country with a comparatively large economy, its history of gross income inequality has been an important factor in mass emigration to the US.[2] With about half of over 121 million people living in poverty,[3] the sheer size of Mexico's poor means that they are unequally disadvantaged.[4] Further, whether for mere survival or as a way out of poverty, many poor people adopt entrepreneurial strategies in the informal economy. As a result, Mexico has a very high self-employment rate of 32%, among the highest of OECD countries as of 2014.[5]

The large number of low-skill, self-employed people in Mexico adds complexity to the class locations of both the urban and the rural poor. Among the under-educated urban poor, a non-exhaustive list of self-employed people would include street performers; street vendors of food, wares, or personal services (manicures/pedicures and massages); small shopkeepers; and the like. Even poor rural folk have varying degrees of experience in buying and selling surplus crops on the market. Further, many small peasants—even those with only usufruct rights to parcels on collective land—have some experience with renting land parcels.[6] It follows that at least some low-skill migrants have had direct experiences with various kinds of self-employment and even small business ownership in their childhoods in Mexico.

THE SCHOLARSHIP ON CULTURAL CAPITAL AND CONCENTRATED DISADVANTAGE

The Pre-migration Transmission of an Entrepreneurial Disposition (A Form of Cultural Capital)

Jan O. Jonsson et al. (2009) argue that specific occupations located within broader, big-class categories, are microclasses that develop, sustain, and transfer their own forms of cultural capital. Therefore, in addition to human capital (educational attainment and work-related skills), financial resources, and specific social networks and opportunities, people also transfer to their children what they call "occupation-specific cultural capital" (Jonsson et al. 2009: 988). These cultural dispositions manifest as *occupation-specific* cultural tastes, judgments, and aspirations. They are not, in other words, national cultural values or categorical (and, therefore, essentializing) cultural traits of entire ethnic groups.[7] Just as there exist identifiable occupation-specific tastes, judgments, and dispositions among, say, university professors, engineers, car mechanics, and plumbers (Jonsson et al. 2009), so such forms of cultural capital also exist among small-scale entrepreneurs.

Not only are specific occupations important conduits of class reproduction across generations (Jonsson et al. 2009: 1019), but the microclass cultural capital that they generate also contributes to the mobility or immobility of the employee's children. In theory, this should be true in Mexico, irrespective of whether the occupations are associated with poor, middle, or wealthy classes. Put differently, the theory of cultural capital applied to microclasses would predict that the children of Mexico's poor do not have identical "propensities for mobility or immobility" (Jonsson et al. 2009: 983). Jonsson et al. explain that microclass differences in the opportunity for mobility or in immobility result from the fact that "the distinctive occupational worlds into which children are born have consequences for the aspirations they develop, the skills they value and to which they have access, and the networks upon which they can draw" (2009: 983). Therefore, what eventual occupations people occupy in a stratification system will partly depend on the microclass locations of their parents.

Research certainly shows that having entrepreneurial parents correlates with the tendency to self-employ.[8] Further, while research indicates a strong positive relationship between the educational attainment of entrepreneurs, especially the college educated among them, and firm prosperity,[9] many studies demonstrate that the children of entrepreneurs have unique advantages in business. Specifically, the children of entrepreneurs have some access to their entrepreneurial parents' financial resources; they also have "easy access" to their parents' business networks.[10] In addition, Fairlie and Robb document that "prior work experience in a family member's business has an independent effect on small business outcomes, which may in part be due to the acquisition of less formal or more general *business human capital*" (2007: 242 emphasis ours; see also Wyrwich 2015; Hoffman et al. 2015). Their argument clearly follows the human capital theory that emphasizes that skills acquired on the job— whether in the home or host country—in addition to formal educational attainment, matter for the success of small businesses.[11] The established scholarship, in short, clearly demonstrates that the businesses of children of entrepreneurs benefit from the material resources, the social networks, and the human capital advantages directly provided or facilitated by their entrepreneurial parents.[12]

Relying on Pierre Bourdieu's notion of cultural capital, we suggest yet another channel for the business advantage of second-generation entrepreneurs. Specifically, we suspect that even people without a college education or even without much of an extensive work history in the family business may still have some entrepreneurial advantages as compared to people without self-employed parents. Parental self-employment, and specifically small business ownership, offers opportunities for the acquisition of occupation-specific cultural capital through informal but intimate and quotidian cultural transfers. The notion of an intuitive business "know-how" allows us to capture some aspects of this type of cultural capital, one which begins to develop when children overhear their entrepreneurial parents "talk shop" or when they observe their parents' transactions with customers or suppliers. Neither formally credentialed nor easy to measure, this entrepreneurial disposition develops through early familial exposure to business, so it develops as a mere "feel for the game" (Bourdieu 1984: 114; Bourdieu and Wacquant 1992: 128–35). This intuitive feel could include, for example, being comfortable with risk taking and haggling; it might include the ability to imagine and then pursue market opportunities in just about any circumstance.[13] Developing this kind of entrepreneurial orientation or proclivity is not only less formal than the education or work-related skills conceptualized as human capital, it is frequently a pre-conscious type of tacit knowledge. It is, in other words, a reflexive disposition that people carry with them wherever they go, even to distant lands where they may live as unwelcome migrants.

We offer an empirical example of this business disposition from Alfonso Morales's (2009) interviews with Mexican immigrant vendors in Chicago. Morales's interview subject, Cecilia, was a successful entrepreneur who recalls that she began learning about buying and selling from her father who gathered firewood and sold it as charcoal from their family home in Mexico. She reported being only seven years old when her father showed her how to weigh charcoal and "from that age, I started selling and to learn about business" (quoted in Morales 2009: 114). Decades later, as an immigrant in Chicago, Cecilia reported seeing sales opportunities in various settings, including at the factory in which she first worked for an hourly wage. According to Morales, Cecilia reported the following story:

> When I first arrived in the United States I was working in the factories (in the middle 1960s) and one of the first things that I sold was lunches in the factories...I would take about thirty lunches a day.... Later, I asked a neighbor who owned a store to sell me a box of oranges and a box of tomatoes. And I would get up early to sell bags of oranges and tomatoes for a dollar and I would stand in front of the door of the factory where I worked and there I would sell them all. (Cecilia, as documented by Morales 2009: 114)

As Morales explains, Cecilia became successful, ultimately leaving wage employment, because of her "entrepreneurial spirit" (2009: 116).Though Max Weber used the notion of an "entrepreneurial spirit," we suggest that the notion of an entrepreneurial disposition is a more precise way of capturing individual-level action, such as Cecilia's. Because of her entrepreneurial cultural capital, she proactively pursued business opportunities in places that would seem unlikely to most people (Morales 2009: 116). Cecilia's entrepreneurial disposition allowed her to imagine a business opportunity among factory workers in Chicago, a place far from her family's business networks in Mexico. Consequently, her first step was to turn to neighbors in Chicago for her initial investments.

Since our survey asked respondents whether their parents were business owners, we can gauge whether those who answered affirmatively differed from those who answered negatively. For example, our data allow us to address whether their motivations for starting a business or their method of obtaining start-up capital differed according to their parents' experiences with small business enterprise. More importantly, given this chapter's focus on business outcomes, we can also determine whether those whose parents are business owners in Mexico have a competitive business advantage in Los Angeles, as suggested by Bourdieu's cultural capital theory. Having business advantages in another country would offer empirical support for arguments about microclass cultural capital, given that our respondents would not—as immigrants in Los Angeles—have had access to the full range of their parents' business networks in Mexico. Further, given that the median age of the immigrants in our study was 19 when they moved to the US, it is fair to assume that those whose parents are entrepreneurs had not had extensive worker or administrative roles in their family's business. In fact, of the 14 respondents who answered the question about whether they had worked in their parents' businesses, 11 said that they had not. Only three respondents said that they worked in their parents business in Mexico, which means that most would have acquired general business knowledge in early childhood or in adolescence. Therefore, significant differences between the business performances of the two groups could indicate the existence of less formal forms of occupation-specific cultural capital among the petty entrepreneurs in our sample. Further, our regression analysis controls for human and financial capital advantages by controlling for levels of education as well as the amounts of start-up capital that our respondents used to start their businesses in Los Angeles. Therefore, whether their parents sold surplus crops, urban street wares, or retail goods from small shops, some Mexican immigrants in our sample may have informally acquired intuitive business "know-how" prior to their emigration in a way that yields benefits in Los Angeles. Our first hypothesis follows:

Hypothesis 1: *Mexican immigrant shopkeepers in Los Angeles will do better in business if at least one parent was self-employed in Mexico (net of education and start-up capital).*

Disadvantaged Neighborhoods Post-migration

If, as Bourdieu argues, cultural capital can convert to material rewards, it does so differently depending on the national and local socio-political-economic contexts, as well as the specific field in which people put their cultural resources into play.[14] As documented in the previous chapter, the national socio-political and economic contexts in the US, including in Los Angeles County, have been especially hard on Mexican immigrants since the late 1990s.[15] We have seen how hardening immigration policies worsened poverty among all Mexican immigrants, including those with the legal right to live and work in the US. The caging effects as well as the massive and rapid influx of newly arrived compatriots increased competition for low-skill jobs, deflating wages for other low-skill immigrants, but especially so for the undocumented.[16] The situation has been especially dire in Los Angeles, a city that is home to more undocumented people than anywhere else in the US,[17] and where poverty among all Mexican immigrants and their US-born children has worsened. As a result of these processes, Mexican immigrants and their families live in the poorest, most segregated, and most densely populated neighborhoods of Los Angeles (Rugh and Massey 2014; Wilkes and Iceland 2004; Jargowsky 2009; Tienda and Fuentes 2014).[18]

The theory of concentrated disadvantage postulates that the hyper-segregation of poor people creates potentially devastating neighborhood dynamics. The theory holds that just as "good" neighborhoods offer multiple and overlapping advantages and opportunities, disadvantaged neighborhoods have many intersecting social problems. As Massey put it, the spatial "concentration of poverty also concentrates any trait correlated with poverty. As the density of poor people rises in a residential area, so does the density of joblessness, crime, family dissolution, substance abuse, disease, and violence" (2007: 204).[19] And it is not just a matter of density, or poor person per square mile. Degrees as well as types of poverty—such as that due to a high percentage of unemployed versus working poor versus foreign-born versus undocumented versus percentage of children in single-parent families, and the like—contribute to the kinds of social problems that challenge disadvantaged neighborhoods (Wilson 1987). In short, the theory of concentrated disadvantage argues that spatially isolating poor people in unstable, high crime neighborhoods that provide inadequate public services is far more conducive to downward than to upward social mobility. Put differently, highly impoverished neighborhoods create many of the circumstances for more permanent, or structural, disadvantage.

With regard to the viability of small business enterprise, research shows that both violent and property crime lower the number of retail employees in neighborhoods over time (Hipp 2010: 221). We suspect that this is so because crime cuts into profits through stolen merchandise and by otherwise raising the costs of security and other self-protective business practices. Other research documents that small businesses in disadvantaged neighborhoods stagnate and even fail due to the customers' weak purchasing power (Waldinger et al. 1990; Aguilera 2009; Trevizo and Lopez 2016). Not only do people in disadvantaged communities have low wages, but also their incomes and employment histories tend to be unsteady. If proprietors cannot rely on a stable demand for their products, it is simply too risky for them to expand their businesses by introducing new products, by investing in more appealing retail spaces, better technology, or other physical capital improvements. Finally, while the challenges of crime and weak markets may be obvious to prospective entrepreneurs, only some shopkeepers have the financial means or the types of merchandise to function outside of impoverished neighborhoods. For such proprietors, the theory of concentrated disadvantage predicts that their businesses will perform worse than will those located in less poor neighborhoods. The second hypothesis follows from this insight:

Hypothesis 2: *High poverty in the neighborhoods in which our respondents operate their shops results in worse business performance for Mexican immigrant entrepreneurs.*

DATA SOURCES AND ANALYTIC STRATEGY

We explore these hypotheses with a unique data set, a random sample of 111 business owners in 20 Latino/a neighborhoods in Los Angeles. As noted in the introduction, because official sources do not produce data about the class backgrounds of immigrants, or even information about where and how they lived pre-migration, we conducted our own survey. Therefore, the first observation made possible by our data set is that the proprietors in our study hailed from 22 out of a possible 31 states (See Appendix B). In addition, many of our respondents are from the Mexico City metropolis, which was not an official state at the time of our survey. A large majority—62% of our respondents—reported that they were raised in an urban area, while a still hefty 38% said that they were raised in a *pueblo* (a rural town/village).

Because our subjects tended to be long-term US residents, with an average of 26 years in the US at the time of the survey and because the average years (the mean) in business at the time of the survey was nine years,[20] most had extensive work histories in the US before becoming entrepreneurs. In her work, María Josefa Santos similarly observed that the entrepreneurs in her study had long labor market histories in the US before they became entrepreneurs (2009: 156). At least among our respondents, such extensive labor market histories were necessary because the vast majority of the shopkeepers in our study first had to become legal residents before they could open up storefronts. As we reported earlier, the majority of our respondents were undocumented when they arrived in the US and, consequently, they worked in the underground economy or with false documents before eventually legalizing their immigration status. Only 7% of our respondents were undocumented at the time of the survey.

Table 3.1 shows the respondents' macro and microclass backgrounds that are relevant to our research questions about occupation-specific cultural capital. Not surprisingly, the vast majority of our respondents were hypo-selected from the upper strata of Mexican society.[21] The overwhelming majority were from disadvantaged backgrounds, with 47% reporting that their fathers were blue-collar workers and an additional 37% reporting that their fathers were in agriculture or ranching. Still, there was some variation in our sample insofar as some immigrants said that their fathers were or had been "civil engineers" (n = 2), a "federal employee" (n = 1), a "technician" (n = 1), a "bookkeeper" (n = 1), a "teacher" (n = 1), a "government worker" (n = 1), or in "management" (n = 1). As reported below, several fathers were also self-employed. The vast majority of the immigrants' mothers, in contrast, did not work outside of their homes (n = 76), though a very small number of immigrants reported that their mothers were or had been "nurses" (n = 3), a "banker" (n = 1), a "school assistant" (n = 1), and a "jeweler" (n = 1).

Table 3.1   Formal and informal cultural capital

	All entrepreneurs %	N^a
Cultural capital		
Father's occupation: Blue collar	47	104
Father's occupation: Agriculture/ranching	37	104
One or both parents were entrepreneurs	14	111
Raised in city (including Mexico City)	62	109
Raised in Pueblo (small town)	38	109
Human capital skills: work skills and formal education		
Work skills		
Prior Mexico experience with business started in LA	25	106
Prior US experience with business started in LA	55	105
Speaks only Spanish at home	74	111
Speaks primarily Spanish to customers	78	111
Formal schooling		
Mean years of schooling	11	110
Median years of schooling	12	110
0–6 years	25	110
7–11 years	15	110
12 or more years	60	110

Source: Authors' survey of Mexican immigrant business owners in Los Angeles, 2007

Notes: [a]Some of our respondents skipped or refused to answer some questions, resulting in varied sample sizes

We defined our respondents' parent(s) as entrepreneurs only if they said that at least one of their parents was a *comerciante* or was otherwise self-employed. *Comerciante* broadly translates to someone who "sells," though the word can also specifically mean "merchant" or "shopkeeper." We identified a total of 13 fathers and mothers as *comerciantes* as well as three additional parents who identified as storeowners (one of whom was a factory owner). We did not treat the one jeweler in the sample as an entrepreneur because she was not identified as self-employed or as owning a business. Notwithstanding the fact that our sample of entrepreneurs came primarily from cities, our rural versus urban respondents were about equally likely to report that at least one of their parents was self-employed. Further, while only 14% of all 111 respondents said that their parents had been business owners in Mexico, 25% reported having some exposure to the type of business that they would someday start in Los Angeles when they still lived in Mexico. The majority—fully 55% of our respondents—

reported that they gained experience with the kind of business that they would eventually start only while living in the US.

Although most of the entrepreneurs in our study report having had disadvantaged backgrounds in Mexico, they also had higher levels of education than is typical for a Mexican immigrant in Los Angeles. Table 3.1 shows that fully 60% of our respondents had 12 or more years of schooling and that, indeed, their median years of schooling was 12 years. This is comparable to official data on Hispanic entrepreneurs in California (from the 2007 Survey of Business Owners), but is considerably higher than what the American Community Survey reported for Mexican immigrant entrepreneurs in Los Angeles (according to Appendix A, only 40% had at least a high school education or more according to the American Community Survey). We suspect that our sample differs from the American Community Survey sample because we did not use as broad of a definition of entrepreneurship as "self-employed" (since such a definition would include, for example, domestic servants, gardeners, painters, plumbers, and the like). We focused instead on shopkeepers in Latino/a neighborhoods because of the greater financial investment required for creating and maintaining their shops.

In the previous chapter, we reported that the vast majority of our respondents (78%) stated that they were operating their very first business at the time of the survey, and that most of these businesses were young, with a median of five years in existence. We also reported that our respondents owned mostly wholesale and retail stores. To be more precise, the latter clustered as hair salons or barbershops, restaurants, party supply stores, clothing stores, markets, auto stores, all of which point to general services and retail. As is typical for small shopkeepers, the entrepreneurs in our study logged long hours in their storefronts—a median of 60 hours per week. Despite such long hours, the profit margins appear small given that nearly half (47%) of the entrepreneurs in our sample did not hire any workers. This finding is consistent with the 2007 official survey data from the Small Business Owners (henceforth SBO) showing that the vast majority of Hispanic small business owners do not hire any paid employees but instead tend to rely on family labor (See Appendix A). Nevertheless, there was some variation in their business performance since about 20% of the entrepreneurs in our sample hired between three and four workers and an additional 6% hired more than five employees.

In order to ascertain whether there were some identifiable financial or cultural capital advantages among our respondents, we first examine whether there were significant differences in the ways that they financed their firms or in their stated rationales for their Los Angeles business ventures. Table 3.2 reports whether there is a difference in the methods by which the entrepreneurs in our sample obtained their start-up capital by whether or not their parents in Mexico were also business owners. Table 3.2 shows that the overwhelming majority of all of our respondents were self-reliant in Los Angeles, tapping into their personal assets to start their businesses ($p = 0.023$, two-tailed test). In addition, the table shows that both groups were about equally likely to borrow from friends and family. This is the case since people with strong ties to one another organize *tandas* and *cundinas*, the informal rotating credit associations that many turn to for easy, free, or inexpensive loans. However, the immigrant shopkeepers whose parents were also entrepreneurs in Mexico were far more likely to borrow from a credit card or from a financial institution than were the petty proprietors whose parents had no business experience. This statistically significant difference between the two groups in their willingness to assume interest-bearing debt suggests more comfort with risk taking among the shopkeepers whose parents were also entrepreneurs in Mexico

Table 3.2 Methods of obtaining start-up capital, by whether parents were business owners in Mexico, 110 entrepreneurs

	Personal savings or assets	Loan from a relative or friend	Cundina, Tanda, Cooperativa	Credit card or financial institution	Other type of loan	Total	N
Parents not in business	71%	7%	4%	5%	12%	99%	94
Parent(s) business owner[a]	63%	0%	13%	25%	0%	101%	16
Total count	77	7	6	9	11		110
Pearson χ^2	11.391** (d.f. = 4)						

Source: Authors' survey of Mexican immigrant business owners in Los Angeles, 2007

Notes: *$p < 0.10$, **$p < 0.05$, ***$p < 0.01$ (two-tailed tests), ^$p < 0.10$ (one-tailed test). Total column may not add up to 100% due to rounding errors

[a]As we observed, it was usually the father who was a business owner

than was manifested by respondents raised by non-entrepreneurs. As observed earlier, risk taking is a cultural disposition of entrepreneurs, one easily transmitted to their children. As such, it suggests a small occupationally specific cultural capital difference, one that may or may not prove useful in their business performance in Los Angeles. Finally, to ascertain whether there are microclass differences in aspirations, Table 3.3 reports whether our respondents differed in their rationale for going into business by whether or not their parents had been entrepreneurs in Mexico. Table 3.3 shows that there is no statistically significant difference in the motivations between the two groups, at least not so in this table ($p = 0.36$, one-tailed test).

Table 3.4 presents the characteristics of the specific neighborhoods in our study. The second column of the table identifies the broader geographic areas—for example, Central versus East versus Southeast Los Angeles versus the San Fernando or San Gabriel Valleys—in which the neighborhoods are nested. As we observe in more detail in the next chapter, the Mexican areas of Los Angeles first developed in response to racial covenants. When these were outlawed, Mexican neighborhoods developed in response to the blue-collar jobs available in Southern California's heavy manufacturing industries. When steel, auto, and rubber production plants and tire factories shut down in the 1970s and 1980s, many white workers abandoned some segments of the city (See Appendix C for area histories). Then, as Mexican immigrants took their place, white parents fled to avoid having their children attend integrated public schools (Schneider 2008). The Mexican population would continue to grow in some of the areas identified in Table 3.4 because of the availability of work in garment, plastics, and food production, that is, the light manufacturing industries of a restructured economy.[22]

In addition to geographic information, Table 3.4 also presents some of the social, economic, and demographic characteristics theorized to affect our respondents' business performance. It is clear from Table 3.4 that more than half of the neighborhoods in our study have levels of poverty that are higher than the average for Los Angeles and that many have high concentrations of immigrants. Indeed, just over half of the neighborhoods in our study had at least as many foreign as native-born people. Business duration also varied by neighborhood so that all businesses in Cypress Park, El Monte, and Pico Union had been in operation for more than ten years. This was not true of businesses in Hollywood, Huntington Park, or South El Monte. Given that the majority of new small firms go out of

Table 3.3 Reasons for starting business, by whether parents were business owners in Mexico, 111 entrepreneurs

	Make more money; better lifestyle; investment; retire early	Be own boss; spend time with family; better working conditions	Lost job; no other option; needed steady job; overcome obstacles	Had experience; all subject knows how to do	Family tradition	Give others job	Inspired by others	Total	N
Parents not in business	39%	26%	18%	11%	3%	2%	1%	100%	95
Parent(s) business owner[a]	44%	19%	6%	19%	6%	6%	0%	100%	16
Total count	44	28	18	13	4	3	1	100%	111
Pearson χ^2	3.728 (d.f. = 6)								

Source: Authors' survey of Mexican immigrant business owners in Los Angeles, 2007

Notes: $*p < 0.10$, $**p < 0.05$, $***p < 0.01$ (two-tailed tests), $^p < 0.10$ (one-tailed test)

[a]As we observed, it was usually the father who was a business owner

Table 3.4 Percent foreign-born and residential poverty, by Los Angeles neighborhood

Neighborhood	Area of LA	Foreign-born %	Residential poverty > LA	Business open 10+ years %	Median number of paid employees	N
Bell	Southeast LA	53	1	29	0	7
Bell Gardens	Southeast LA	50	1	50	2	6
Boyle Heights	East LA	52	1	31	0	16
Cudahy	Southeast LA	53	1	40	0	5
Cypress Park	Northeast LA	53	0	100	2	1
El Monte	San Gabriel Valley	51	1	100	3	1
El Sereno	East LA	43	1	14	0	7
Highland Park	Northeast LA	45	0	14	2	7
Hollywood	Central LA	54	1	0	7	3
Huntington Park	Southeast LA	56	1	0	1	5
La Puente	San Gabriel Valley	44	0	17	0	12
Maywood	Southeast LA	55	1	25	2	4
Pacoima	San Fernando Valley	47	1	0	3	4
Panorama City	San Fernando Valley	55	1	33	2	3
Pico Rivera	Southeast LA	34	0	56	0	9
Pico Union	Central LA	65	1	100	4	1
San Fernando	San Fernando Valley	43	0	60	3	10
Silver Lake Adjacent "Central City West"	Central LA	41	1	50	0	2

(*continued*)

Table 3.4 (continued)

Neighborhood	Area of LA	Foreign-born %	Residential poverty > LA	Business open 10+ years %	Median number of paid employees	N
South El Monte	San Gabriel Valley	52	0	0	2	3
South Gate	Southeast LA	49	0	60	1	5

Source: Authors' survey of Mexican immigrant business owners in Los Angeles, 2007

Notes: Entrepreneurs lived in neighborhoods with a 48% average foreign-born population and 58% of the neighborhoods in the sample had poverty rates higher than the poverty rate for Los Angeles

businesses within four to five years of launching,[23] this ten-year minimum threshold is already a marker of business success. But the businesses located in Pico Union and Hollywood seem even more successful given that they hired more employees than the average number of employees hired for the entire sample. This employment pattern contrasts sharply with businesses located in Pico Rivera, Cudahy, La Puente, El Sereno, Boyle Heights, Bell, and an area adjacent to Silver Lake referred to as "Central City West," which had zero paid employees.

What explains such variant patterns of business performance? We turn to this question next.

Models, Measurement, and Regression Technique

To discern how pre- and post- migration stratification variables affect the business performance of the entrepreneurs in our sample, we estimate the following baseline equation:

$$Y_{i,n} = \alpha + \beta_1 GENDER_{i,n} + \beta_2 MARR_{i,n} + \beta_3 EDUC_{i,n}$$
$$+ \beta_4 YRSINUS_{i,n} + \beta_5 RETAIL_{i,n} + \beta_6 SERVICE_{i,n}$$
$$+ \beta_7 HRS_{i,n} + \beta_8 DUR_{i,n} + \beta_9 STARTUP_{i,n} + \beta_{10} FB_n + \varepsilon_{i,n}$$

where Y represents the number of paid employees for entrepreneur i operating a business in neighborhood n. We use paid employees as our outcome variable because several of our respondents refused to answer specific questions about their business sales or profits. The "number of paid employees" is a variable regularly used in the business literature to gauge business performance. It is reliable insofar as there is less incentive to misreport the number of paid employees than there is about sales, receipts, and profits. Data from the 2007 SBO help make the case for the empirical validity of our measure in showing that while Hispanics with paid employees comprised only 11% of all Hispanic-owned businesses, they accounted for fully 80% of the total sales for their group.[24] The inordinate discrepancy in sales among those with paid employees as compared to those without paid employees is evidence of better profit margins (on average) for those who hire more labor. Research on Asian small business owners also indicates that those who employ more people are more likely to survive over time (Bates 1994: 680). We are thus confident that our dependent variable, number of paid employees, is a good indicator of business performance among Mexican immigrant entrepreneurs in Los Angeles.

The baseline model includes the following standard demographic and human capital variables: GENDER represents the respondent's gender (female = 1; male = 0), MARR represents whether the respondent is married, (married = 1; not married = 0), EDUC is a continuous variable accounting for the number of years of schooling. Since our sample consists of immigrant entrepreneurs, we also include the variable YRSINUS, which represents the number of years the immigrant has resided in the US. The longer an immigrant has resided in the US, the more familiar he or she may be with the US labor market and entrepreneurial opportunities. We also include industry control variables. RETAIL is a dummy variable indicating whether the subject's business is in the retail sector and SERVICE is a dummy variable capturing entrepreneurship in the service sector. The omitted category is businesses in the professional sector. We control for the industry category since the financial return to entrepreneurship can vary across industries. The variable HRS records the natural log of weekly hours spent in the business.[25] DUR is a dummy variable that represents whether a respondent's business has been open for more than ten years. This variable captures business longevity, which has been shown to be a determinant of business outcomes. The variable STARTUP captures the natural log of the amount of each respondent's financial start-up capital. Theoretically, higher levels of start-up capital should result in better business outcomes. FB represents the percentage of foreign-born residents in each of our 20 neighborhoods, as reported in the 2000 Census. We do not introduce legal status in the model because the vast majority of our respondents reported that they legalized their immigration status before opening their small businesses. Most, in fact, would not have been able to be store-front proprietors without having legal status, as we discuss in a later chapter where we examine how the timing of their legalization vis-à-vis the timing of their business matters for business outcomes. Finally, "ε" is the error term in the model.

To explore our hypotheses, we begin by including two additional variables in our baseline model. The variable PARBUS is a dummy variable capturing whether or not the respondent's parent(s) were self-employed in Mexico (1 = if at least one parent was self-employed or 0 = no self-employed parents). The coefficient associated with this variable speaks directly to our first hypothesis predicting that our respondents have a business advantage from their parents' experience with self-employment in Mexico. As such, we expect that the coefficient for the PARBUS variable should be positive. To assess our second hypothesis about post-migration neighborhood effects, we add a poverty variable (POV), a dummy variable measuring whether the business is located in a neighborhood where the poverty rate is greater than that for the entire city of Los Angeles (residential poverty>LA = 1 and 0 otherwise). As we observed in the previous chapter, the rate of poverty in Los Angeles is higher than California's and the national average. Therefore, our POV variable reflects extremely poor neighborhoods. In addition, as shown in Table 3.4, there is variation in poverty levels across the neighborhoods in our sample. If our second hypothesis predicting worse business outcomes in high poverty neighborhoods is correct, then the coefficient associated with the POV should be negative.

We employ a Poisson regression because our data are comprised of count variables (non-negative integers), which have a high degree of skewness. The Poisson estimation is better than a traditional Ordinary Least Squares (OLS) estimation since count variables can result in negative predicted values or violate assumptions of normality. Finally, because our sample is small, we do not focus our discussion on the magnitude of the coefficients because we do not want to over-interpret them. Although we do not discuss the magnitude of the coefficients outside of parenthetical references, we report them in the next table along with the standard errors, as per standard practice. Our analysis, in other words, focuses on the signs of the relevant coefficients and on whether they are statistically significant. We are confident in the signs and the statistical significance of our tables because our data are based on a random sample, as described in the introductory chapter of this book.

Main Results

Column 1 in Table 3.5 presents the results for the baseline model. They suggest that gender, level of formal education, operating in the services sector, and the log of number of hours spent in the business per week are not statistically significant. Although these null results are counterintuitive, other statistically significant variables in the model likely reduced their explanatory power. For example, being married may have trumped the effects of the gender variable. We explore this possibility in detail in Chap. 5. The number of years migrants live in the US positively affects their business performance and the literature certainly treats the time invested by migrants in the host country as important human capital (Li 2001). This is so because the longer they live in a host country, the greater their work experience, the better their new language skills, and the deeper their knowledge about their host society. Therefore, while formal education in the home country is not relevant to business performance in LA, the human capital skills acquired at work and simply the length of time living in the US positively affect business performance, net of other variables. Given the literature's emphasis on the volume of financial resources at people's disposal, it is not surprising that the amount of start-up capital invested in a business predicts better business performance among Mexican entrepreneurs in our sample, all else equal. It is surprising, however, that operating in the retail sector and having survived in business for more than ten years resulted in fewer hires. The coefficients associated with these last two variables were negative and statistically significant. The negative coefficient associated with having been in business for more than ten years suggests that many small shops in Mexican neighborhoods endure, but that they stagnate and tend, on average, to remain small.

As predicted by our first hypothesis, the results in column 2 of Table 3.5 show clearly that Mexican immigrant shopkeepers in Los Angeles do better when at least one parent operated his or her own business in Mexico ($p < 0.01$, two-tailed test). Despite being no older than their late teens when they migrated to the US, their childhood exposure to their parents' businesses in Mexico contributed to their business performance. The evidence shows that they hired more paid workers in their Los Angeles shops than did the small business owners without such exposure to a family business in Mexico. Since this finding is net of all other variables in the model, including human and start-up (financial) capital, we now have better evidence of a type of microclass cultural capital at work: The business know-how informally acquired in childhood via parental self-employment in Mexico clearly converted into material rewards for small business owners in Los Angeles. This suggests that even small differences in the microclass cultural capital of co-ethnics indeed contribute to the viability of and success with their businesses across the US-Mexico border.

Beyond such pre-migration microclass differences among our respondents, the results presented in Table 3.5 also show that the neighborhood characteristics in which the migrants manage their businesses matter. First, the table shows across all three models a small but positive relationship between the percent foreign-born (FB) in a neighborhood and the business performance of shopkeepers. Across the models, the positive relationship remains statistically significant even after we introduce the poverty variable, POV. Although the percentage of foreign-born does not indicate where people were born, or how many are without legal status, it is still a neighborhood characteristic. It shows a small but positive relationship between immigrant neighborhoods and the business performance of Mexico-born shopkeepers. However, as noted, not all immigrant neighborhoods are disadvantaged (Jargowsky 2009), and those that are disadvantaged are not equally poor.

Therefore, a better indicator of neighborhood disadvantage is its degree of poverty. As predicted by hypothesis 2, column 3 of Table 3.5 clearly shows that entrepreneurs whose shops are in highly impoverished neighborhoods hire fewer employees than those in less impoverished neighborhoods ($p < 0.01$). This was true net of all control variables. Our findings, thus, are consistent with the thesis that neighborhoods that concentrate poverty are unconducive to the success of small business. We specifically find that such neighborhoods undermine the business performance of shopkeepers. Some of our respondents' comments shed light on how this is so. As we demonstrated in a previous analysis, many small Mexican entrepreneurs in high poverty areas report that their co-ethnics "haggle" or otherwise ask for too many discounts (Trevizo and Lopez 2016). When haggling is effective, it cuts into already small profit margins even if discounted sales also lead to good will among customers. Spatially concentrated poverty not only blocks the mobility of the very individuals who have taken entrepreneurial steps to move out of poverty, but in doing so, it also reduces job opportunities for local residents. Our findings thus illustrate how disadvantage begets other disadvantage, creating downward cycles that make it difficult to break out of poverty.

In sum, the negative and statistically significant coefficient associated with poverty is consistent with the neighborhood disadvantage thesis that identifies the spatial concentration of poverty as a harsh and undercutting circumstance from which to attempt upward mobility (Fischer and Massey 2000; Aguilera 2009). We know from past research that both violent and property crime drive away retail stores (Hipp 2010). Our results here indicate that the weak purchasing power of the poor negatively impinges on

Table 3.5 The impact of class and neighborhood on business performance (Poisson regression)

	Model (1)	Model (2)	Model (3)
Gender (GENDER)	−0.108	−0.059	−0.170
	(0.167)	(0.169)	(0.172)
Married (MARR)	0.662***	0.671***	0.728***
	(0.207)	(0.209)	(0.211)
Years of schooling (EDUC)	0.005	−0.005	−0.007
	(0.021)	(0.021)	(0.021)
Years in the US (YRSINUS)	0.026***	0.030***	0.036***
	(0.010)	(0.010)	(0.011)
Retail sector (RETAIL)	−0.631^	−0.560	−0.670^
	(0.448)	(0.446)	(0.452)
Services sector (SERVICE)	0.137	0.143	0.057
	(0.440)	(0.438)	(0.444)
Log hours worked per week (HRS)	0.193	0.347	0.209
	(0.314)	(0.320)	(0.318)
Business open more than 10 years (DUR)	−0.324^	−0.392*	−0.513**
	(0.233)	(0.237)	(0.235)
Log start-up capital (STARTUP)	0.182**	0.182***	0.170**
	(0.073)	(0.070)	(0.070)
Neighborhood's percent foreign-born (FB)	0.041***	0.043***	0.079***
	(0.014)	(0.014)	(0.019)
Parent business owner (PARBUS)		0.599***	0.645***
		(0.223)	(0.226)
Residential poverty > LA (POV)			−0.679***
			(0.224)
N	99	99	99
Psuedo R-square	0.134	0.150	0.174

Source: Authors' survey of Mexican immigrant business owners in Los Angeles, 2007

Notes: *$p < 0.10$, **$p < 0.05$, ***$p < 0.01$ (two-tailed tests), ^$p < 0.10$ (one-tailed test), standard errors in parentheses

Dependent variable is the number of paid employees

business performance. Further, as documented here, aggregate neighborhood poverty not only blocks the mobility of small shopkeepers, but it also results in lost job opportunities for other residents in the neighborhood. Under these circumstances, it becomes difficult to break out of poverty both for small shopkeepers and for their unemployed neighbors.

Conclusion

This chapter began with evidence about microclass differences in the family backgrounds of mostly low-skill immigrants from Mexico. Consistent with Bourdieu's stratification theory that holds that a family's class standing matters for the upward or downward mobility of their children over time, we found that even microclass advantages that immigrant shopkeepers may have had in their Mexican upbringings affect the odds of social mobility, however minimal, in the host country. We add to the scholarship by showing that informal forms of tacit business know-how acquired in their Mexican childhoods contribute to the overall positive effects of having entrepreneurial parents; and that they especially do so in the least deprived neighborhoods in which they manage their storefronts. While consistent with other research showing the benefits of having entrepreneurial parents, we highlight the role of an entrepreneurial cultural disposition among low-skill immigrants as a small competitive advantage in another country. The research addressing immigrant mobility and entrepreneurship has generally glossed over the role of this kind of occupation-specific cultural capital. First, the classic sociological literature addressing culture focused on broad values (writ large) that purportedly explain inter-ethnic differences in entrepreneurship between entire immigrant groups. Second, the scholarship examining intra-ethnic differences in the proclivity for and success with entrepreneurship emphasizes the role of human capital, such as formal educational attainment, as well as skills acquired at work, whether in Mexico or the US. Even the research on the transferability of human capital skills across borders ignores how occupation-specific cultural capital may operate as entrepreneurial dispositions in a host society. Similarly, the research on entrepreneurial families treats the family business as a wellspring for material resources or for social capital. These factors, however, are less relevant to the social mobility of low-skilled immigrants in a host society because the customer or supplier bases of their family businesses are located in the migrant's country of origin. In sum, because we controlled for human, social, and financial capital, our research highlights the role of tacit cultural disposi-tions as entrepreneurial advantages in a host country.

However, while microclass origins in Mexico are clearly important to the immigrants' business prospects, we also found strong evidence sup-porting the view that neighborhood characteristics in the host society are powerful stratifying forces. We specifically found that extreme neighbor-hood poverty in Los Angeles blocks the mobility even of those who have positioned themselves to move up the rungs of the economic ladder by undermining the viability of small businesses. Therefore, if historically working-class immigrants found that small business proprietorship was the way out of poverty, those rungs appear broken for Mexican immigrants who tend to live in the poorest neighborhoods of Los Angeles. The con-centration of poverty and other forms of disadvantage connected to it contributes to the dynamics that make it difficult to succeed in business, irrespective of the financial resources and labor invested by small business proprietors.

To be clear, the concentrated disadvantage thesis further specifies that the interaction effects of poverty and ethnic segregation compound a neighborhood's social problems. We examine this particular possibility in the next chapter. Here, we simply point out that neighborhood poverty undermines the businesses of Mexican immigrant shopkeepers because it is associated with the weak purchasing power of residents within the neighborhood.

To conclude, this chapter offers evidence of two distinct types of class effects: those cultivated pre-migration and those operating at the neigh-borhood level post-migration. These double findings have implications not only for entrepreneurship and mobility studies, but also for all research focusing on Mexican immigrants. This is because much scholarship treats Mexicans as a relatively homogenous ethnic group in the US, reducing any variation among them to gender and, increasingly, to racial or ethnic distinctions (e.g., between indigenous groups or as distinct from mesti-zos). This chapter, in contrast, observes some class variation, focusing on microclass differences among poor Mexicans. We specifically demonstrate that such microclass differences among poor people contribute to their economic trajectories. We further show that not all poor Mexican neigh-borhoods in Los Angeles are disadvantaged equally. Some neighborhoods are poorer than others are and, as shown in the next chapter, some are more ethnically and racially diverse than others.

NOTES

1. Gary Becker (1993) offers a foundational statement on human capital theory.
2. Mexico's Revolution of 1910 as well as various protest movements since the 1960s also result from extreme social inequality. While improving some in the last 100 years, Campos et al. (2012) document that inequality rose between 1989 and 1994 and then declined between 1994 and 2006. The decline of inequality lost momentum between 2006 and 2010. Recent data show that the annual income share going to the top 1% of the population is 47 times more than what goes to the poorest decile of the same, while the annual income share of the top 10th percentile of the population is 17 times more than what it is for the bottom decile of the population (Krozer and Moreno-Brid 2014).
3. This 2012 estimate is based on a food-based definition of poverty, which is different from the "asset-based" definition of poverty. If we used the latter definition, then the 2012 poverty estimate would be 47% of the population living in poverty, according to the CIA World Factbook (February 2016).
4. Mexico has historically not had much of a middle class and what middle strata exist today are vulnerable to falling back into poverty. A class structure that is missing an established and robust middle class actually contributes to the economic insecurity of the most vulnerable by increasing the spatial segregation and social distance between the urban rich and urban poor.
5. OECD Factbook 2015–2016, Economic, Environmental, and Social Sciences, DOI:https://doi.org/10.1787/factbook-2015-en
6. Collective property in the countryside usually takes the form of *ejidos*. Among indigenous groups, *comunidades* may be more common. Before 1992, neither collective land nor *ejido* parcels worked by families could be sold or rented. After the constitutional reforms of 1992, they can be (See Trevizo 2011).
7. For the classic articulation of this view, see Light (1972). For a recent account of national cultural values, see Vinogradov and Kolvereid (2007). For a critique of culturalist explanations of the entrepreneurial differences between ethnic migrants in a host society, see Waldinger et al. (1990), Sanders and Nee (1996) and Valdez (2011).
8. See Robb and Fairlie (2007), Dunn and Holtz-Eakin (2000). For a review of the literature documenting the greater likelihood of becoming a small business owner among the children of the self-employed, see Wyrwich (2015) as well as Hoffman et al. (2015).
9. See Doms et al. (2010), Robb and Fairlie (2009), and Anderson and Miller (2003).

10. See Dunn and Holtz-Eakin (2000), Anderson and Miller (2003), Fairlie and Robb (2007), and see Wyrwich on "easy access" (2015).

11. For a review of human capital theory as applied to immigrants and self-employment, see Kanas, van Tubergen, and van der Lippe (2009). This recent literature summarizes the debates about the role of origin-country education in migrant self-employment in the host country. Also see Vinogradov and Kolvereid (2007).

12. For a more detailed discussion of the advantages of "human capital/class resources" as provided by the family, see Sanders and Nee (1996).

13. Some economists identify informal learning about the family business as a "general" form of human capital that develops entrepreneurial ability (See Wyrwich 2015: 192).

14. On Bourdieu's theory of fields, see Fligstein and McAdam (2011) and Benson (1999).

15. As Gonzales explains, many of the City of Los Angeles's efforts at integrating immigrants are "undercut by a lack of federal [immigration] reforms" (2016: 225). This is because employers at the local level have to follow federal immigration law. Their doing so affects the wages of the undocumented and, thus, the wages of authorized low-skill legal immigrants.

16. Nationwide, the foreign-born population doubled between 1990 and 2010, from nearly 20 million to 40 million, and both legal and unauthorized migrants comprise this most recent wave. For a good graphic of immigration data over time, see Haeyoun Park and Alicia Parlapiano (June 23, 2016, online edition of New York Times). María Enchautegui (1998) argues that the recent wave of immigration lowered wages for all low-skilled immigrant workers. Consequently, their poverty rate grew faster than the poverty rate for U.S. native groups (pp. 811–812). For research on how large inflows of low-skill immigrants affect other low-skill immigrants, see also Bean and Stevens (2003), Bean et al. (2004), Borjas (2006), Smith and Edmonston (1997).

17. See Gonzales (2016: 224). At the time of the survey in 2007, there were 10 million people living in Los Angeles County, 71% of whom were ethnic minorities.

18. This may partially explain why the self-employment rate in Mexico is higher than it is among Mexicans living in the United States (Fairlie and Woodruff 2007).

19. See also Harding (2009), Hipp (2007, 2010), Feldmeyer (2010), and Wodtke et al. (2011).

20. Table 2.2 reported a median number of 5 years in business at the time of the survey, but it is also accurate to say that the mean number is 9 years in business, as reported here.

21. See Lee and Zhou (2014) for an analysis of immigrants who are hyper-versus hypo-selected from the upper economic strata of their home societies.
22. The aerospace industry was the last to close its doors in the first half of the 1990s.
23. See Waldinger et al. (1990: 30).
24. See https://www.census.gov/library/publications/2007/econ/2007-sbo-hispanic.html for a summary of the characteristics of Hispanic businesses and business owners from the 2007 Survey of Business Owners.
25. Taking the natural log of a variable with a lot of variation can improve the overall fit of the model.

REFERENCES

Aguilera, Michael Bernabé. 2009. Ethnic Enclaves and the Earnings of Self-employed Latinos. *Small Business Economics* 33: 413–425.

Anderson, Alistair R., and Claire J. Miller. 2003. "Class Matters": Human and Social Capital in the Entrepreneurial Process. *Journal of Socio-Economics* 32: 17–36.

Bates, Timothy. 1994. Social Resources Generated by Group Support Networks May Not Be Beneficial to Asian Immigrant-Owned Small Business. *Social Forces* 72 (3): 671–689.

Bean, Frank D., and Gillian Stevens. 2003. *America's Newcomers and the Dynamics of Diversity*. New York: Russell Sage.

Bean, Frank D., Mark Leach, and B. Lindsay Lowell. 2004. Immigrant Job Quality and Mobility in the United States. *Work and Occupations* 31 (4): 499–518.

Becker, Gary S. 1993. *Human Capital: A Theoretical and Empirical Analysis, with Special Reference to Education*. 3rd ed. Chicago: The University of Chicago Press.

Benson, Rodney. 1999. Field Theory in Comparative Context: A New Paradigm for Media Studies. *Theory and Society* 28 (3): 463–498.

Borjas, George J. 2006. Making It in America: Social Mobility in the Immigrant Population. *Future of Children* 16 (2): 55–71. http://files.eric.ed.gov/fulltext/EJ1042192.pdf

Bourdieu, Pierre. 1984 (1979). *Distinction: A Social Critique of the Judgement of Taste*. Cambridge, MA: Harvard University Press.

Bourdieu, Pierre, and Loïc J.D. Wacquant. 1992. *An Invitation to Reflexive Sociology*. Chicago: University of Chicago Press.

Campos, Raymundo, Gerardo Esquivel, and Nora Lustig. 2012. *The Rise and Fall of Income Inequality in Mexico: 1989–2010*. WIDER Working Paper, No. 2012/10. ISBN 978-929-230-473-7

Doms, Mark, Ethan Lewis, and Alicia Robb. 2010. Local Labor Force Education, New Business Characteristics, and Firm Performance. *Journal of Urban Economics* 67: 61–77.

Dunn, Thomas, and Douglas Holtz-Eakin. 2000. Financial Capital, Human Capital, and the Transition to Self-Employment: Evidence from Intergenerational Links. *Journal of Labor Economics* 18 (2): 282–305.

Enchautegui, María E. 1998. Low-Skilled Immigrants and the Changing American Labor Market. *Population Development Review* 24 (4): 811–824.

Fairlie, Robert, and Alicia Robb. 2007. Families, Human Capital, and Small Business: Evidence From the Characteristics of Business Owners Survey. *Industrial and Labor Relations Review* 60 (2): 225–245.

Fairlie, Robert, and Christopher Woodruff. 2007. Mexican Entrepreneurship: A Comparison of Self-Employment in Mexico and the United States. In *Mexican Immigration to the United States*, ed. George Borjas, 123–158. Chicago: University of Chicago Press.

Feldmeyer, Ben. 2010. The Effects of Racial/Ethnic Segregation on Latino and Black Homicide. *The Sociological Quarterly* 51 (4): 600–623.

Fischer, Mary J., and Douglas S. Massey. 2000. Residential Segregation and Ethnic Enterprise in U.S. Metropolitan Areas. *Social Problems* 47 (3): 408–424.

Fligstein, Neil, and Doug McAdam. 2011. Toward a General Theory of Strategic Action Fields. *Sociological Theory* 29 (1): 1–26.

Gonzales, Robert G. 2016. *Lives in Limbo: Undocumented and Coming of Age in America*. Oakland: University of California Press.

Harding, David J. 2009. Collateral Consequences of Violence in Disadvantaged Neighborhoods. *Social Forces* 88: 757–784.

Hipp, John R. 2007. Income Inequality, Race and Place: Does the Distribution of Race and Class Within Neighborhoods Affect Crime Rates? *Criminology* 45 (3): 665–697.

———. 2010. A Dynamic View of Neighborhoods: The Reciprocal Relationship Between Crime and Neighborhood Structural Characteristics. *Social Problems* 57 (2): 205–230.

Hoffman, Anders, Martin Junge, and Nikolaj Malchow-Moller. 2015. Running in the Family: Parental Role Models in Entrepreneurship. *Small Business Economics* 44: 79–104.

Jargowsky, Paul A. 2009. Immigrants and Neighborhoods of Concentrated Poverty: Assimilation or Stagnation? *Journal of Ethnic and Migration Studies* 35: 1129–1151.

Jonsson, Jan O., David B. Grusky, Matthew Di Carlo, Reinhard Pollak, and Mary C. Brinton. 2009. Microclass Mobility: Social Reproduction in Four Countries. *American Journal of Sociology* 114 (4): 977–1036.

Kanas, Agnieszka, Frank van Tubergen, and Tanja van der Lippe. 2009. Immigrant Self-Employment: Testing Hypotheses About the Role of Origin- and Host-

Country Human Capital and Bonding and Bridging Social Capital. *Work and Occupations* 36 (3): 181–208.

Krozer, Alice, and Juan Carlos Moreno-Brid. 2014. Inequality in Mexico. *World Economics Association Newsletter* 4 (5). ISSN 2049-3274. http://www.worldeconomicsassociation.org/files/newsletter/Issue-4-5.pdf

Lee, Jennifer, and Min Zhou. 2014. From Unassimilable to Exceptional: The Rise of Asian Americans and 'Stereotype Promise'. *New Diversities* 16 (1): 7–22.

Li, Peter S. 2001. Immigrants' Propensity to Self-Employment: Evidence from Canada. *The International Migration Review* 35 (4): 1106–1128.

Light, Ivan. 1972. *Ethnic Enterprise in America: Business and Welfare Among Chinese, Japanese, and Blacks*. Berkeley: University of California Press.

Massey, Douglas S. 2007. *Categorically Unequal. The American Stratification System*. New York: Russell Sage Foundation.

Massey, Douglas S., and Stefanie Brodmann. 2014. *Spheres of Influence: The Social Ecology of Racial and Class Inequality*. New York: Russell Sage Foundation.

Morales, Alfonso. 2009. A Woman's Place Is on the Street: Purposes and Problems of Mexican American Women Entrepreneurs. In *An American Story: Mexican American Entrepreneurship and Wealth Creation*, ed. John S. Butler, Alfonso Morales, and David L. Torres, 99–126. West Lafayette: Purdue University Press.

Newman, Katherine S., and Rebekah Peeples Massengill. 2006. The Texture of Hardship: Qualitative Sociology of Poverty, 1995–2005. *Annual Review of Sociology* 32: 423–446.

Robb, Alicia, and Robert Fairlie. 2007. Access to Financial Capital Among U.S. Businesses: The Case of African-American Firms. *The Annals of the American Academy of Political and Social Science* 613: 47–72.

———. 2009. Determinants of Business Success: An Examination of Asian-Owned Businesses in the USA. *Journal of Population Economics* 22: 827–858.

Rugh, Jacob S., and Douglas S. Massey. 2014. Segregation in Post-Civil Rights America: Stalled Integration or End of the Segregated Century. *DuBois Review: Social Science Research on Race* 11 (2): 205–232.

Sanders, Jimy M., and Victor Nee. 1996. Immigrant Self-Employment: The Family as Social Capital and the Value of Human Capital. *American Sociological Review* 61 (2): 231–249.

Santos, Maria Josefa. 2009. Knowledge and Networks: Mexican-American Entrepreneurship in Southwestern Michigan. In *An American Story: Mexican American Entrepreneurship and Wealth Creation*, ed. John S. Butler, Alfonso Morales, and David L. Torres, 151–174. West Lafayette: Purdue University Press.

Schneider, Jack. 2008. Escape from Los Angeles: White Flight from Los Angeles and Its Schools, 1960–1980. *Journal of Urban History* 34 (6): 995–1012.

Smith, James P., and Barry Edmonston. 1997. *The New Americans: Economic, Demographic, and Fiscal Effects of Immigration.* Washington, DC: National Academies Press.

Tienda, Marta, and Norma Fuentes. 2014. Hispanics in Metropolitan American: New Realities and Old Debates. *Annual Review of Sociology* 40: 499–520.

Trevizo, Dolores. 2011. *Rural Protest and the Making of Democracy in Mexico, 1968–2000.* University Park: The Pennsylvania State University Press.

Trevizo, Dolores, and Mary Lopez. 2016. Neighborhood Segregation and Business Outcomes: Mexican Immigrant Entrepreneurs in Los Angeles County. *Sociological Perspectives* 59 (3): 668–693.

Valdez, Zulema. 2011. *The New Entrepreneurs: How Race, Class, and Gender Shape American Enterprise.* Stanford: Stanford University Press.

Vinogradov, Evgueni, and Lars Kolvereid. 2007. Cultural Background, Human Capital and Self-Employment Rates Among Immigrants in Norway. *Entrepreneurship and Regional Development* 19 (4): 359–376.

Waldinger, Roger, Howard Aldrich, and Robin Ward. 1990. *Ethnic Entrepreneurs: Immigrant Business in Industrial Societies.* Newbury Park: Sage.

Wilkes, Rima, and John Iceland. 2004. Hypersegregation in the Twenty-First Century: An Update and Analysis. *Demography* 4: 23–36.

Wilson, William Julius. 1987. *The Truly Disadvantaged: The Inner City, the Underclass, and Public Policy.* Chicago: University of Chicago Press.

Wodtke, Geoffrey T., David J. Harding, and Felix Elwert. 2011. Neighborhood Effects in Temporal Perspective: The Impact of Long-Term Exposure to Concentrated Disadvantage on High School Graduation. *American Sociological Review* 76 (5): 713–736.

Wyrwich, Michael. 2015. Entrepreneurship and the Intergenerational Transmission of Values. *Small Business Economics* 45: 191–213.

CHAPTER 4

Mexican Segregation: Good or Bad for Business?

INTRODUCTION

As we saw in the preceding chapters, both economic restructuring and harsh immigration policies that grew the size of the undocumented population contributed to blocking the mobility of Mexicans. In a city like Los Angeles where housing costs are among the highest in the nation, Mexican families live in some of the most segregated and impoverished urban neighborhoods in the US. While the previous chapter documented that impoverished neighborhoods are not conducive to the success of small businesses, the present chapter explores whether, how, and the degree to which spatial segregation matters to business outcomes. We show that serving ethnic enclaves is not good for business, and, in contrast, that branching out to serve a more multiethnic customer base is better for business outcomes. In a slightly different way, this chapter confirms what we found in the previous chapter: neighborhood poverty is the driving mechanism of poor business outcomes. Our findings thus contribute to the debate about the relative benefits of ethnic enclaves as against mixed economies for immigrant entrepreneurs. While our regression analysis tends to support the mixed economy thesis, qualitative comments captured in our survey appear consistent with at least some of the mechanisms described by the ethnic enclave thesis. This chapter concludes that the concentrated disadvantage theory better accounts for the partial and

© The Author(s) 2018   85
D. Trevizo, M. Lopez, *Neighborhood Poverty and Segregation in the (Re-)Production of Disadvantage*,
https://doi.org/10.1007/978-3-319-73715-7_4

seemingly contradictory findings described by either the ethnic enclave or mixed economy theories.

We begin this chapter by describing the different ways in which place concentration and racial segregation are conceptualized. We do this to introduce both the ethnic enclave versus the mixed economy debate and the main propositions of the theory of concentrated disadvantage. We then show our regression findings before presenting some comments from the small business owners in our study. The combination of quantitative and qualitative evidence supports our conclusion that the theory of concentrated disadvantage best accounts for the contradictory findings that report sometimes positive and sometimes negative immigrant business performance in ethnic enclaves.

RACIAL SEGREGATION, ETHNIC ENCLAVES, AND BUSINESS OUTCOMES

There is no consensus in the scholarly literature about whether immigrants voluntarily segregate into ethnic communities or are segregated by social forces outside of their control. Nor is there a definitive view about whether the business outcomes of small immigrant firms benefit from or are handicapped by their spatial concentration in ethnic enclaves. Part of the difficulty in reaching consensus stems from the way in which scholars conceptualize segregation. Many scholars, for example, observe that the spatial concentration of immigrant groups in specific neighborhoods results from their search for affordable housing near their extended families and/or co-ethnics.[1] Other scholars, however, emphasize that the historic legacy and continued enactment of racial discrimination in housing markets also contribute to the racial-ethnic spatial clustering of neighborhoods (Ochoa and Ochoa 2005: 11–12).

The scholarship on Mexicans in Los Angeles finds evidence consistent with all of these perspectives. Research shows that their segregation in LA results from both historic and contemporary racial discrimination against them in housing markets; it also results from the fact that while they are financially poor, they have rich networks of social contacts in existing Mexican neighborhoods. To illustrate some of the dynamics at work, neighborhoods in Los Angeles were explicitly advertised as White communities in the 1920s. Racially restrictive housing covenants formalized discrimination so that by the 1950s, segregation had increased (Ochoa and Ochoa 2005: 11–12). Although Mexican *barrios*, or neighborhoods, in Los Angeles, developed in areas east of the Los Angeles River, their segregation was not conspicuous outside of East LA in 1960, given that the city was still predominantly White and the foreign-born population was under 10% (Waldinger and Bozorgmehr 1996). It was not until the post-1965 immigration surge that a significant number of neighborhoods experienced White Flight, with parents of school-aged children fleeing the city's increasingly integrated public schools (Schneider 2008).[2] By the 1980s, the White population had declined (see Schneider 2008), and Mexican immigrants continued to settle in both mature Mexican *barrios* and new areas of the county where there had been few co-nationals. Such areas include the San Fernando Valley and Santa Clarita Valley, as well as the historically Black areas of Watts and Compton (Ortiz 1996). By 1990, more than half of the immigrants arriving in Los Angeles were from Mexico, El Salvador, and Guatemala (Waldinger and Bozorgmehr 1996), though at nearly 4 million, Mexicans constituted the largest group (Logan et al. 2002: 303). In this period, the exposure index fell: Mexicans had less exposure to Whites in their LA neighborhoods than previously, and Los Angeles became one of the most segregated cities in the US (see Wilkes and Iceland 2004; Tienda and Fuentes 2014; Rugh and Massey 2014).

The extensive scholarship on network effects demonstrates how social capital contributes to ethnic clustering in the process of neighborhood (re-)formation. Migrant networks contribute to place concentration insofar as friends, family, or simply people from the same hometowns in Mexico offer essential support to newly arrived immigrants.[3] For example, many family members of prospective migrants "sponsor" their relatives by providing food and housing for them when they arrive in their US destinations, and they do so until the migrants obtain work and become self-sufficient. They also help newly arrived migrants with information about job opportunities. Some families might pay the so-called *coyote* smugglers who assist[4] people in crossing the border illegally (i.e., without authorization) (Malpica 2005).[5] Friends and family extend solidarity even when they cannot guarantee jobs for newly arrived migrants. Bachmeier's work (2013) documents this phenomenon at the macro level when observing that Mexican migrant streams continue to flow to long-established immigrant communities (i.e., to "mature settlements") even when the labor market is saturated. For indigenous Mexican migrant streams, these dynamics result in something that looks like subnational ethnic-indigenous clustering in specific neighborhoods, as documented by Malpica for Los Angeles (2005: 128). For mestizos—the non-indigenous or mixed-"race" Mexicans—the support that they receive upon arrival from their networks also contributes to the demographic profile of specific neighborhoods in Los Angeles.

Finally, other scholars emphasize that irrespective of the specific reasons—whether poverty, racial discrimination, or because of their social networks—the spatial concentration of immigrants is essentially adaptive. Place concentration simply lowers many of the immigrants' transition costs and some research even suggests health benefits associated with Mexican *barrios*.[6] According to this school of thought, place concentration helps immigrants to mobilize co-ethnic solidarity, a cultural resource that is necessary to build the institutions that support the community (Malpica 2005; Logan et al. 2002). In this view, immigrants support one another by living in close proximity until they can afford to move to less impoverished neighborhoods (Jargowsky 2009).[7] Robert E. Forman (1971: 6), for example, argued that immigrants segregate voluntarily in order to reduce their transition costs and thus to

> minimize 'culture shock'. Immigrants established their own church with services in their own languages, developed their own native-language newspapers, and established their own clubs and mutual-aid societies. If the immigrant faced difficulties, it was with the support of the centuries-old culture and traditions that he and his neighbors had carried to the new American urban environment. (as cited in Jargowsky 2009: 1131)

Small Businesses in Ethnic Enclaves

With regard to small businesses, the ethnic enclave literature similarly holds that the spatial segregation of ethnic communities can benefit new immigrants. According to this theory, ethnic enclaves create opportunities for immigrants who are not competitive in the US labor market because they have not yet mastered English or because their educational credentials or labor market skills are devalued in the US. Immigrants with sufficient financial resources may respond to their blocked opportunities by starting small businesses that cater to a co-ethnic market. Immigrants without sufficient financial capital may still benefit from the opportunity to work for co-ethnic entrepreneurs, according to this theory. As such, the ethnic enclave literature argues that place segregation benefits both the entrepreneurs and the co-ethnic workers that they hire. While critics of this theory demonstrate that co-ethnic workers in enclaves are easily exploited (i.e., that they give more than they get),[8] our study focuses only on two propositions, those that hold that both (i) co-ethnic markets and (ii) neighborhood solidarity benefit small immigrant proprietors (not their workers) who are spatially clustered in one place.

To be clear, the ethnic enclave concept has a specific meaning not to be confused with everyday notions. In the words of Alejandro Portes, ethnic enclaves exist when "immigrant groups which *concentrate in a distinct spatial location* and organize a variety of enterprises serving their own ethnic market and/or the general population" (Portes 1981: 290–291; our emphasis). While the emphasis on the spatial concentration of ethnic enclaves is not conceptually identical to neighborhood racial segregation,[9] Portes and his colleagues point to the clear benefits of spatially concentrating a variety of ethnic firms, and one benefit is the ease of selling to nearby co-ethnics (Portes and Jenson 1992). What is more, the very spatial concentration of co-ethnics creates demand for culturally specific products. Ethnic places not only create specialized markets, but immigrant entrepreneurs have a cultural and linguistic advantage in catering to them. Their intimate knowledge about what is culturally authentic along with their ability to communicate in their customers' native language gives immigrant entrepreneurs an advantage, one amounting to having a protected ethnic market (Zhou 2004; Portes and Zhou 1993; Light 1972; Aldrich et al. 1985).

The theory of ethnic enclaves further emphasizes that immigrants benefit from shared ethnicity because cultural and linguistic identity engenders trust. Zhou argues, for example, that the spatial concentration of ethnic enclaves is "organized around the symbols of a common nationhood, familiar cultural environment, and densely knit networks" (Zhou 2004: 41). For many, a shared cultural identity inspires a sense of duty to support co-ethnics who collectively form a part of a generalized exchange system, one based on a mutual obligation for assistance and support. Ivan Light and Carolyn Rosenstein (1995) argue that the extent of such intra-ethnic solidarity varies by group, and that such differences are observable in the degree to which distinct ethnic groups mobilize cultural resources. At a minimum, however, ethnic identity tends to create networks in which people implicitly trust one another, and the trust networks of which they form a part, in turn, create opportunities.[10] Hiring co-ethnics because they are co-ethnics is one example, and this is easier to do when they are spatially concentrated.[11] In addition, some co-ethnic networks share business information (Gold 1994). Further, generalized ethnic trust facilitates the vertical integration of firms and, in some cases, the formation of ethnic guilds (Bonacich and Modell 1980).[12] Some people may even capitalize ethnic trust by borrowing money from their co-ethnics at little to no interest and without having to put down collateral.[13] The rotating credit associations

that we described in previous chapters are an example, but how they operate and whether they charge interest varies by ethnic group. Among
Mexicans, free or low-interest loans are generally available only to friends
and family. In these situations, strong ties mitigate risk because trust is
enforceable through close relations.

Some of the distinctive features of ethnic enclaves emphasized by
Portes' definition are harder to apply to Mexicans in Los Angeles who
constitute the majority of all Latino/as in a city that is nearly half Hispanic.
Put simply, because there are many segregated Mexican neighborhoods in
Los Angeles county, no one Mexican neighborhood is so distinct as to
fully capture a market for ethnic goods or hold a monopoly on ethnic
solidarity. Nevertheless, Mexico is a territorially large, multiethnic country,
and research indicates that immigrant networks are geographically and
ethnically diverse in ways that affect which migrant streams flow to which
US regions, cities, and even neighborhoods (Massey et al. 1994; Malpica
2005). It follows that regionally and ethnically diverse migrant streams
from Mexico help to constitute the demographic profile of specific
neighborhoods of a large and densely populated city like Los Angeles.
Recent research certainly finds that clusters of immigrants in some Mexican
neighborhoods in Los Angeles identify as Zapotec, Mixtec, or another
indigenous Mexican group (Rivera-Salgado 2016; Malpica 2005).[14]
Because Mexicans are segregated in specific neighborhoods that frequently
track with their networks, they are spatially concentrated in ethnically specific (Malpica 2005: 118) or perhaps in other subcultural or regional ways.
As such, the propositions about spatial clustering derived from the ethnic
enclave thesis would predict the following hypothesis:

Hypothesis 1: *Mexican-owned storefronts located in highly segregated residential neighborhoods comprised primarily of co-ethnics will benefit from
the demand for ethnic products and the supply of co-ethnic solidarity.*

In direct opposition to the theory of ethnic enclaves, the mixed economy thesis argues that a multiethnic clientele is better for ethnic businesses
because customer homogeneity discourages experimentation with goods,
services, or new business practices. Nee and his colleagues (1994) argue
that entrepreneurs who sell to ethnically diverse customers expand their
products to accommodate the tastes of broader groups of people, ultimately performing better in business than those who primarily sell to co-
ethnics.[15] To illustrate with a hypothetical example, *carnicerías* (Mexican

meat shops) that also sell American-style barbeque sauces and ketchup would attract some American customers in addition to Mexican customers. In the real world, the business model suggested by mixed economy scholars is well illustrated by the Mexican immigrant owners of La Monarca Mexican bakery. The owners of La Monarca adopted a "bicultural" business strategy of locating their bakeries in predominantly Latino working-class immigrant neighborhoods as well as the more affluent and White neighborhoods of Santa Monica and South Pasadena (Gonzalez 2015). In the ten years since opening their first shop in 2006, the owners recently opened their seventh bakery. They attribute their success to a combination of selling authentic products that are "Mexican in essence" (see Gonzalez 2015) but also appealing to "a larger demographic" (see Silva, September 10, 2015). To give an example of their strategy to appeal to broad groups of people in Los Angeles, La Monarca sells vegetarian chorizo quiches alongside artisanal, yet authentically Mexican, pan dulce (Mexican sweet bread). Gonzalez (2015) describes their strategy to appeal to a larger demographic by stating: "To appeal to both Latinos and non-Latinos,... La Monarca maintains a careful cultural balancing act, right down to design. The colors and décor in each bright and airy store are picked to suggest Mexico, ... but not look too Mexican."

Diversifying the products or services is important for the long-term survival of small firms because product redundancy saturates markets, reduces demand, and leads to lower profits for ethnic proprietors. As Waldinger and his colleagues observe, ethnic markets have a high failure rate both because they are tiny and because they offer similar goods and services (1990: 23). Further, following Granovetter's (1973) argument about the strength of weak ties, Anderson and Miller argue that trading widely, that is, with people with whom entrepreneurs have only weak connections also expands the variety of information flows and connects to broader business communities (Anderson and Miller 2003: 29). By extension, ethnically diverse customers should offer entrepreneurs a competitive advantage in business if they are numerous enough to comprise an extensive "weak tie" network. In sum, co-ethnic markets are limited to a smaller range of goods and services that can quickly saturate markets. Catering exclusively to co-ethnics rarely encourages innovation, and this is especially so if the proprietors are isolated from broader business communities with more diverse sources of information or opportunities. The foregoing suggests that ethnic enclaves are essentially mobility traps for small entrepreneurs.

A recent edited volume addressing this debate with regard to Mexican immigrants offers evidence consistent with the mixed economy thesis. To illustrate, a history chapter in that edited collection shows that entrepreneurs in the 1940s in Texas—a period in which the immigrant community was much smaller than it is today—were indeed more successful in business when they accessed "Euro-American networks" (Villarreal 2009: 47). Their working-class Mexican establishments made it possible for some proprietors to "participate in mainstream business organization" (Villarreal 2009: 47,53). Others proved successful by proactively targeting English-speaking Americans in their sales pitches even when what they sold was Spanish language newspapers or tortillas (Villarreal 2009: 53). Similarly, a small qualitative study on twenty-first-century immigrant entrepreneurs in rural Michigan reports that Mexican-owned restaurants "adapt" their menus—that is, the type of food served at the Mexican restaurants—to cater to "American tastes." In other words, they Americanize the food at their restaurants because, in the words of one immigrant restauranteur, "With only [a] Mexican clientele, we cannot sustain the business" (Santos 2009: 164).

The mixed economy theory argues, in short, that a multiethnic clientele is better for the long-term performance of ethnic businesses. If this theory is correct, we would expect that co-ethnic segregation in Los Angeles is bad for business, all else equal. The following hypothesis follows:

Hypothesis 2: *Mexican-owned storefronts located in highly segregated residential neighborhoods comprised primarily of co-ethnics will be less successful relative to their co-ethnic counterparts operating in neighborhoods with more diverse clienteles, all else equal.*

Given the immigration history that we outlined in Chap.2, it is not surprising that between 1980 and 1990, the number of households speaking Spanish at home increased by 74%, according to Lopez (1996). Lopez (1996) further argues that Spanish is spoken throughout Los Angeles as low-wage workers commute from their homes to jobs in the suburbs as well as to other parts of the city. Precisely because many people in Los Angeles speak Spanish, many natives as well as non-Latin immigrants also learn the language, or at least they learn enough of the language to get by in Los Angeles. Similarly, Mexican immigrants who do not speak English well may still learn enough of the language to communicate with non-Spanish-speaking customers in their transactions. Therefore, proprietor reports that they speak more English than Spanish at their shops could indicate that they have a more multiethnic clientele. According to the mixed thesis, they should do better in business if this is the case. The following hypothesis follows.

Hypothesis 3: *Mexican-owned storefronts in which the proprietors speak both English and Spanish to their customers will be more successful relative to their predominantly Spanish speaking co-ethnic counterparts, all else equal.*

With regard to the debate discussed thus far, the theory of concentrated disadvantage would argue that whether ethnic enclaves generate positive or negative business outcomes depends on the economic and social circumstances of the particular ethnic group in question. As observed in the previous chapter, the theory of concentrated disadvantage argues that people's life chances are determined by whether or not segregation spatially concentrates advantages that improve people's access to various opportunities (educational, employment, and more) as well as coveted resources (if so, a positive prediction) or the opposite (if so, a negative prediction). As such, this theory maintains that the spatial concentration of co-ethnics is detrimental when it concentrates poor and negatively racialized groups of people. These details, or caveats, are important because immigrant groups vary by educational levels, individual access to financial capital, as well as by the aggregate wealth of the ethnic community itself. Immigrant groups are also racialized differently. The context of reception is much harsher for some immigrant groups as compared to others. This is because some are presumed to be deficient—whether in intelligence, moral integrity, work ethic, or because of their religion. This theory, then, predicts that the mechanisms that prove socially noxious result from the interaction of racism and poverty among those who are spatially segregated. The theory of concentrated disadvantage specifically states that segregation proves toxic when it isolates poor and negatively racialized minorities in unstable, high-crime neighborhoods that provide inadequate public services. In short, the theory of concentrated disadvantage focuses on the intersectional dynamics involved in socioeconomic mobility and immobility, and such dynamics would indeed help to explain business outcomes. Further, intersectional dynamics are not fixed but rather vary over time and place. Massey and Brodmann (2014), for example, thus argue that the restructuring of the political economy in the US in the last 50 years not only worsened income inequality but also transformed the American stratification system away from an additive allocation of people to social spheres on the basis of strong racial effects and weak class effects, and toward a new one that allocated people to spheres on the basis of an *interaction* between still potent racial effects and increasingly powerful class effects. As a result, in the United States today we observe steadily fewer pure race and class effects *but a growing kaleidoscope of race-class interactions.* (Massey and Brodmann 2014: 334; emphasis added)

The case of Mexican immigrants illustrates some of the race-class inter-actions highlighted by Massey and Brodmann. To begin with, Mexican communities in the US are not simply ethnically concentrated places. They are simultaneously negatively racialized and grossly impoverished communities whose very unfortunate circumstances reinforce the racism against them as well as their poverty. Further, as documented in Chap. 2 of this book, racism against Mexicans intensified since the 1970s, as evi-denced in California's Proposition 187, the rise of border vigilantes (or Minutemen), as well as the increasingly alarmist and essentialist political rhetoric about the migrants (and their children).[16] These political and cul-tural movements betray a hardened stance against Mexican immigrants in the twenty-first century, one that increasingly defines them as violent criminals and, thus, as a threat to the nation that requires urgent security measures (such as a wall along the US-Mexico border). Finally, the race-class interaction is observable in the stringent immigration policies that since the 1990s penalized both legal and unauthorized Mexican immigrants with lower wage returns to their human capital. Since most Mexican immigrants saw greater poverty because of punitive immigration policies, it is not surprising that they remained stuck in high poverty neighborhoods during the same period in which other (non-Mexican) immigrants were able to move to less poor neighborhoods (Jargowsky 2009). Thus if, as Jargowsky finds, "Mexican immigrants seem to remain in impoverished neighbourhood contexts for decades" (Jargowsky 2009: 1148), it is partly because their communities grew poorer since the 1990s, when racial hostility against them increased in the context of a growing undocumented population.

The theory of concentrated disadvantage predicts that the marginalized neighborhoods in which Mexicans live are not conducive to small business development. At a minimum, poverty decreases buying power both because of the low wages in the community and because of poor people's greater likelihood of experiencing irregular employment. Further, since poverty increases crime, the loss of merchandise and costs associated with increased security also cut into profits. As Waldinger and his colleagues observe (1990), the ethnic market limits growth since it "can support only a restricted number of businesses because it is quantitatively small and because the ethnic population is too impoverished to provide sufficient buying power" (Waldinger et al. 1990: 23). Similarly, Aguilera's (2009) research finds that self-employment in impoverished areas

> does not provide economic benefits to self-employed Mexican immigrants in California or Texas. Rather, such self-employed immigrants earn significantly lower earnings relative to those self-employed within the ethnic economy outside the enclave. (p. 422)

For his part, David Torres concludes that ethnic concentration matters to wealth creation only when it combines with high levels of economic resources (2009: 38).

These scholars clearly emphasize how poverty affects small businesses in racially segregated communities. In addition to the limited purchasing power of some immigrant groups, ethnic solidarity does not yield equal or even comparable rewards to all groups even when their cultural identity and intra-ethnic solidarity are strong. In the context of high poverty, ethnic ties can lead some shopkeepers to experience what Aguilera described as "overburdening obligations" (2009: 423). Finally, when racial or ethnic segregation concentrates poor people, it isolates entrepreneurs from very successful businesses from whom smaller proprietors might learn about new opportunities, receive new information and concrete advice, or simply mirror in business practices. In sum, the concentrated disadvantage school of thought would predict that small businesses will stagnate and even fail if they operate in neighborhoods that spatially concentrate poor and negatively racialized groups. As Mexicans immigrants are negatively stereotyped, the fourth hypothesis follows.

Hypothesis 4: *Mexican-owned businesses located in highly segregated residential areas comprised primarily of co-ethnics will perform better in the least poor neighborhoods.*

We explore these competing hypotheses with data from our survey next.

FINDINGS

Table 4.1 presents select, individual, firm, and neighborhood characteristics for the 20 communities represented in our sample.[17] The table shows that the proprietors in our study were long-term immigrants, with some in business longer than ten years. However, firm maturity as well as the average number of people hired by the shopkeepers also varies by neighborhood. So does poverty. As noted previously, the table shows that more than half of the neighborhoods in our study have poverty rates worse than LA's already high poverty level. In addition, with the exception of the community called Pico Rivera, upwards of 40% of the residents in most neighborhoods is foreign-born. Indeed, the proprietors in our sample reported that many of their customers emigrated from Central or South America, Armenia, Philippines, South Korea, and Iran; they also refer to some of their foreign-born customers in general terms, such as "*Asiaticos,*" "Middle Eastern," or "*Arabes.*" Given the preponderance of immigrants from other parts of Latin America, it makes sense that Spanish is the language that dominates in business in some LA neighborhoods. Still, English prevailed in others. For example, less than half of the proprietors in Pico Rivera spoke primarily Spanish to their customers, whereas all proprietors in Cudahy, Cypress Park, El Monte, Huntington Park, Maywood, and Pico Union spoke primarily Spanish to their customers.

Finally, Table 4.1 shows that some residential areas had upwards of 70–80% Mexican concentration. Other neighborhoods—for example, Silver Lake Adjacent (Central City West) and Hollywood—are far more diverse. Indeed, the *Los Angeles Times* used census data to calculate a diversity index for various neighborhoods and cities within Los Angeles County. The index measures the probability that any two residents, chosen at random, would be of different ethnicities. If all residents are of the same group, the index is zero and if all residents are different, then the index is 1. For example, Hollywood had a diversity index of 0.644. However, many of the other neighborhoods in our sample such as El Sereno, Pico Rivera, San Fernando, and Bell Gardens had indices less than 0.3.[18] We contend that the highly segregated neighborhoods in our sample come close to Portes' classic definition (1981) of an ethnic enclave insofar, as they spatially cluster a variety of Mexican firms that primarily serve co-ethnic Mexican customers. Further, 16 of the 20 neighborhoods were at least 50% "Mexican," the criterion set by Logan et al. 2002 for the Mexican neighborhood designation (p.305). Our sample, therefore,

Table 4.1 Additional summary statistics by neighborhood (select characteristics)

Neighborhood	Area of Los Angeles	Foreign born %	Residential poverty> LA	Business open 10+ years %	Median number of paid employees	Median years of schooling	Primarily Spanish spoken to clients %	Mexican %	Median start-up capital	N
Bell	Southeast LA	53	1	29	0	10	86	68	$15,000	7
Bell Gardens	Southeast LA	50	1	50	2	9	83	78	$22,500	6
Boyle Heights	East LA	52	1	31	0	12	94	82	$7,500	16
Cudahy	Southeast LA	53	1	40	0	12	100	70	$5,000	5
Cypress Park	Northeast LA	53	0	100	2	2	100	71	$10,000	1
El Monte	San Gabriel Valley	51	1	100	3	12	100	62	$10,000	1
El Sereno	East LA	43	1	14	0	12	86	67	$15,000	7
Highland Park	Northeast LA	45	0	14	2	12	43	52	$10,000	7
Hollywood	Central LA	54	1	0	7	12	67	17	$2,000	3
Huntington Park	Southeast LA	56	1	0	1	12	100	76	$25,000	5
La Puente	San Gabriel Valley	44	0	17	0	13	67	69	$20,000	12
Maywood	Southeast LA	55	1	25	2	12	100	77	$20,000	4
Pacoima	San Fernando Valley	47	1	0	3	10	75	71	$20,000	4
Panorama City	San Fernando Valley	55	1	33	2	12	67	47	$16,000	3
Pico Rivera	Southeast LA	34	0	56	0	11	44	78	$13,000	9
Pico Union	Central LA	65	1	100	4	9	100	43	$30,000	1
San Fernando	San Fernando Valley	43	0	60	3	11	80	80	$15,000	10
Silver Lake Adjacent "Central City West"	Central LA	41	1	50	0	12	50	20	$12,500	2
South El Monte	San Gabriel Valley	52	0	0	2	12	67	74	$15,000	3
South Gate	Southeast LA	49	0	60	1	9	80	72	$28,000	5

Source: Authors' survey of Mexican immigrant business owners in Los Angeles (2007) and the 2000 census

Notes: This table adds information first presented as Table 3.4. New variables are shown after the red line

clearly represents a range, from the more multiethnic neighborhoods to those that are extremely segregated—for example, Boyle Heights and San Fernando, with upwards of 80% Mexican.

Yet, even the neighborhoods that appear to be mono-cultural Mexican enclaves in Table 4.1 do not reveal the full subnational extent of their social homophily. Recall that Mexico is a territorially large and ethnically diverse country. While we do not have data on indigenous groups by neighborhood, we do have data on the states in which our proprietors were born. The data show that they were born in 22 out of a possible 31 states (see Appendix B), yet small clusters were born in the following Mexican *estados*: Durango (n = 6), Guerrero (n = 5), Jalisco (n = 22), Michoacán (n = 13), Nayarit (n = 8), Zacatecas (n = 7) and Mexico City[19] (n = 16). Appendix D shows whether their natal states correlate with the neighborhoods in which they operate their businesses. At first pass, the evidence does not appear to show the subnational clustering at the neighborhood level that we might expect from the various studies on immigrant networks. However, because the neighborhoods of Southeast Los Angeles literally abut one another (see Fig. 1.1, which shows a map of the neighborhoods in our sample) and because there are so many Mexican states and LA neighborhoods in our study, we regrouped the data by the broader geographic areas of Los Angeles County (see the second column of Table 4.1). These new geographic units scale up from the local neighborhood level but remain socially meaningful (emic) place markers.[20] The evidence on these larger geographic areas shows a small but positive and statistically significant correlation, indicating that immigrants from specific Mexican states set up businesses in specific geographic areas of Los Angeles (r = 0.14; p = 0.081; see Appendix D). This subnational type of ethnic clustering in some general areas of Los Angeles appears more significant than the length of the migrants' US residency or whether the migrants cohabitate with their spouses. This statistically significant correlation, then, is additional evidence of Mexican spatial homophily in the commercial districts of LA's urban immigrant areas. Our evidence indicates that while Mexicans in Los Angeles live in many segregated communities, the general areas in which their small shops are located loosely correlate with the proprietors' sending states. This subnational type of co-ethnic clustering suggests more social homophily among Mexicans than what is indicated by their national Mexican identification alone. This finding, then, constitutes more evidence of ethnic enclaves.

Our sample, thus, offers urban geographic as well as workplace evidence that the shopkeepers in our study operate in the ethnic economy, and that some Mexican-owned firms indeed spatially cluster in ethnic enclaves, though others operate in less segregated neighborhoods. As such, we can now turn to the central question of this chapter: How does racial segregation or ethnic enclaves affect business outcomes? As noted in the previous chapter, because our respondents would not report their annual profits or receipts, the dependent variable in our study is the number of paid employees. This variable is common in the business literature because research shows that it correlates with sales receipts and profits. As such, the number of paid employees is a good indicator of better or worse business performance among Mexican immigrant proprietors in Los Angeles.

In the previous chapter, we established that the baseline model would control for gender (GENDER), whether the respondent was married (MARR), level of education (EDUC), years of US residency (YRSINUS), business sector (RETAIL, SERVICE), the log of weekly hours invested in the storefront (HRS), business duration longer than ten years (DUR), and the amount of start-up capital (STARTUP). The PARBUS variable controls for whether the respondents' parent(s) had business experience in Mexico (coded 1 for yes). We also control for neighborhood characteristics, such as the percent foreign-born (FB) and the level of neighborhood poverty (POV). We provide a detailed discussion of how we operationalized each of these variables in the previous chapter, and in the notes associated with our results table for this chapter.

To test our hypotheses that the spatial concentration of Mexican co-ethnics has a positive (H_1:+) or negative (H_2:−) impact on the business outcomes of Mexican immigrant entrepreneurs, we add the variable COETHNIC to our baseline model. As shown in Table 4.2, COETHNIC is the percentage of Mexicans in each of the neighborhoods in our study. This is a good variable to test the hypotheses about how co-ethnic Mexican segregation affects business outcomes because it is negatively correlated with the proprietors' self-assessments that they have a "multiethnic clientele" (correlation coefficient −0.228; $p < 0.05$, two-tailed test). The COETHNIC variable in our model is a more objective measure than the proprietors' self-reports since we used the 2000 census for the information. We also include the dummy variable SPAN (1 = speaks only Spanish at work; 0 = speaks Spanish and English at work) to our baseline model to explore the third hypothesis (H_3) derived from the mixed economy thesis. While fully 78% of our respondents reported that they spoke primarily

Spanish to their clients, nearly a quarter (22%) reported that they spoke both English and Spanish to their customers. Although it might seem logical that speaking Spanish to customers is evidence consistent with ethnic enclaves, this assumption may not work as neatly in a city like Los Angeles whose residents are from all over Latin America. In addition, many non-immigrant Angelinos get by with a limited vocabulary in Spanish (or in "Spanglish") while shopping, as noted previously. However, even if speaking Spanish while shopping is an inaccurate measure for estimating enclave effects in a city like Los Angeles, speaking more English than Spanish could indicate that the proprietors serve a more multiethnic clientele. As such, a negative coefficient associated with the SPAN variable could indicate strong support for the mixed economy hypothesis (H_3). A positive coefficient, however, is not enough to reject the mixed economy thesis precisely because, as noted, many non-Mexicans and non-Hispanics speak Spanish, or Spanglish, in Los Angeles.

To interrogate our fourth and final hypothesis (H_4), we add an interaction variable, COETHNIC *POV to the baseline model. Recall that the concentrated disadvantage theory specifically predicts that the effects of racial segregation—of the kind that concentrates poor and negatively racialized people—lead to especially negative neighborhood outcomes. This should also be true for shopkeepers. We follow standard practice by including the COETHNIC and POV variables in the model to gauge their additive effects independently of their interaction effects. As shown in Table 4.2, the POV variable is a dummy that captures whether the business is located in a neighborhood where the poverty rate is greater than the average for Los Angeles (if so, it is coded 1).

Table 4.2 reports the results of a Poisson regression and, since we have already discussed the control variables in the previous chapter, our discussion here focuses on the theoretical debate presented in this chapter.[21] Although the effect is small, the evidence from the Table shows a negative and statistically significant COETHNIC coefficient (column 1). This finding is consistent with the mixed economy hypothesis (H_2) that the spatial segregation of co-ethnics is bad for the business performance of Mexican immigrant entrepreneurs. These results, therefore, are inconsistent with the first hypothesis (H_1) derived from the ethnic enclave theory. The table clearly shows that storefronts located in highly segregated Mexican neighborhoods perform slightly worse, not better, than those in less segregated neighborhoods do. This suggests that Mexican proprietors find it hard to develop their businesses solely on the demand for co-ethnic products and services. Nor can entrepreneurs expand their firms from the co-ethnic solidarity that inheres through Mexican neighborhoods. The negative segregation effects identified in our model are net of the poverty effects and all control variables, including gender, level of education, start-up capital, as well as the industry of each firm.

At the same time, our regression results show that those entrepreneurs who predominantly spoke Spanish to their customers did better than those who spoke more English at work (column 1). Recall that we interpret the predominance of English at work as evidence that Mexican proprietors serve a more multiethnic clientele. Although the regression results associated with the SPAN variable are inconsistent with one of the mixed economy hypotheses (H_3), on balance, our regression results remain more consistent with the mixed economy thesis than with the ethnic enclave prediction. This is because the negative coefficient associated with co-ethnic Mexican segregation is statistically significant and its meaning is unambiguous. The meaning we attach to the Spanish language coefficient, however, is difficult to interpret in the Los Angeles context. The positive coefficient associated with the Spanish language variable could reflect that other immigrants from Latin America, as well as many US-born Americans, speak Spanish in Los Angeles.

Although the interaction term in our model was not statistically significant, our regression results remain consistent with the concentrated disadvantage thesis that emphasizes that high levels of poverty and racial segregation are bad for business. We see this clearly from Column 1 in Table 4.2 that shows that business owners in high poverty neighborhoods hire fewer employees than those in less impoverished neighborhoods.[22] The evidence, in short, remains consistent with the concentrated disadvantage thesis, predicting negative business outcomes for spatially segregated poor and negatively racialized people. Further, the fact that the negative coefficients associated with the poverty and ethnic segregation variables are statistically significant indicates powerful effects in light of the small size of our sample. That the regression results did not show a statistically significant coefficient associated with the interaction term could mean that there is no unique interaction effect independent of the additive poverty and racial effects. Alternatively, the non-significance of the interaction term could simply mean that our data set was too small to capture the interaction effect. This is possible given that our interaction variable was constituted by the POV and COETHNIC variables also in the model.

Table 4.2   The impact of class on business performance (Poisson regression)

	Model (1)	Model (2)
Gender (GENDER)	−0.110	−0.131
	(0.183)	(0.185)
Married (MARR)	0.744***	0.768***
	(0.214)	(0.214)
Years of schooling (EDUC)	−0.015	−0.013
	(0.022)	(0.022)
Years in the US (YRSINUS)	0.045***	0.046***
	(0.012)	(0.012)
Retail sector (RETAIL)	−0.584^	−0.566
	(0.453)	(0.454)
Services sector (SERVICE)	0.048	0.089
	(0.448)	(0.449)
Log hours worked per week (HRS)	0.247	0.266
	(0.320)	(0.324)
Business open more than 10 Years (DUR)	−0.621**	−0.677***
	(0.243)	(0.247)
Log start-up capital (STARTUP)	0.147**	0.128*
	(0.065)	(0.068)
Neighborhood's percent foreign-born (FB)	0.068***	0.070***
	(0.019)	(0.019)
Parent business owner (PARBUS)	0.580**	0.488**
	(0.234)	(0.248)
Residential poverty > LA (POV)	−0.766***	0.530
	(0.230)	(1.100)
Mexican concentration (COETHNIC)	−0.013**	0.003
	(0.005)	(0.015)
Primarily Spanish spoken to clients (SPAN)	0.669**	0.646**
	(0.273)	(0.272)
Interaction (COETHNIC*POV)		−0.019
		(0.016)
N	99	99
Psuedo R-square	0.202	0.206

Source: Authors' survey of Mexican immigrant business owners in Los Angeles, 2007

Notes: *p < 0.10, **p < 0.05, ***p < 0.01 (two-tailed tests), ^p < 0.10 (one-tailed test), standard errors in parentheses

The dependent variable is the number of paid employees. GENDER (female = 1; male = 0) MARR (married = 1; not married = 0). EDUC represents the number of years of schooling. YRSINUS represents the number of years the immigrant has resided in the US. RETAIL is a dummy variable for operating in the retail sector, SERVICE is a dummy variable for operating in the services sector. The professional sector is the omitted group. The variable HRS is the log of weekly hours devoted to the business. DUR is a dummy variable that represents whether a respondent's business has been open for more than ten years. The variable STARTUP is the log of the amount of start-up capital reported by the subject. FB represents the percent foreign-born by neighborhood as reported in the 2000 census. PARBUS controls for whether the respondents' parent(s) had business experience in Mexico (coded 1 for yes)

Finally, our respondents' comments help us understand the regression results better. Of the people in our study who offered additional comments at the time of the survey, several proprietors emphasized that their ability to conduct business in Spanish was, in fact, an advantage of working with co-ethnics and other Latinos/as, and these comments are consistent with our regression results. In a brief sentence, one of our respondents captured most of the causal mechanisms described by the ethnic enclave theory when he listed the advantages of having co-ethnic customers at his restaurant as the "language, types of food, and customs."[23] Another proprietor was quite specific about ethnic specialties when explaining that *paisanos* from his home state of Nayarit are particularly discerning in the case of *mariscos* (or seafood).[24] Yet another proprietor (also from the state of Nayarit) explained that the merchandise from his botánica "brings back memories to customers."[25] Many other proprietors observed that serving their co-ethnics was "easy" (*"fácil"*) or "comfortable," and several specified that their co-ethnics are "understanding," share "customs," are "loyal," can be "trusted," or that they "understand the product." The majority of the respondents—specifically 69% said that there is solidarity among their compatriots. Almost as many (62%) said that co-ethnics "help one another," including by helping each other with business recommendations, a job offer, friendship, or interpreting paper work. Three proprietors simply observed that their compatriots are "good people," while four other proprietors added that they appreciate the strong family relationships of the Mexican community.

However, a good number of respondents complained when stating that their co-ethnic customers haggle or request too many discounts. One of our respondents reported that co-ethnic customers "want everything at low prices" (in Spanish, *"quieren todo barato"*)[26]; another said, "they ask for many impossible discounts" (*"piden muchos descuentos imposibles"*);"[27] while still another described them as "cheap" while also taking note of their "loyalty."[28] One proprietor whose auto-repair shop is in Boyle Heights, an established Mexican community, explained that the "community does not have money."[29] In addition, several proprietors mentioned that they themselves help (or support) the community by selling at "good prices." While it is quite common for businesses to donate goods and services for special community events, our respondents regularly discount their prices or are simply careful about how they price their merchandise because they operate in the context of co-ethnic poverty. Given the sensitivity that merchants in our study expressed about their approach to pricing, it became clear to us that the line between fair pricing and deep discounts is blurred, so much so that it likely cuts into already small profit margins. This, then, helps to explain why the co-ethnic segregation variable was negative, indicating worse business outcomes for Mexican proprietors operating in mono-cultural or highly segregated Mexican neighborhoods. In sum, their statements illuminate why the poverty coefficient proves so important in our regression models.

One of our respondents who owns a pet shop in Hollywood, one of the more multiethnic neighborhoods in our study, expresses the point about race and class interactions succinctly as follows. After describing his customers as being primarily Latinos (broadly) but also a growing number of Asians, he said that an advantage of working with people from Mexico is that they share a common culture (which he simply called "*raza*") and language. At the same time, he answered affirmatively when asked, "How important is it for the future of your business to have a diverse clientele?" The shopkeeper responded: "It is very important because the *gringos* [White people] have the dough." (In Spanish, his exact words were, "*Es muy importante p/q [por que] los gringos tienen la feria.*").[30] Another entrepreneur made the same point, if less colorfully, as follows: "it would be very important because there would be greater profits and the business would grow. I'm ready to serve clients from other ethnicities." (In Spanish, her words were "*sería muy bueno porque obtendría más ganacias y crecería el negocio. Esta [sic] preparada para atender clientela de otras etnicas*").[31] The vast majority (88%) of the proprietors in our sample agreed, stating that having multiethnic clients would grow or improve the business. One respondent went so far as to state that it would expand merchandise from other countries.[32] Only 12% of the entrepreneurs in our study said that having a multiethnic clientele was not important for the development of their business.

In sum, while the mechanisms described by the enclave thesis—for example, the demand for specialty products, the ability to conduct business in their native language, the sense of loyalty, co-ethnic trust, and affinity—are valued by the proprietors in our study, our evidence suggests that neither specialty markets nor co-ethnic solidarity are enough to overcome the limitations of poverty. The evidence suggests that despite being cognizant of and actively engaging in co-ethnic solidarity, Mexican immigrants operate in markets where co-ethnics are too poor to help them to develop their firms. Many of our respondents clearly recognized that operating in more multi-ethnic contexts would be helpful for the long-term growth of their businesses, and their views are consistent with our regression results.

CONCLUSION

This chapter offers new, if suggestive, evidence that the commercial areas out of which Mexican shopkeepers operate in Los Angeles loosely correlate with the proprietors' home sending states in Mexico. Yet, despite the social homophily and even clear evidence of ethnic enclaves in some of the neighborhoods represented in our sample, the regression results still proved more consistent with the mixed economy thesis than with the ethnic enclave thesis. Small business owners in highly segregated Mexican neighborhoods hire fewer workers than those whose businesses operate in more multicultural areas. Therefore, independently of poverty, co-ethnic segregation among Mexicans is bad for business. High levels of co-ethnic segregation thwarts the development of Mexican-owned shops, in part because ethnic markets of similar goods and services saturate quickly. The redundancy of goods and services sold by co-ethnics is simply not good for business expansion or wealth creation. Also, as Anderson and Miller observe, "a relatively dense social network...does not allow for a variety of information flows" (2003: 29).

That said, our evidence also shows that a driving force behind poor business performance is neighborhood poverty. Our conclusion is supported not only by the statistical significance of the poverty coefficient, but also by comments from the shopkeepers themselves. Although many of our respondents reported benefiting from clients who "understand" their merchandise (or services) and from co-ethnic solidarity, cultural affinity cannot mobilize material resources where there are few to mobilize. To the contrary, some Mexican proprietors felt overburdened by their sense of duty to help co-ethnics who ask for discounts. Given the negative results associated with the poverty coefficient, we conjecture that during economic downturns, such businesses have a greater likelihood of business failure because their customers are too impoverished to sustain their businesses when disposable income diminishes. Finally, this study could not definitively address whether there is an interaction effect independently of poverty and race-based segregation because our data set is small. Future research might determine whether and how interactions matter.

Our findings, however, do suggest that the business outcomes of ethnic firms vary by ethnic enclave for many reasons. First, migrants from different countries emigrate to the US with varying levels of financial resources, education, personal access to capital, as well as density and wealth of their broader co-ethnic community, and so on. As Jennifer Lee and Min Zhou (2014) observe, some immigrants are hyper-selected from the upper strata of their home societies while others are hypo-selected from the upper strata of theirs. Given that immigrants arrive in the US from distinctly privileged or variously disadvantaged social backgrounds and with marked differences in their access to risk capital or even the right kinds of social capital (or network connections), it is not surprising that foreign-born people would engage self-employment at distinct rates and with different degrees of business success. It is hardly astonishing that people from financially privileged or from highly educated backgrounds can leverage their financial or educational assets to (re-)create wealth through new and creative business ventures across international borders (see also Bates 1994). The more enlightening story is about people from disadvantaged backgrounds who create for themselves pathways, albeit small paths, for upward mobility, however modest. Our findings tell this story and further contribute to the stratification literature by emphasizing how local neighborhood contexts matter for intra-ethnic variation in business outcomes. Our study begins to suggest that social capital contributes to the reproduction of advantage and disadvantage partly by contributing to the demographic profile or spatial composition of neighborhoods. The regression results in this chapter specifically support the theory of concentrated disadvantage that emphasizes the negative outcomes—in this case, negative business outcomes—associated with spatially concentrating poor and racialized people.

Despite these negative results, our findings suggest reasons for optimism about the prospects for upward mobility through small business enterprise. Our evidence shows that when people in multiethnic neighborhoods shop in Mexican-owned shops, the businesses of the immigrant entrepreneurs do better. Multiethnic customers not only create markets for more diverse goods, but they simply have more buying power than Mexicans do. Although our study captured qualitative comments consistent with the notion that ethnic enclaves offer both market opportunities and ethnic support to business proprietors, we concur with Morales (2009) and others that ethnic solidarity does not lead to business success when the ethnic market is comprised primarily of very poor people.

A policy implication that follows from this research is that local governments can encourage Mexican entrepreneurs to select business locations closer to multiethnic markets, or at least help them to develop long-term business strategies with an eye toward expansion. Municipal government programs that assist prospective entrepreneurs with site selection and business plans already exist. Our research adds information about better business locations for Mexican immigrant entrepreneurs, and informed planning might be especially helpful to people who might not perceive such opportunities given the social hostility against them. Negatively racialized groups might find it inconceivable to locate their businesses to more multiethnic neighborhoods given their awareness of the racial discrimination against them. That said, they might welcome additional information backed by research, especially considering that the issues we have addressed here are debated at the practical level among the small business proprietors themselves. To illustrate, petty vendors associated with "El Mercadito" in Boyle Heights have recently debated the purported benefits of ethnically diverse customers, with some vendors arguing that they would not create more demand for their goods and services (see Mejia July 14, 2016, Los Angeles Times). Other vendors, however, see a business opportunity in multiethnic clients. For example, the US-born son of a Mexican immigrant entrepreneur who recently inherited his father's restaurant stated that he plans to add a liquor license to organize "tequila-tasting events." His goal is to "try and evolve with the tastes of our customers, but at the same time stay true to our identity as an authentic Mexican place....but at the same time evolving and changing things to meet the needs of these new customers" (as quoted by Mejia, July 14, 2016 *L.A. Times*). Our research suggests that his viewpoint is "on the money." Diverse customers indeed yield better business outcomes.

Notes

1. For an early account, see Thomas and Znaniecki (1974 [1927]). See also Jargowsky (2009), Portes and Zhou (1993). Logan et al. (2002) specifically argue that "The ethnic neighborhood for some groups is a springboard, but for others it is a destination" (p. 321).

2. According to Schneider (2008), Whites specifically fled the Los Angeles Unified School district because they objected to Black and Latino students sharing classrooms with their children.
3. See Massey et al. (1987, 1991), Hernández-León (2008), Waldinger and Lichter (2003), Elliott and Sims (2001), Portes and Bach (1985), Portes (1995), Malpica (2005: 123), Hagan (1994), Boyd (1989), Gurak and Caces (1992).
4. Many coyote smugglers exploit the people they are paid to help and, certainly, some women report having been raped during their passage. It is beyond the scope of this work to offer a typology of abuses or determine the frequency with which they happen.
5. Although not as common, even *paisanos*—people from the same sending states—will assist new migrants (Malpica 2005) who are not family members. Some paisanos may even front the money necessary for the passage as a loan. In addition, there are local organizations in Los Angeles and beyond that are sometimes helpful to new migrants. For example, as of 2002, there were over 200 Hometown Associations in Los Angeles alone, and these are just some of the local organizations that may offer minimal support to newly arrived migrants. While these associations formed with the express purpose of supporting the people in their hometowns *in Mexico*, they clearly reflect a *patria chica* identity (i.e., an identity with the people of their local regional states). This identity and the organizations that form as hometown clubs or associations may also mobilize support for migrants from the same states. Finally, Los Angeles is not alone in the creation of these organizations. There are about 600 such home clubs in 30 U.S. cities during the same period according to a PBS report "The Sixth Section," September 2, 2003. http://www.pbs.org/pov/thesixthsection/mexican-hometown-associations/
6. On the '*barrio* advantage', see Eschbach et al. (2004).
7. Jargowsky (2009) refers to the movement into less poor neighborhoods as geographic integration.
8. See Bonacich (1987), Sanders and Nee (1987), and Johnson (1988).
9. See Portes and Jenson (1992). Briefly, the concept "ethnic enclave" specifically refers to a diverse number of vertically and horizontally integrated businesses owned by immigrants who sell goods and services to spatially clustered co-ethnics (IBID). Therefore, while the definition of ethnic enclaves emphasizes spatial concentration, a true enclave has a variety of firms engaging in different types of business activities.
10. As socialization is always imperfect, these sets of expectations are not universally internalized. As such, there are many instances of individuals, even family members, who exploit others. Despite the evidence of intra-ethnic

conflict and exploitation, on balance, more people report on their sense of solidarity than about their concerns with intra-ethnic exploitation.

11. Portes and Bach (1985) and Portes and Manning (1991) make this point.
12. Some research even suggests that when ethnic solidarity is weak, ethnic businesses will tend to fail (Light 1972).
13. See Light (1972), Bonacich and Modell (1980), Ndofor and Priem (2011), and Light and Rosenstein (1995). Although all groups have their fair share of exploitative people who charge usurious rates, there is an abundance of evidence of helpful ethnically based informal rotating credit associations as well as other forms of co-ethnic organizations (such as mutual aid societies).
14. According to Arturo Warman, there are more indigenous Mexicans in Los Angeles than in any other city outside of Mexico City. In his ethnographic study, Malpica (2005) found that there are about 120,000 Zapotecs in Los Angeles.
15. See also Light and Gold (2000: 127) as well as Aldrich and Reiss (1976). Bates (1994) demonstrates that small firms operating outside the Asian enclave do better than those that operate primarily inside the enclave. He adds that the much-lauded success of Asian firms is due to the "impressive educational credentials" of the proprietors as well as their large financial investments. The firms that rely on ethnic solidarity tend to typify "the less profitable, more failure-prone small business of Asian immigrants" (1994: 671).
16. Recall that during the campaign for the 2016 U.S. presidential election the Republican Party candidate, Donald Trump, referred to Mexicans as rapists and criminals. To nuance his claims he added that "some" are good people. See the previous chapter for an analysis of the heightened racism against Mexicans in the 21st century. For a nuanced ethnographic account of border vigilantes, see Shapira (2013).
17. We did not have sufficient grant money to pursue 25 respondents per neighborhood, which would have been much better for gauging neighborhood effects (See Footnote #7, in Sampson et al. 2002).
18. See http://maps.latimes.com/neighborhoods/diversity/neighborhood/list/ for a list of neighborhoods and their diversity indices.
19. The Distrito Federal was not a state at the time of our survey.
20. People from Los Angeles identify as being from "East Los Angeles" or from the "San Fernando Valley," and so on. See Appendix C for a brief historical overview of the general areas of Los Angeles that are represented in our study.
21. Poisson regressions are used with count variables because they tend to skew. Our dependent variable cannot have fewer than zero paid employees.

22. In a regression analysis not demonstrated here, we first ran the regression with the co-ethnic variable only. Then, we added the poverty variable in a second estimation to see how the coefficient on co-ethnics would change across models. The coefficient for co-ethnics stayed the same once we controlled for poverty, indicating that poverty is not driving the ethnic results. So without poverty, the ethnic coefficient is -0.136239 ($p = 0.10$); when we add the poverty variable, the ethnic coefficient remains (-0.132442, $p = 0.10$).

23. Because we did not assign pseudonyms to our survey respondents, we identify the people whom we quote by their case number. In this case, it was Proprietor #10.

24. Proprietor #105.

25. Proprietor #116.

26. Proprietor # 102.

27. Quotation from Proprietor #172 (Similar viewpoints are from proprietor #115, #128, and #131).

28. Quotation from Proprietor #109. Proprietor # 174 had a similar opinion.

29. Proprietor #119.

30. Proprietor #53.

31. Proprietor # 50.

32. Proprietor #110.

References

Aguilera, Michael Bernabé. 2009. Ethnic Enclaves and the Earnings of Self-employed Latinos. *Small Business Economics* 33: 413–425.

Aldrich, Howard, and Albert Reiss. 1976. Continuities in the Study of Ecological Succession: Changes in the Race Composition of Neighborhoods and Their Businesses. *American Journal of Sociology* 81: 846–866.

Aldrich, H., J. Cater, T. Jones, D. McEvoy, and P. Velleman. 1985. Ethnic Residential Concentration and the Protected Market Hypothesis. *Social Forces* 63 (4): 996–1009.

Anderson, Alistair R., and Claire J. Miller. 2003. "Class Matters": Human and Social Capital in the Entrepreneurial Process. *Journal of Socio-Economics* 32: 17–36.

Bachmeier, James D. 2013. Cumulative Causation, Coethnic Settlement Maturity and Mexican Immigration to the U.S. Metropolitan Areas, 1995–2000. *Social Forces* 91 (4): 1293–1317.

Bates, Timothy. 1994. Social Resources Generated by Group Support Networks May Not Be Beneficial to Asian Immigrant-Owned Small Business. *Social Forces* 72 (3): 671–689.

Bonacich, Edna. 1987. "Making It" in America: A Social Evaluation of the Ethics of Immigrant Entrepreneurship. *Sociological Perspectives* 30 (4): 446–466.

Bonacich, Edna, and John Modell. 1980. *The Economic Basis of Ethnic Solidarity: Small Business in the Japanese American Community.* Berkeley: University of California Press.

Boyd, Monica. 1989. Family and Personal Networks in International Migration: Recent Developments and New Agendas. *International Migration Review* 23: 638–680.

Elliott, James R., and Mario Sims. 2001. Ghettos and Barrios: The Impact of Neighborhood Poverty and Race on Job Matching Among Blacks and Latinos. *Social Problems* 48 (3): 341–361.

Eschbach, Karl, Glenn V. Ostir, Kushang V. Patel, Kyriakos S. Markides, and James S. Goodwin. 2004. Neighborhood Context and Mortality Among Older Mexican Americans: Is There a Barrio Advantage? *American Journal of Public Health* 94 (10): 1807–1812.

Forman, Robert E. 1971. *Black Ghettos, White Ghettos, and Slums.* Englewood Cliffs: Prentice Hall.

Gold, Steve. 1994. Patterns of Economic Cooperation Among Israeli Immigrants in Los Angeles. *International Migration Review* 28: 114–135.

Gonzalez, Saul. 2015. Inside an LA Bakery That Crosses Bicultural Borders. *PRI's The World and Globalpost,* November 24. https://www.pri.org/stories/2015-11-24/inside-la-bakery-crosses-bicultural-borders

Granovetter, Mark S. 1973. The Strength of Weak Ties. *American Journal of Sociology* 78 (6): 1360–1380.

Gurak, Douglas T., and Fe Caces. 1992. Migration Networks and the Shaping of Migration Systems. In *International Migration Systems: A Global Approach,* ed. Mary M. Kritz, Lin Lean Lim, and Hania Zlotnick. Oxford/New York: Clarendon Press/Oxford University Press.

Hagan, Jacqueline. 1994. *Deciding to Be Legal. A Maya Community in Houston.* Philadelphia: Temple University Press.

Hernández-León, Rubén. 2008. *Metropolitan Migrants: The Migration of Urban Mexicans to the Unites States.* Berkeley: University of California Press.

Jargowsky, Paul A. 2009. Immigrants and Neighborhoods of Concentrated Poverty: Assimilation or Stagnation? *Journal of Ethnic and Migration Studies* 35: 1129–1151.

Johnson, Phyllis. 1988. The Impact of Ethnic Communities on the Employment of Southeast Asian Refugees. *Amerasia Journal* 14 (1): 1–22.

Lee, Jennifer, and Min Zhou. 2014. From Unassimilable to Exceptional: The Rise of Asian Americans and 'Stereotype Promise'. *New Diversities* 16 (1): 7–22.

Light, Ivan. 1972. *Ethnic Enterprise in America: Business and Welfare Among Chinese, Japanese, and Blacks.* Berkeley: University of California Press.

Light, Ivan, and Steven J. Gold. 2000. *Ethnic Economies.* San Diego: Academic Press.

112   D. TREVIZO AND M. LOPEZ

Light, Ivan, and Carolyn Rosenstein. 1995. *Race, Ethnicity, and Entrepreneurship in Urban America*. New York: Aldine De Gruyter.

Logan, John R., Wenquan Zhang, and Richard D. Alba. 2002. Immigrant Enclaves and Ethnic Communities in New York and Los Angeles. *American Sociological Review* 67: 299–322.

Lopez, David E. 1996. Language: Diversity and Assimilation. In *Ethnic Los Angeles*, ed. Roger Waldinger and Mehdi Bozorghmehr, 139–164. New York: Russell Sage Foundation.

Malpica, Melero Daniel. 2005. Indigenous Mexican Migrants in a Modern Metropolis: The Reconstruction of Zapotec Communities in Los Angeles. In *Latino Los Angeles: Transformations, Communities, and Activism*, ed. Enrique C. Ochoa and Gilda L. Ochoa, 2005. Tucson: University of Arizona Press.

Massey, Douglas S., and Stefanie Brodmann. 2014. *Spheres of Influence: The Social Ecology of Racial and Class Inequality*. New York: Russell Sage Foundation.

Massey, Douglas S., Rafael Alarcón, Jorge Durand, and Humberto González. 1987. *Return to Aztlan: The Social Process of International Migration from Western Mexico*. Berkeley: University of California Press.

Massey, Douglas S., Andrew Gross, and Mitchell Eggers. 1991. Segregation, the Concentration of Poverty, and the Life Chances of Individuals. *Social Science Research* 20: 397–420.

Massey, Douglas, Luin Goldring, and Jorge Durand. 1994. Continuities in Transnational Migration: An Analysis of Nineteen Mexican Communities. *American Journal of Sociology* 99 (6): 1492–1533.

Morales, Alfonso. 2009. A Woman's Place Is on the Street: Purposes and Problems of Mexican American Women Entrepreneurs. In *An American Story: Mexican American Entrepreneurship and Wealth Creation*, ed. John S. Butler, Alfonso Morales, and David L. Torres, 99–126. West Lafayette: Purdue University Press.

Ndofor, Hermann Achidi, and Richard L. Priem. 2011. Immigrant Entrepreneurs, the Ethnic Enclave Strategy, and Venture Performance. *Journal of Management* 37 (3): 790–818.

Nee, Victor, Jimmy M. Sanders, and Scott Sernau. 1994. Job Transitions in an Immigrant Metropolis: Ethnic Boundaries and the Mixed Economy. *American Sociological Review* 59: 849–872.

Ochoa, Enrique C., and Gilda L. Ochoa, eds. 2005. *Latino LA: Transformation, Communities, and Activism*. Tucson: The University of Arizona Press.

Ortiz, Vilma. 1996. The Mexican-Origin Population: Permanent Working Class or Emerging Middle Class? In *Ethnic Los Angeles*, ed. Roger Waldinger and Mehdi Bozorghmehr, 247–278. New York: Russell Sage Foundation.

Portes, Alejandro. 1981. Modes of Structural Incorporation and Present Theories of Labor Immigration. In *Global Trends in Migration*, ed. Mary Kritz, Charles

B. Keeley, and Silvano Tomasi, 279–297. New York: Center for Migration Studies.

———. 1995. Economic Sociology and the Sociology of Immigration: A Conceptual Overview. In *The Economic Sociology of Immigration: Essays on Networks, Ethnicity, and Entrepreneurship*, ed. A. Portes. New York: Russell Sage Foundation.

Portes, Alejandro, and Robert L. Bach. 1985. *Latin Journey: Cuban and Mexican Immigrants in the United States*. Berkeley/Los Angeles: University of California Press.

Portes, Alejandro, and Lief Jenson. 1992. Disproving the Enclave Hypothesis: Reply. *American Sociological Review* 57 (3): 418–420.

Portes, Alejandro, and Robert D. Manning. 1991. The Immigrant Enclave: Theory and Empirical Examples. In *Majority and Minority*, ed. Norman R. Yetman, 319–332. Boston: Allyn and Bacon.

Portes, Alejandro, and Min Zhou. 1993. The New Second Generation: Segmented Assimilation and Its Variants Among Post-1965 Immigrant Youth. *Annals of the American Academy of Political and Social Science* 530: 74–96.

Rivera-Salgado, Gaspar. 2016. From Hometown Clubs to Transnational Social Movement: The Evolution of Oaxacan Migrant Associations in California. *Social Justice* 42 (3/4): 118–136.

Rugh, Jacob S., and Douglas S. Massey. 2014. Segregation in Post-Civil Rights America: Stalled Integration or End of the Segregated Century. *DuBois Review: Social Science Research on Race* 11 (2): 205–232.

Sampson, Robert J., Jeffrey D. Morenoff, and Thomas Gannon-Rowley. 2002. Assessing 'Neighborhood Effects': Social Processes and New Directions in Research. *Annual Review of Sociology*. 28: 443–478.

Sanders, Jimy M., and Victor Nee. 1987. Limits of Ethnic Solidarity in the Enclave Economy. *American Sociological Review* 52 (6): 745–773.

Santos, Maria Josefa. 2009. Knowledge and Networks: Mexican-American Entrepreneurship in Southwestern Michigan. In *An American Story: Mexican American Entrepreneurship and Wealth Creation*, ed. John S. Butler, Alfonso Morales, and David L. Torres, 151–174. West Lafayette: Purdue University Press.

Schneider, Jack. 2008. Escape from Los Angeles: White Flight from Los Angeles and Its Schools, 1960–1980. *Journal of Urban History* 34 (6): 995–1012.

Shapira, Harel. 2013. *Waiting for Jose: The Minutemen's Pursuit of America*. Princeton: Princeton University Press.

Thomas, William, and Florian Znaniecki. 1974 [1927]. *The Polish Peasant in Europe and America*. New York: Octagon. Reprint.

Tienda, Marta, and Norma Fuentes. 2014. Hispanics in Metropolitan American: New Realities and Old Debates. *Annual Review of Sociology* 40: 499–520.

Torres, David. 2009. The Mexican American Self-Employed Population. In *An American Story: Mexican American Entrepreneurship and Wealth Creation*, ed. John S. Butler, Alfonso Morales, and David L. Torres, 9–42. West Lafayette: Purdue University Press.

Villarreal, Mary Ann. 2009. Life on the 'Hill': Entrepreneurial Strategies in 1940s Corpus Christi. In *An American Story: Mexican American Entreprneurship and Wealth Creation*, ed. John Sibley Butler, Alfonso Morales, and David L. Torres. West Lafayette: Purdue University Press.

Waldinger, Roger, and Mehdi Bozorgmehr. 1996. *Ethnic Los Angeles*. New York: Russell Sage Foundation Press.

Waldinger, Roger, and Michael I. Lichter. 2003. *How the Other Half Works: Immigration and the Social Organization of Labor*. Berkeley: University of California Press.

Waldinger, Roger, Howard Aldrich, and Robin Ward. 1990. *Ethnic Entrepreneurs: Immigrant Business in Industrial Societies*. Newbury Park: Sage.

Wilkes, Rima, and John Iceland. 2004. Hypersegregation in the Twenty-First Century: An Update and Analysis. *Demography* 4: 23–36.

Zhou, Min. 2004. The Role of the Enclave Economy in Immigrant Adaptation and Community Building: The Case of New York's Chinatown. In *Immigrant and Minority Entrepreneurship: The Continuous Rebirth of American Communities*, ed. J.S. Butler and G. Kozmetsky, 37–60. Westport: Praeger Publishers.

CHAPTER 5

Gendered Differences Among Mexican Immigrant Shopkeepers

Introduction

The preceding chapters showed that gender does not have an independent effect on the business performance of small proprietors with shops in the Mexican neighborhoods of Los Angeles. Given that the scholarly litera-ture has established that women tend to have worse business outcomes compared to men, a more careful gender analysis is warranted. This chap-ter specifically explores whether the statistically significant predictors of business outcomes discussed in previous chapters are gender neutral or whether men and women are differentially affected by neighborhood pov-erty and segregation as well as other variables, such as early microclass differences in Mexico. Intersectional theory has long questioned the notion that independent variables are, in reality, fully autonomous. Instead, theorists from this school of thought argue that race, class, and gender intersect to produce multiple and complex experiences, relations, exclu-sions, and, indeed, business outcomes.[1]

Although qualitative analyses can capture much of this complexity by situating lived experiences contextually, quantitative intersectional analy-ses are also useful. To do more than treat gender merely as an independent control variable, we re-estimate the regression equations separately for both men and women. We do this to gauge the extent to which the returns to distinct variables in our model differ for men and women. In other words, we re-examine our original hypotheses to better understand how

© The Author(s) 2018   115
D. Trevizo, M. Lopez, *Neighborhood Poverty and Segregation in the (Re-)Production of Disadvantage*,
https://doi.org/10.1007/978-3-319-73715-7_5

racially segregated and impoverished neighborhoods specifically affect Mexican immigrant entrepreneurs by gender. The thesis of this chapter is that while Mexican immigrant women are more disadvantaged as compared to their male counterparts, mitigating factors help them to narrow the gender gap in business performance or at least do so for small immigrant proprietors in Los Angeles.

Understanding the business experiences of women relative to men is important because small firms owned by women are an increasingly important source of economic growth in the US. Between 1997 and 2007, the number of women-owned businesses increased by 44%, a rate of growth that is twice as fast as that of men's (Blank 2010: 6). In addition, between 1997 and 2002, minority women accounted for more than half of the increase in women-owned firms (Blank 2010: 7). Finally, while women business owners have historically hired fewer people than have men, these gendered employment patterns are starting to change, as Blank observes (2010: 12).

This chapter begins by introducing the intersectional theoretical framework and applying it specifically to entrepreneurship. Our empirical findings follow, with descriptive statistics presented before two separate regressions, one for men and one for women. We then offer intersectional analyses of gendered class and ethnic dynamics that lead us to conclude that class mitigates some gender effects. Specifically, the fact that some women in our study had parent business owners made them more competitive, and this helped them to narrow the gender gap in the business performance of Mexican immigrants in Los Angeles.

ANALYZING BUSINESS PERFORMANCE THROUGH AN INTERSECTIONAL LENS

An intersectional analysis that takes some cues from Pierre Bourdieu's sociology observes that gendered outcomes are always class and field specific. As Toril Moi explains,[2]

[A] Bourdieuian perspective ... assumes that gender is always a socially *variable* entity, one which carries different amounts of symbolic capital in different contexts. Insofar as gender never appears in a "pure" field of its own, there is no such thing as pure "gender capital." The capital at stake is always the symbolic capital relevant for the specific field under examination. We may nevertheless start from the assumption that under current social conditions and in most contexts maleness functions as positive and femaleness as negative symbolic capital. (Moi 1991: 1036; emphasis in original)

Applied to the field of small-scale entrepreneurship, the empirical research on how gender affects business performance indeed shows that self-employed women tend to perform worse than men do (Fairlie and Robb 2009a; Loscocco et al. 1991). Research not only shows that women tend to have lower profits and hire fewer employees than men, but that they are considerably more likely to fail (12.9% more likely). As of 2007, women owned about 30% of privately held businesses in the US but accounted only for 11% of sales and slightly less than 13% of the employment generated by such businesses (Blank 2010).

Most scholarship explains these gendered outcomes by focusing on the variation in financial, human, and social capital between individual proprietors; others examine their differences in risk tolerance or in the profitability of the specific industries (product markets) in which men and women concentrate. Fairlie and Robb (2009a), for example, find that women have lower levels of start-up capital, fewer years of family business experience, or that they have less experience in general. Women work fewer hours then men—for example, self-employed women work an average of 40.1 hours per week as compared to men who work 46.2 hours per week (see also Blank 2010; Robb and Coleman 2009). Further, Loscocco et al. (1991) find that women's concentration in services contributes to their underperformance because the service sector tends to be comprised of small and less profitable firms. This is true even of firms owned by highly qualified women. Still other research shows that women are less likely to apply for bank loans and that when they do apply, they tend to borrow less capital than men do (Treichel and Scott 2006). For their part, Davis and Long (1999) suggest that women are simply more risk averse, generally choosing business opportunities that are likely to survive even if with modest economic returns (i.e., profits). Finally, research suggests that women have fewer and less diverse social networks than men do, fewer connections to other business owners, and, consequently, fewer opportunities.

While identifying these differences is important, treating gender strictly as an independent variable among other controls tends to overlook how context and intersections matter. According to Mirchandani (1999), the differences between male and female entrepreneurs have "*not* been contextualized within theoretical understandings of the ways in which entrepreneurial work is situated within gendered processes..." (p. 225; emphasis in original). Instead, research on entrepreneurship simply compares male and female entrepreneurs to identify advantages or disadvantages, whether by individuals or by groups (1999: 233). In other words, while identifying gender differences in start-up capital, education, and industry choice is an important part of the story, it is equally important to examine entrepreneurship as "gendered, racialized and class-based processes" (Mirchandani 1999: 233). Beginning holistically, from the standpoint of lived experiences in the context of social power structures, is different than attempting to isolate the independent factors that have made men more successful than women in business (Stevenson 1990). So, while adding a gender variable to quantitative analyses of entrepreneurship is a substantial improvement over research that only looks at men's experiences, it is only a beginning. A deeper analysis involves exploring how broader contextual forces and intersectional dynamics affect people's choices and how and why these forces and dynamics systematically lead to divergent outcomes and life-chances for men and women.

Greene and Brush (2004) observe, for example, that despite the gains that women have achieved, they still experience discrimination and occupational segregation in employment, are still primarily responsible for home and children, and do not have access to the same kinds of information networks available to men. These scholars maintain that the role that gender plays in work, family, and organized social life is more important in explaining gender differences in business outcomes than are such factors as financial and human capital. They further observe that due to occupational segregation in the labor market, women concentrate in service or retail industries and generally do so in non-managerial positions. As a result, women have less opportunity to acquire managerial experience. Neither do they have much labor experience in male-dominated occupations that can be instrumental in business ownership and success.

Crucially, these gendered experiences also vary by ethnicity, which, like gender itself, is both racialized in distinct ways and has class-specific cultural expressions. Focusing on women entrepreneurs of Afro-Caribbean descent in Canada, for example, Knight (2016) finds that black women's history of working in domestic care, and the fact that many are single income-earners, affects their entrepreneurial experiences. These women have fewer financial resources to devote to their businesses than men do and, as single income-earners, they cannot afford to abandon waged employment completely. These findings have clear parallels in the US where African-American and Mexican immigrant female entrepreneurs have higher rates of business failure relative to non-Hispanic white women (Mora and Davila 2014).

Complicating matters further still is the fact that some gender scripts vary within the same racial-ethnic group in class-specific ways. As observed in previous chapters, Mexican immigrant women shopkeepers perform better or worse depending on both their class background and their marital status. However, the relationship between class advantages and successful business outcomes is not always linear or at least not in the short run. Valdez (2016), for example, finds that middle-class Mexican parents expect their daughters to postpone business ventures until they complete college, get married, and have children. Their poor co-ethnic counterparts do not face the same set of sequenced expectations. Certainly, many poor Mexican women work full-time jobs even when they have young children at home. However, despite the fact that middle-class Mexican women are expected to have children before launching a business venture, their cultural, financial, and social capital advantages yield better business opportunity relative to their poorer counterparts over time.

Even though some ethnic gender scripts vary by class, patriarchy both in Mexico and in the US remains a powerful ideology, one that continues to prescribe a caregiving role to women and a breadwinning role to men. Even if strict gender roles are not universally accepted, they remain dominant, appearing "commonsensical" to many people and even biologically determined, or "natural," to others. Consequently, Mexican business owners are more likely to bequeath their businesses to their sons instead of their daughters.[3] Patriarchal ideology and caregiving norms also help to explain why research finds that self-employed women's earnings drop with marriage, with family size, and with hours invested in housework (Hundley 2000). The exact opposite holds for self-employed males. In other words, married self-employed women entrepreneurs devote less time to their businesses than their married male counterparts do because they spend more time engaging in household and caregiving work (Hundley 2000). So, while many women see entrepreneurship as more flexible than wage and salary employment, the fewer hours of labor that they invest in their businesses results in lower earnings (Hundley 2000). According to Hundley (2000), the earnings penalty that self-employed women pay for doing more caregiving and household work is actually larger than the earnings penalty that women pay in wage and salary employment for their double duty.

Finally, mothering and household responsibilities exact such a time commitment, and the norms are so culturally prescriptive that Mexican immigrant women's networks tend not to scale up from family, church, or their children's schools (Granberry and Marcelli 2011: 123; see also Hagan 1998). This means that Mexican immigrant men have broader work and recreational networks, and these yield more information, whether about legalizing one's status or about better paying jobs, than do Mexican immigrant women's networks (Hagan 1998). So, whereas the men's broader networks of "weak ties" exposes them to more diverse sources of information, Mexican immigrant women's networks tend to supply redundant information. This is especially the case for Mexican women who work in isolation as domestics and even more so for unmarried women with even fewer ties to people who are not family or of the same ethnicity. With fewer networks of weak ties, Mexican immigrant women simply have less access to information about available business opportunities.

To illustrate how social networks are mobilized as business opportunities, consider how one male restaurateur, Ruben, acquired his start-up capital. According to Zulema Valdez (2011), who interviewed him in Houston, Ruben's parents brought him to the US without legal authorization when he was only 16. Though he eventually graduated from a state university, because he was undocumented when he wanted to start his business, he believed himself ineligible for a bank loan. So, he turned to friends instead, as described below:

> I approached my [wealthy Guatemalan male] friend with my idea. I knew his father very well and I put a business plan together and it looked good. I was in a conversation with this friend of mine and another [Guatemalan] friend... The other guy approached me later and said, "You know what, I want to do it with you." He didn't have any money so he went to his father. (as quoted in Valdez 2011: 79)

Not only do Mexican immigrant women have fewer networks but even those who are already entrepreneurs face gender discrimination in financial markets, and this affects their business performance over time. Mijid (2015) finds that even after controlling for the typical variables that explain successful loan applications, banks discriminate against female business owners who apply for business loans. This discrimination in financial markets, in turn, is discouraging to women who are subsequently less likely than are men to apply for loans.

In sum, only a small part of the role that gender plays in business performance is revealed with regression analyses that control for gender. Greene and Brush (2004) suggest that analyses of entrepreneurial phenomena would illuminate more by understanding women's business choices in the context of their families, occupational segregation, and social lives. Intersectional theorists agree. Yet, while scholars have fruitfully applied the framework to the labor market experiences of women and immigrants,[4] only recently have some applied the perspective to entrepreneurship. In advocating for intersectional analyses, Romero and Valdez (2016) explain that social context is not merely background information. Rather, intersectionality refers to those power structures in everyday life that are shaped by race, class, gender, legal status, and ethnicity. As they put it,

> studies that use an intersectional framework to examine the conditions for starting businesses, the role of the family and community in this endeavor, barriers to success or even the meaning of success itself, motivations for owning a business, and experiences of running or managing a business suggest more complex relationships between individual and collective agency and structural inequality. (Romero and Valdez 2016: 1556)

As the preceding chapters have already demonstrated some general class effects among Mexican immigrants, we next address some descriptive intersectional analyses in the form of simple cross-tabulations. These percentage distributions show not only how some class effects are gendered, but also how some gender differences are classed. We conclude our empirical findings with two distinct regression analyses that separately model men's and women's business outcomes. This allows us to determine the degree to which our earlier findings are gender neutral or are gendered in specific ways.

FINDINGS

Table 5.1 presents the characteristics of our respondents as well as that of their businesses by gender. The third column in Table 5.1 indicates whether the differences between men and women are statistically significant. The table clearly shows that the difference in our measure of business performance, the number of paid workers, is not significant. There are, however, important gender differences depending on marital status, the wholesale/resale and service business sectors, the number of years in business (or, simply, business duration) as well as whether the proprietor purchased an existing business or started the firm from scratch. In the first

Table 5.1 Characteristics of Mexican immigrants and of their Los Angeles businesses by gender

	Men	Women	t-test[a]	N
Demographic characteristics				
Married	76	56	2.121***	108
Mdn. age @ time of survey	41	43	0.401	106
Mdn. age when opened business	35	36	−0.930	106
Migration characteristics				
Mdn. age at entry	20	18	0.940	105
Mdn. years in the US at time of survey	29	24	0.600	108
Currently undocumented	6	9	−0.626	108
Cultural capital: informal and formal				
Father's occupation in agriculture or ranching	40	30	1.000	109
One or both parents were entrepreneurs	13	16	−0.420	109
Prior Mexico experience with business they would start in LA	30	20	1.124	104
Prior US experience with business they would start in LA	56	56	−0.012	103
Speaks only Spanish at home	81	68	1.597	109
Speaks primarily Spanish to customers	79	79	0.085	109
Mean years of schooling	10	11	−0.883	108
Median years of schooling	12	12	−0.694	
Educational categories				
0–6 years	30	20	1.216	108
7–11 years	13	16	−0.459	108
12 or more years	57	64	−0.741	108
Business types and business history				
Wholesale and retail stores	72	55	1.783*	109
Services (restaurants, hair salons, dry cleaners, welder services)	25	41	−1.854*	109
Other professional service	4	4	0.056	109
First business opened in the US	76	79	−0.381	109
Duration of business (median years)	8	4	2.480***	109
Mdn. hours a week spent on business	56	60	−0.088	109
Purchased an existing business	32	55	−2.498***	109
Start-up capital				
Mean start-up capital	$24,583	$25,876	−0.175	104
Median start-up capital	$12,500	$15,000	−1.109	104
Start-up capital acquired through:				
Personal savings or assets	75	64	1.045	108
Loan from relative or friend	8	5	0.460	108
Cundina, tanda, cooperativa	4	7	−0.772	108
Credit card or from financial institution	8	9	−0.260	108
Other	6	14	−1.512	108

(*continued*)

Table 5.1   (continued)

	Men	Women	t-test[a]	N
Business outcome: paid workers				
Mean paid workers	1.6	1.5	0.377	107
Median paid workers	0.5	1	−0.215	107
Paid workers quartiles				
No employees	50	46	0.458	107
1–2 employees	25	27	−0.267	107
3–4 employees	15	24	−1.075	107
More than 5 employees	10	4	1.117	107

Source: Authors' survey of Mexican immigrant business owners in Los Angeles, 2007

Notes: [a]A z-score is shown when the differences in medians was tested for statistical significance. $*p < 0.10$, $**p < 0.05$, $***p < 0.01$

part of this section, we focus on the statistically significant differences between men and women and then offer more hypotheses about how gender might matter to business outcomes.

Table 5.1 shows that while Mexican immigrant men are more likely to have storefronts in the wholesale and retail industries, their female counterparts are more likely to open storefronts in services. This difference is likely due to occupational segregation, where women work in feminized industries before launching their own businesses. The fact that the women in our sample are more likely to operate in the less profitable service industry might lead us to expect that their businesses are disadvantaged relative to male-owned firms. However, the regression results presented in the preceding chapters showed that operating a retail business (relative to other industries) had a negative and statistically significant impact on business outcomes, but that owning a business in the services industry (as compared to other industries) did not. Running our regression analysis separately for men and women will allow us to see if these earlier regression findings remain the same or if they vary by gender. Based on the research reviewed in this chapter, we specifically hypothesize *that women (but not men) entrepreneurs will experience a negative return to having their business in either the retail or the service industry.*

As noted, Table 5.1 also shows that men have been in business twice as long as women have (eight years for men, four years for women). We saw in earlier chapters that entrepreneurs who had been in business for more than ten years actually had worse business outcomes—that is, they hired fewer employees—as compared to small proprietors in business for less than ten years. In a previous analysis (Trevizo and Lopez 2016), we conceptualized the negative outcomes associated with firms in business longer than ten years as "stagnation." Because men have been in business much longer than women have, Table 5.1 suggests that they should realize a larger penalty. Our regression analysis by gender will allow us to determine whether this is the case.

Finally, Table 5.1 clearly indicates that the men in our sample are more likely than the women to be married (76% compared to 56%, respectively). This difference is important because our regression analyses in prior chapters showed that being married is helpful to business performance. However, it is not clear whether the positive impact of marriage on business performance holds for both men and women equally. The question is worth pursuing considering that Hundley (2000) shows that only male business owners benefit from marriage. He specifically found that women's self-employed earnings decline with marriage and with the size of their families. The weekly hours logged by the entrepreneurs in our sample suggest that men benefit from marriage only when compared to single men. Married men invest about 5 hours more per week in their small firms than single men do (married men work a median of 60 hours per week in their shops, whereas single men work a median of 56 hours per week of single men). The story differs for women. Whether married or single, Mexican female entrepreneurs in our sample logged a median of 60 hours per week in their small shops. Put differently, we do not see any indication that the married women in our sample reduce the number of hours that they invest in their firms per week as compared to the non-married women in our sample or even as compared to the married men in our sample.

Table 5.2 is the percent distribution of the reasons for going into business provided by the women in our sample. The table shows statistically significant differences between married and non-married women's reasons for going into business ($p = 0.064$). The third column in Table 5.2 shows the percentage of women who reported that they opened shop because they lost their job, had no other option, needed a steady job, or sought to overcome barriers. These answers point to the harsh labor market conditions that we have previously referred to as blocked mobility. That the non-married women proprietors in our sample appear to face greater financial insecurity than do the married women suggests that the latter benefit from a different kind of marriage boost—for example, by pooling financial resources with their spouses in a way that

Table 5.2   Percent distribution of reasons for going into business, by marital status among women, 55 entrepreneurs

Marital status	Make more money; better lifestyle; investment; retire early	Be own boss; spend time with family; better working conditions	Lost job; no other option; needed steady job; overcome obstacles	Had experience; all subject knows how to do	Family tradition	Give others job	Total	N
Non-married women	21%	25%	38%	13%	0%	4%	101%	24
Married women	45%	26%	7%	13%	7%	3%	101%	31
Total count	19	14	11	7 ·	2	2		55
Pearson χ^2	10.42* (d.f. = 5)							

Source: Authors' survey of Mexican immigrant business owners in Los Angeles, 2007

Notes: *$p < 0.10$, **$p < 0.05$, ***$p < 0.01$ (two-tailed tests), ^$p < 0.10$ (one-tailed test). The "Inspired by Others," category present in Table 2.4 is not listed here because no respondents reported this as a reason for starting their business. Totals may not add up to 100 percent due to rounding error

unmarried women cannot. If married women are able to pool resources with their spouses to start or to develop their businesses, it is also possible that their firms benefit from their partner's labor. This is plausible given that descriptive statistics from our sample indicate that all married respondents—male and female alike—reported that they lived with their spouses. Our baseline regression estimations have controlled for the marriage boost possibility by controlling for start-up capital as well as for whether our respondents are married. We cannot control for the number of children or their ages since we did not collect information on dependents. Still, based on these descriptive characteristics in our sample, *we hypothesize that married women in our sample will perform better in business than unmarried women.*

Table 5.3 introduces a new variable, one that describes how the proprietors in our study acquired their businesses, and it indicates some statistically significant gendered differences in their proprietary patterns ($p = 0.086$). The table clearly shows that a larger percentage of women than men purchased their business from another proprietor

Table 5.3   Percent distribution in how the business was obtained, by gender, 109 entrepreneurs

Gender	Bought from another owner	Established from the beginning	Inherited	Other	Rented	Total	N
Women	55%	43%	0%	2%	0%	100%	56
Men	32%	60%	4%	2%	2%	100%	53
Total count	48	56	2	2	1		109
Pearson χ^2	8.150**						
	(d.f. = 4)						

Source: Authors' survey of Mexican immigrant business owners in Los Angeles, 2007

Notes: *$p < 0.10$, **$p < 0.05$, ***$p < 0.01$ (two-tailed tests), ^$p < 0.10$ (one-tailed test)

(55% women vs. 32% men), while a larger percentage of men than women built their firms from the bottom up (60% men vs. 43% women). This statistically significant gendered pattern is consistent with prior research suggesting that women are more risk averse than men are in the field of entrepreneurship (Davis and Long 1999). Purchasing an existing business is a more prudent strategy than starting a business from the ground up because even in the worst-case scenario—say, purchasing a business on the brink of failure—an existing shop is likely to have some customers, stock, and perhaps some equipment. In fact, banks are more likely to lend to entrepreneurs who purchase existing businesses as compared to those who start new businesses given the existing assets and better odds of realizing profit more quickly.[5] Even if the initial purchasing price of the business is greater than the costs of starting a firm from scratch, the benefits of having an established customer base, easier access to loans, and having some sort of cash flow might outweigh the initial purchase price. In addition, women with children may simply prefer to save time by purchasing existing businesses given how much more time consuming it is to start firms from scratch. Finally, the immediate cash flow that comes with purchasing an existing business may be attractive to single women who do not have financial support from a spouse.

At the same time, research also suggests that there are greater economic returns connected to higher levels of entrepreneurial risk, though it is possible that such findings apply to larger firms rather than to the small storefronts in our study (Knight 1921; Kuratko 2014). To understand better if there are gendered returns to higher and lower risk business ventures, we interrogate the business outcomes associated with these distinct proprietary patterns in our regressions. Following previous studies that show that purchasing existing businesses carry less risk but offer lower returns as compared to new business start-ups, *we hypothesize that women who purchased existing shops will tend to hire fewer employees than those owned by female shopkeepers who start a business from the ground up.* To test this hypothesis, we add the variable EXIST to our baseline model. This dummy variable is coded as 1 if the entrepreneur purchased the business from another owner (0 indicates otherwise).

The preceding chapters of this book have consistently demonstrated class effects, whether by highlighting how microclass advantages in Mexico translate into better business performance in the US context or how operating in the most impoverished LA neighborhoods undermines business performance over time. While we do not find statistically significant class differences by gender, we did observe significant class differences *among* women as well as *among* men. Table 5.4 displays these differences by showing how start-up capital levels vary by educational attainment for men and women separately. The sample is split between those with less than 12 years of schooling (low skilled) and those with 12 or more years of schooling (high skilled). Not surprisingly, higher skill women entrepreneurs report more start-up capital relative to their low skill counterparts ($p = 0.05$ one-tailed test). Table 5.4 shows a similar pattern for men ($p = 0.09$ one-tailed test). There are, in short, clear class differences *among* the women and *among* the men in our sample, and this variation within gender could affect the performance of their tiny firms. So, just as in previous analyses, the regressions presented in this chapter continue to control for educational level.

Given the gender, marital, and class differences indicated by these bivariate relationships (as well as those in Table 5.1), the next section estimates regressions separately for men and women to re-examine old as well as to explore new hypotheses. We revisit our original hypotheses to determine whether men and women are affected by neighborhood poverty, neighborhood segregation, and early life (in Mexico) class differences in gendered or in gender-neutral ways. Intersectional theory predicts that the deleterious effects of neighborhood poverty, co-ethnic segregation as well as early family class resources that we observed in earlier chapters will affect women more negatively than men. Based on the literature, we also expect that women will perform worse than men do in the retail and service

Table 5.4 Percent distribution in start-up capital levels, by educational attainment and gender, 51 women and 51 men entrepreneurs

Years of schooling	0–$3 K	$3 K–$8 K	$8 K–$15 K	$15 K–$30 K	$30 K–$50 K	$50 K–$70 K	$70 K +	Total	N
Women									
Less than 12 years	16%	16%	26%	32%	5%	0%	5%	100%	19
12 or more years	0%	13%	41%	16%	19%	9%	3%	101%	32
Total count	3	7	18	11	7	3	2		51
Pearson χ^2	10.75** (d.f. = 6)								
Men									
Less than 12 years	18%	18%	27%	23%	0%	9%	5%	100%	22
12 or more years	14%	14%	28%	14%	28%	3%	0%	101%	29
Total count	8	8	14	9	8	3	1		51
Pearson χ^2	8.938^ (d.f. = 6)								

Source: Authors' survey of Mexican immigrant business owners in Los Angeles, 2007

Notes: *$p < 0.10$, **$p < 0.05$, ***$p < 0.01$ (two-tailed tests), ^$p < 0.10$ (one-tailed test). Total column may not sum to 100% because of a rounding error

sectors because their stores tend to be in feminized areas, such as party and beauty supply shops. Examining the impact of the business sector on firm outcomes allows us to test the expectation of differential returns by gender. To determine if men and women are rewarded differently for their risk-taking patterns, we also examine whether the returns on purchasing an existing business as compared to starting a business from scratch vary sharply. In sum, a comparison of separate regression analyses for men and women test the following hypotheses:

H_1: *Neighborhood poverty will have a worse effect on women than on men.*

H_2: *Neighborhood co-ethnic segregation will have a worse effect on women than on men.*

H_3: *Early family class privileges will benefit men more than they will benefit women.*

H_4: *Women and men will experience a premium to marriage.*

H_5: *Women will perform worse than men do in the retail and service sectors because they are in more feminized types of businesses.*

H_6: *Women will be penalized for purchasing extant businesses.*

REGRESSION RESULTS

One way to attempt an intersectional analysis with quantitative data is to interact all explanatory variables with the gender dummy variable. As this is not feasible, we opted instead to re-estimate the regression equations separately for both men and women and included all the same control variables that we had in the baseline model (see Chap. 3 for the equation). Doing so makes it possible to discern whether any of the key variables discussed thus far influenced entrepreneurial outcomes differently depending on the proprietor's gender. Table 5.5 shows the regression results for women and Table 5.6 shows the regression results for men. In contrast to our hypotheses, both the degree of poverty and racial segregation per neighborhood affect men and women entrepreneurs in comparable ways. Men and women alike have slightly better outcomes in neighborhoods with more foreign-born so long as the neighborhoods are not highly segregated by co-nationals (from Mexico). So, while foreign-born neighborhoods are good for immigrant businesses, too much co-ethnic segregation contributes to redundancy and is bad for business. The businesses of both men and women are also negatively affected by greater poverty levels, and

Table 5.5   Determinants of business outcomes for women (Poisson regression)

	Model
Married (MARR)	0.392^
	(0.284)
Years of schooling (EDUC)	−0.019
	(0.040)
Years in the US (YRSINUS)	0.049***
	(0.017)
Retail sector (RETAIL)	−1.205**
	(0.524)
Services sector (SERVICE)	−0.526
	(0.502)
Log hours worked per week (HRS)	−0.324
	(0.560)
Business open more than 10 years (DUR)	−0.378
	(0.381)
Log start-up capital (STARTUP)	−0.178^
	(0.111)
Neighborhood's percent foreign-born (FB)	0.073**
	(0.035)
Parent business owner (PARBUS)	1.007**
	(0.428)
Residential poverty > LA (POV)	−0.526^
	(0.364)
Mexican concentration (COETHNIC)	−0.019*
	(0.012)
Primarily Spanish spoken to clients (SPAN)	0.327
	(0.499)
Prior existing business (EXIST)	0.543*
	(0.305)
N	50
Pseudo R-square	0.234

Source: Authors' survey of Mexican immigrant business owners in Los Angeles, 2007

Notes: *$p < 0.10$, **$p < 0.05$, ***$p < 0.01$ (two-tailed tests), ^$p < 0.10$ (one-tailed test), standard errors in parentheses

Dependent variable is the number of paid employees. GENDER (female = 1; male = 0). MARR (married = 1; not married = 0). EDUC represents the number of years of schooling. YRSINUS represents the number of years the immigrant has resided in the US. RETAIL is a dummy variable for operating in the retail sector, SERVICE is a dummy variable for operating in the services sector. The professional sector is the omitted group. The variable HRS is the log of weekly hours devoted to the business. DUR is a dummy variable that represents whether a respondent's business has been open for more than 10 years. The variable STARTUP is the log of the amount of start-up capital reported by the subject. FB represents the percent foreign-born by neighborhood as reported in the 2000 Census. PARBUS controls for whether the respondents' parent(s) had business experience in Mexico (coded 1 for yes). POV is a dummy variable for whether poverty was greater than the poverty level for LA. COETHNIC is a measure of Mexican concentration in the area. SPAN is a dummy variable indicating whether the business owner spoke predominately Spanish to clients. EXIST is a dummy variable if the business owner purchased an existing business or not

Table 5.6   Determinants of business outcomes for men (Poisson regression)

	Model
Married (MARR)	0.775*
	(0.419)
Years of schooling (ED)	0.014
	(0.031)
Years in the US (YRSINUS)	0.037*
	(0.021)
Retail sector (RETAIL)	13.71
	(1129.2)
Services sector (SERVICE)	14.40
	(1129.2)
Log hours worked per week (HRS)	0.474
	(0.466)
Business open more than 10 years (DUR)	−0.141
	(0.417)
Log start-up capital (STARTUP)	0.324***
	(0.108)
Neighborhood's percent foreign-born (FB)	0.104***
	(0.032)
Parent business owner (PARBUS)	−0.043
	(0.416)
Residential poverty > LA (POV)	−0.856**
	(0.335)
Mexican concentration (COETHNIC)	−0.014*
	(0.008)
Primarily Spanish spoken to clients (SPAN)	0.713*
	(0.382)
Prior existing business (EXIST)	0.065
	(0.326)
N	49
Pseudo R-square	0.302

Source: Authors' survey of Mexican immigrant business owners in Los Angeles, 2007

Notes: *$p < 0.10$, **$p < 0.05$, ***$p < 0.01$ (two-tailed tests), ^$p < 0.10$ (one-tailed test), standard errors in parentheses

The dependent variable is the number of paid employees. GENDER (female = 1; male = 0). MARR (married = 1; not married = 0). EDUC represents the number of years of schooling. YRSINUS represents the number of years the immigrant has resided in the US. RETAIL is a dummy variable for operating in the retail sector, SERVICE is a dummy variable for operating in the services sector. The professional sector is the omitted group. The variable HRS is the log of weekly hours devoted to the business. DUR is a dummy variable that represents whether a respondent's business has been open for more than 10 years. The variable STARTUP is the log of the amount of start-up capital reported by the subject. FB represents the percent foreign-born by neighborhood as reported in the 2000 Census. PARBUS controls for whether the respondents' parent(s) had business experience in Mexico (coded 1 for yes). POV is a dummy variable for whether poverty was greater than the poverty level for LA. COETHNIC is a measure of Mexican concentration in the area. SPAN is a dummy variable indicating whether the business owner spoke predominately Spanish to clients. EXIST is a dummy variable if the business owner purchased an existing business or not

men may even be slightly more negatively affected by poverty than are women (compare the negative coefficients reported in the two distinct tables, −0.526 for women vs. −0.856 for men). Thus, our hypotheses that women's businesses would be more vulnerable in less than ideal settings are not supported by our LA data. In addition, there appear to be no statistically significant returns to education in our sample of small shopkeepers and this is so irrespective of the proprietor's gender. Further, both male and female immigrant entrepreneurs benefit in roughly the same way from the number of years that they have lived in the US. As we discussed in previous chapters, both men and women have better business outcomes the longer they live in the US.

However, while these new analyses show that male and female Mexican immigrant entrepreneurs have comparable business outcomes in ways that are consistent with our findings from the preceding chapters, not all variables are gender neutral. While it is not surprising that female retailers are disadvantaged relative to more professional women entrepreneurs (the omitted category is professional services), women in retail are disadvantaged as compared to their male counterparts (in retail). The table clearly shows that in contrast to men, women receive a negative return for operating in the retail sector (but not services), and these findings are net of all controls. We do not, however, observe that women in the services realize a penalty. Even though women are more likely than are men to concentrate in the service industry, doing so does not negatively affect their business outcomes as we originally hypothesized. We also see that larger amounts of start-up capital have a negative impact on women's business performance but a positive impact on men's (compare the coefficients reported in the two distinct tables, −0.178 for women vs. 0.324 for men). Thus, the positive and statistically significant impact of start-up capital on business outcomes that we observed in earlier chapters appears to be consistent with what we find here for men, but not for women. Finally, a comparison of the regressions shows that while men clearly benefit from speaking Spanish to their customers, the results for women are statistically insignificant. A larger sample would help us to determine whether the bilingual advantage that we reported in the previous chapter only benefits men and not women.

Given that separate regressions indicate some gendered results even if not always as hypothesized, why did we not see significant gender differences in the complete regression analyses of the previous chapters (that did not split the sample by gender)? Table 5.5 suggests an answer. As noted, in this chapter, we added the variable EXIST to our baseline model to measure whether or not respondents purchased the business from a previous owner. The results presented in Table 5.5 suggest that women's more conservative, risk-avoiding strategies in addition to any childhood microclass advantages that they may have are mitigating factors that help some women outperform some men. As Table 5.5 suggests, at least in our sample, Mexican immigrant women who purchased existing firms from other proprietors are more successful than women who start their businesses from the bottom up. This finding is contrary to our expectations but still reveals an important gendered difference, at least among the petty proprietors in our study. Recall that we had hypothesized that purchasing an existing business results in less risk but also lower returns as compared to starting a business from scratch. Given that more women in our sample purchased existing businesses than did men, we also hypothesized that women would receive larger negative returns. Our findings suggest, in contrast, that there is a positive return to purchasing existing business since assuming less risk actually paid off for the women in our sample. Clearly, more research is necessary to illuminate the dynamics at work.[6] What is evident from our data is that the success of the more prudent women appears to compensate partially for the underperformance of women's retail stores; it also compensates for the negative impact of additional start-up capital. Men, however, are unaffected by their decision to purchase an existing firm or to start their businesses from scratch.

Further, Table 5.5 shows that women's businesses appear to do better when they had a parent in Mexico who was also a business owner. This is another gendered result insofar as having a self-employed parent has a strong, positive, and statistically significant impact on the business performance of women but not of men. The reason why early life microclass advantages would affect women more than men could have to do with women's more limited labor market experiences relative to their male counterparts. Put another way, Mexican immigrant men spend more years in the US labor force than their female counterparts do, and they have a more diverse array of job experiences that, undoubtedly, increase different kinds of human capital. Given their smaller range (or set) of job-related skills, the business acumen acquired informally from their families in Mexico would matter more for women. Employing Pierre Bourdieu's concept, we observed in Chap. 3 that children of entrepreneurs acquire microclass cultural capital that can prove advantageous in some contexts

(Bourdieu 1984; see also Jonsson et al. 2009; Robb and Fairlie 2007; Dunn and Holtz-Eakin 2000; Wyrwich 2015; Hoffman et al. 2015).We specifically argued that an entrepreneurial disposition makes people more or less comfortable with haggling or risk taking or simply gives people perspective about potential market opportunities in seemingly improbable places. Our data here suggest that while entrepreneurial risk taking does have some gendered manifestations, women raised by business-owning parents indeed have an entrepreneurial disposition, and their intuitive "feel for the game" gives them a competitive advantage, as suggested in Table 5.5.

Our finding that the entrepreneurial disposition acquired early in their family life with business-owning parents in Mexico benefits women more than it does men is inconsistent with Valdez's (2011) argument that having self-employed parents is only helpful for middle-class men but not for middle-class women (pp. 50–53).Through her interviews of restaurateurs, Valdez found that the Latina women in her sample who had self-employed parents and who had prior experience in the family business were successful if they also married into middle-class families. In other words, the positive return to having a self-employed parent was only realized if women had husbands in the US who offered support for their businesses, whether financial or through access to his networks. Our findings show that once we control for start-up capital, men are actually less likely than are women to benefit from their entrepreneurial cultural capital. The benefit to Mexican female entrepreneurs is net of the initial start-up capital and of educational levels, as well as all other controls. The men, in contrast, saw much greater returns to their financial capital investments than the women did.

And, there are still other important gendered differences, as indicated by comparing Tables 5.5 and 5.6. As we found all along, both men's and women's businesses receive a small boost when the proprietors are married. However, Mexican men benefit more than Mexican women do from the marriage boost to business, as indicated by the fact that the size of the coefficients is larger for the marriage variable in the men's table (Table 5.6), as compared to the women's table (Table 5.5). These findings then allow us to nuance Hundley's original argument (2000), rather than simply contradict him. His study documented that married self-employed female entrepreneurs were financially less successful than their male counterparts were because women have a double shift, at their firm and then at home. He argued that married women proprietors invest less time in their businesses because they do more of the household chores and caregiving work than self-employed men do (Hundley 2000). Although our dependent variable is the number of paid employees rather than earnings, we observe that even though Mexican female shopkeepers in our sample benefit from being married, they are still less successful than their married male counterparts are. Though we did not control for whether they had children at home, we do control for the hours that they log in their businesses. So, net of weekly hours invested, Mexican married women entrepreneurs perform less well than their married male counterparts do, even though they perform better than unmarried Mexican women entrepreneurs do.

In sum, though not all of our hypotheses were correct, this chapter still demonstrates important intersectional outcomes, including how some gendered outcomes are contingent on class. In demonstrating how the returns to variables indeed vary in gendered and classed ways, our quantitative intersectional analyses highlight the utility of going beyond treating gender as a control dummy variable.

DISCUSSION AND CONCLUSION

This chapter applied an intersectional lens to explain the business performance of Mexican immigrant entrepreneurs in Los Angeles. Since we are only looking at one racial-ethnic group, racial discrimination is mostly already (held) constant in our analyses. Future research could, however, determine whether darker skin or indigenous features penalize Mexican immigrant proprietors. Although our data could not detect whether these types of racialized differences are relevant to business outcomes, we could interrogate how and when gender matters by running separate regressions for men and women. As expected from the intersectional perspective, we found that while some results are gender neutral, others are gendered and that some gendered differences are actually class specific. Therefore, in a way that is consistent with a Bourdieuian perspective, we show that the way gender matters varies by class. We further show that gender effects also vary by marital status and even the subindustries within the general field of entrepreneurship.

The regression comparisons suggest that each of our neighborhood variables—specifically the extent of poverty, the degree of neighborhood segregation, and the extent of foreign-born—are gender neutral in terms of their impact on business outcomes. As we demonstrated in previous chapters, both male- and female-owned businesses do worse in poorer and more segregated neighborhoods. They also benefit in comparable ways from the percent foreign-born in their neighborhoods so long as the immigrants are internationally diverse enough as to not create high levels of co-national segregation.

Still, as would be expected from the intersectional theory, the regressions indicate some gendered results. They strongly suggest that Mexican immigrant women are indeed disadvantaged as compared to their male counterparts in two important respects. First, the men's business performance does not hinge on the business sector in the way that women's business performance does. Specifically, women in retail have statistically significant lower odds of hiring more employees than women in other business sectors. Further, although married women do better than non-married women in our sample, married men benefit more from the marriage boost to business than do married women. Though we did not ask about children, we have no doubt that women's household and caregiving duties limit how they invest in their businesses and, thus, the extent to which they can be successful. Mexican immigrant men clearly have some advantages in business as compared to their female counterparts. If we combine these results with our knowledge of the discrimination that women face in financial markets, it is hard not to concede that Mexican immigrant women are at a disadvantage as compared to their male counterparts.

That said, the women in our sample were not always less successful than the men and not all women are equally disadvantaged. The women's class backgrounds mitigate some of the disadvantages that they experience as women. Specifically, Mexican immigrant women who grew up with business-owning parents in Mexico performed better than women whose parents were not entrepreneurs. In addition, women who purchased an already existing firm did better than women who started their businesses from the bottom up. So, if the larger models that combined information for both men and women did not show that gender matters in the first chapters of this book, it is because gender matters in complex and intersecting ways for the people in our study.

Our data, then, begin to suggest that some gender gaps may be narrowing (which is not the same thing as reaching parity) at least for small shopkeepers in Latino neighborhoods in Los Angeles. A recent report indicates that minority women—with Hispanic women among them—are not only engaging self-employment more than they had in the past, but are in fact closing the earnings gap between men and women (Roche

2014). In the "Monthly Labor Review" report by the US Bureau of Labor Statistics, Kristen Roche (2014) documents that Hispanic and other non-traditional women more than doubled their self-employment rate between 1993 and 2012; they also narrowed the self-employment earnings differential between men and women.[7] The evidence from our sample is consistent with Roche's finding and suggests that the gap in business performance is not as great as expected given prior scholarship showing that self-employed women hire fewer employees than their male counterparts (see Fairlie and Robb 2009a). Our data may have captured these relatively recent trends. Future studies can determine whether Mexican immigrant women entrepreneurs are really doing as well as men are because they hire more employees based on greater profit margins or because immigrant men are doing worse than they had previously.

To conclude: What explains that Mexican immigrant women in our sample do not appear to have significantly worse business experiences than their male counterparts? We suggest that specific microclass advantages from Mexico help some women compensate for a few of the disadvantages that they would face as female immigrants in the US. As noted, they seem to benefit more than the men do from the cultural capital acquired in their childhoods while living with parents who are themselves business owners. This classed, yet gendered, dynamic combines with women's more conservative strategy (of buying extant businesses) in a way that mitigates their disadvantages in LA business. Future studies can determine whether the intersectional dynamics documented here help Mexican immigrant female entrepreneurs over the long run or if they operate in similar ways in other cities.

Notes

1. For a foundational statement on intersectionality, see Kimberle Crenshaw (1991). For recent works summarizing the intersectional experiences of immigrant women, see Salcido and Menjívar (2012).
2. Pierre Bourdieu is certainly an intersectional theorist whose work is relevant to the study of gender and even race and ethnicity. In an essay on masculine domination, Bourdieu explained "I am going to try to show that... masculine domination...is a particular and particularly effective form of symbolic violence (other examples of which might be found in the domination of one ethnicity over another or of one class over another through culture, for example)" (2002: 227; Translation, Warren Montag).

3. We see some evidence for this type of pattern in our data. Although our data do not indicate the benefactors, two men in our sample said that they inherited their business. None of the women in our sample reported an inheritance.

4. Sociologists (see Irene Browne and Joya Misra 2003; Patricia Hill Collins 2015; Salcido and Menjívar 2012) and, to a lesser extent, economists (see Brewer et al. 2002 for a review of the literature) have pursued intersectional analyses. An intersectional approach examines the interconnectedness of race, gender, and/or class in creating unique labor market experiences. For example, Kim (2009) finds evidence that black women in the US suffer from three earnings penalties: gender, race, and the intersection of race and gender. The author similarly finds that black women experience a 15% earnings penalty due to gender, a 9% penalty due to their race, but a separate 3% penalty as a result of the intersection of race and gender. This last penalty is due to the unique experience of being a black woman. Thus, the total amount of labor market discrimination is greater than the sum of the race and gender components.

5. See https://linkbusiness.com.au/knowledge-center/Starting-a-New-Venture-vs-Buying-an-Existing-Business for a summary of the costs and benefits of purchasing an existing business.

6. One possibility might be that women purchase businesses in which they once worked.

7. The self-employment rates of other atypical agents, such as divorced women or those without young children, also rose in this period, as did the earnings from their businesses.

REFERENCES

Blank, Rebecca. 2010. *Women-Owned Businesses in the 21st Century*. US Department of Commerce, Economics and Statistics Administration.

Bourdieu, Pierre. 1984 (1979). *Distinction: A Social Critique of the Judgement of Taste*. Cambridge, MA: Harvard University Press.

———. 2002. Nouvelles réflexions sur la domination masculine. *Cahiers du Genre* 33 (2): 225–233. https://doi.org/10.3917/cdge.033.0225.

Brewer, Rose, Cecilia Conrad, and Mary King. 2002. The Complexities and Potential of Theorizing Gender, Caste, Race and Class. *Feminist Economics* 8 (2): 3–18.

Browne, Irene, and Joya Misra. 2003. The Intersection of Gender and Race in the Labor Market. *Annual Review of Sociology* 29: 487–513.

Collins, Patricia Hill. 2015. Intersectionality's Definitional Dilemmas. *Annual Review of Sociology*. 41: 1–20.

Crenshaw, Kimberle. 1991. Mapping the Margins: Intersectionality, Identity Politics, and Violence Against Women of Color. *Stanford Law Review* 43: 1241–1299.

Davis, Susan E.M., and Dinah D. Long. 1999. Women Entrepreneurs: What Do They Need? *Business and Economic Review* 45 (4): 25–26.

Dunn, Thomas, and Douglas Holtz-Eakin. 2000. Financial Capital, Human Capital, and the Transition to Self-Employment: Evidence from Intergenerational Links. *Journal of Labor Economics* 18 (2): 282–305.

Fairlie, Robert, and Alicia Robb. 2009a. Gender Differences in Business Performance: Evidence from the Characteristics of Business Owners Survey. *Small Business Economics* 33: 375–395.

Granberry, Phillip J., and Enrico A. Marcelli. 2011. Social Capital Is Associated with Earnings Among Foreign-Born Mexican Men but Not Women in Los Angeles County. *International Migration* 49 (6): 113–128.

Greene, Patricia G., and Candida S. Brush. 2004. Women Entrepreneurs: An Explanatory Framework of Capital Types. In *Immigrant and Minority Entrepreneurship*, ed. J.S. Butler and G. Kozmetsky. Westport: Praeger.

Hagan, Jacqueline. 1998. Social Networks, Gender and Immigrant Settlement: Resource and Constraint. *American Sociological Review* 63 (1): 55–67.

Hoffman, Anders, Martin Junge, and Nikolaj Malchow-Moller. 2015. Running in the Family: Parental Role Models in Entrepreneurship. *Small Business Economics* 44: 79–104.

Hundley, Greg. 2000. Male/Female Earnings Differences in Self-Employment: The Effects of Marriage, Children, and the Household Division of Labor. *Industrial and Labor Relations Review* 54 (1): 95–114.

Jonsson, Jan O., David B. Grusky, Matthew Di Carlo, Reinhard Pollak, and Mary C. Brinton. 2009. Microclass Mobility: Social Reproduction in Four Countries. *American Journal of Sociology* 114 (4): 977–1036.

Kim, Marlene. 2009. Race and Gender Differences in the Earnings of Black Workers. *Industrial Relations* 48 (3): 466–488.

Knight, Frank H. 1921. *Risk, Uncertainty, and Profit*. New York: Houghton Mifflin Company.

Knight, Melanie. 2016. Race-ing, Classing and Gendering Racialized Women's Participation in Entrepreneurship. *Gender, Work, and Organization* 23 (3): 310–327.

Kuratko, Donald F. 2014. *Entrepreneurship: Theory, Process, and Practice*. 9th ed. Boston: Cengage.

Loscocco, Karyn, Joyce Robinson, Richard Hall, and John K. Allen. 1991. Gender and Small Business Success: An Inquiry into Women's Relative Disadvantage. *Social Forces* 70 (1): 65–85.

Mijid, Naranchimeg. 2015. Why Are Female Small Business Owners in the United States Less Likely to Apply for Bank Loans Than Their Male Counterparts? *Journal of Small Business and Entrepreneurship* 27 (2): 229–249.

Mirchandani, Kiran. 1999. Feminist Insight on Gendered Work: New Directions in Research on Women and Entrepreneurship. *Gender, Work, and Organization* 6 (4): 224–235.

Moi, Toril. 1991. Appropriating Bourdieu: Feminist Theory and Pierre Bourdieu's Sociology of Culture Author(s). *New Literary History* 22 (4). Papers from the Commonwealth Center for Literary and Cultural Change (Autumn, 1991), pp. 1017–1049.

Mora, Marie T., and Alberto Davila. 2014. Gender and Business Outcomes of Black and Hispanic New Entrepreneurs in the United States. *American Economic Review* 104 (5): 245–249.

Robb, Alicia, and Susan Coleman. 2009. A Comparison of New Firm Financing by Gender: Evidence from the Kauffman Firm Survey Data. *Small Business Economics* 33 (4): 397–411.

Robb, Alicia, and Robert Fairlie. 2007. Access to Financial Capital Among U.S. Businesses: The Case of African-American Firms. *The Annals of the American Academy of Political and Social Science* 613: 47–72.

Roche, Kristen. 2014. Female Self-Employment in the United States: An Update to 2012. *Monthly Labor Review, U.S. Bureau of Labor Statistics*, October. https://www.bls.gov/opub/mlr/2014/article/female-self-employment-in-the-united-states-an-update-to-2012.htm

Romero, Mary, and Zulema Valdez. 2016. Introduction to the Special Issue: Intersectionality and Entrepreneurship. *Ethnic and Racial Studies* 39 (9): 1553–1565.

Salcido, Olivia, and Cecilia Menjívar. 2012. Gendered Paths to Legal Citizenship: The Case of Latin-American Immigrants in Phoenix, Arizona. *Law & Society Review* 46 (2): 335–365.

Stevenson, Lois. 1990. Some Methodological Problems Associated with Researching Women Entrepreneurs. *Journal of Business Ethics* 9: 439–446.

Treichel, Monica Zimmerman, and Jonathan A. Scott. 2006. Women-Owned Businesses and Access to Bank Credit: Evidence from Three Surveys Since 1987. *Venture Capital* 8 (1): 51–67.

Trevizo, Dolores, and Mary Lopez. 2016. Neighborhood Segregation and Business Outcomes: Mexican Immigrant Entrepreneurs in Los Angeles County. *Sociological Perspectives* 59 (3): 668–693.

Valdez, Zulema. 2011. *The New Entrepreneurs: How Race, Class, and Gender Shape American Enterprise*. Stanford: Stanford University Press.

————. 2016. Intersectionality, the Household Economy, and Ethnic Entrepreneurship. *Ethnic and Racial Studies* 39 (9): 1618–1636.
Wyrwich, Michael. 2015. Entrepreneurship and the Intergenerational Transmission of Values. *Small Business Economics* 45: 191–213.

CHAPTER 6

From "Illegal" to Neighborhood Shopkeeper: How Legal Capital Affects Business Performance

INTRODUCTION

Undocumented Mexican immigrants are not only a racialized ethnic minority, but they face the additional disadvantage associated with illegal status. Further, since being undocumented is itself generally associated with lower levels of education (Jasso et al. 2008), the combination of their relative lack of education, racism, and being undocumented generally leads to the worst possible employment prospects. In Chap. 2, we demonstrated that the increasingly punitive immigration legislation of the twentieth and twenty-first centuries added to the disadvantages faced by the undocumented by producing "caging effects." As observed, hundreds of thousands of people felt compelled to establish roots in the US because they were too afraid to return to Mexico, whether in a traditional seasonal (or circular) migration pattern or for a longer period (Massey et al. 2002; Argueta 2016). Both the caging effects and the continued inflows of large numbers of unauthorized migrants through the 1990s led to a significant increase in the undocumented population in the US (Massey et al. 2002) and both patterns, we argue, contributed to their blocked social mobility. However, whereas prior research has demonstrated the harsh labor market conditions these workers endure, along with the social and legal penalties that they face, this chapter illuminates some benefits of overcoming illegality.

Our data provide a window into what some immigrants do after they adjust their immigration status from undocumented to legal permanent

© The Author(s) 2018   143
D. Trevizo, M. Lopez, *Neighborhood Poverty and Segregation in the (Re-)Production of Disadvantage*,
https://doi.org/10.1007/978-3-319-73715-7_6

resident (henceforth, "legal" or LPR). This chapter not only shows some of the potential economic benefits linked to the transition from undocumented to legal migrant but demonstrates that such benefits also depend on what people do with their new status as well as *when* they do it. More specifically, we show that the benefits of legal status depend not only on which opportunities are seized but also on *when* prospective entrepreneurs make use of their new legal rights as small shopkeepers. So, whereas prior research shows that undocumented status cuts off access to good paying jobs (see Hall et al. 2010; Massey and Gelatt 2010; Donato and Sisk 2012; Flippen 2012), we show that social mobility is affected by the length of time spent conducting business under the auspices of legal status. As such, this analysis—like those in the preceding chapters—also contributes to the stratification literature.

Because the acquisition of LPR status brings more rights, it is a major turning point for anyone who is undocumented,[1] and not least for people in the labor market. Obtaining legal status makes it possible for labor market participants to pursue either better jobs or new types of economic opportunity. We contend that the business outcomes of (previously undocumented) aspiring immigrant entrepreneurs with legal status—the people on whom we focus this chapter—are better or worse, depending on the length of time between their legalization and the start of their entrepreneurial venture. We show, for example, that the benefits of legalizing depend partly on how quickly prospective entrepreneurs make use of their newly acquired legal status in the pursuit of small business enterprise.

This chapter thus addresses how legal status shapes business people's experiences in the formal economy. We demonstrate that the specific combination of early business experience with legal status creates advantages over those who remain in the labor market for a longer period before starting their business. Figure 6.1 illustrates these two pathways, one for people who start early in business and the second for people who linger in the labor market before opening up their business. Our regression analysis

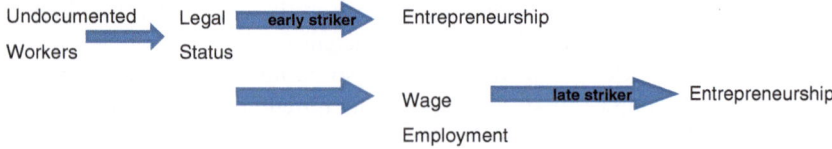

Fig. 6.1   Timing of entrepreneurship among legalized migrants

shows that for a group of what we call "early strikers," the accumulated experiences of petty proprietorship under the auspices of legal status positively affect their business performance over the long term. This chapter thus demonstrates the advantage enjoyed by immigrant entrepreneurs who launch a business soon after legalizing their immigration statuses (i.e., "early strikers"). Building on the scholarly literature, we call this premium *legal capital* (discussed below). By extension, we also demonstrate that there is a penalty for those entrepreneurs who wait too long to open up shop after legalizing their immigration status (so, the "late strikers") relative to early strikers. Since our regression results control for individual differences in education and start-up capital, as well as for other social and demographic variables, we are confident that idiosyncratic differences between people are not the only factors explaining the business performance of their small firms.

We find that early strikers restructured their economic trajectory by risking capital earlier in their career span in order to start their own businesses and, we conjecture, by sharpening their business acumen and learning the intricacies of the formal economy earlier. We demonstrate that radically retooling earlier in the span of their working careers yields better business outcomes as compared to shopkeepers who postponed entrepreneurship for more labor market experience upon legalization. Therefore, a second general point derived from our findings is that social mobility among once undocumented immigrants who are aspiring entrepreneurs depends not only on what they do with their legal status but also on how soon after legalization they try their hands at entrepreneurship. In other words, timing matters to the benefits of what has been called legal capital.

We make our case in this chapter first by presenting the scholarship that conceptualizes the notion of legal capital. Our empirical findings of how the timing of petty proprietorship vis-à-vis legalization matters for aspiring entrepreneurs follows. This chapter concludes with an analysis of how legal capital, the knowledge and skills acquired in the formal economy under the auspices of legal status, contributes to the accumulation of business advantage over time.

LEGAL CAPITAL, THE CONCEPT

Research shows that immigration status—whether someone has the legal right to live and work in the US, has a temporary work permit, is a permanent legal resident, or is a naturalized citizen—affects labor market outcomes

(Tienda and Singer 1995; Rivera-Batiz 1999; Kossoudji and Cobb-Clark 2002; Bratsberg et al. 2002; Hall et al. 2010). This research clearly establishes that the undocumented are among the most vulnerable and exploited of all workers in the US, getting considerably less pay as compared to Americans or even other immigrants with legal status and the same labor market skills.[2]

Precisely because their socio-legal status forces them into harsh workplace conditions, many long-term undocumented people sell their labor services, or inexpensive wares, in the informal economy—that is, the part of the economy not subject to the purview of the state. Sometimes referred to as "survivor entrepreneurs," many low-skilled immigrants are self-employed freelance housekeepers, gardeners, dog-walkers, painters, handymen, and the like. Others engage in petty merchant activities, whether as pushcart street or swap-meet vendors. If they do not file taxes that report their earnings, they operate in the informal economy. Whatever the specific job or trade, these survival activities do not generally lead to upward mobility. Even swap-meet vendors are survivor entrepreneurs who, like the others, tend not to experience meaningful upward mobility. Due to their low earnings, many survivor entrepreneurs lack sufficient savings or financial capital to start a viable business. In other words, the movement from the wage sector to self-employment as an undocumented migrant does not generally lead to substantially higher earnings. While some undocumented migrants manage, with the help of close friends or family, to skirt the law and open storefronts, the economic growth potential of such quasi-legal firms is also limited, so long as the proprietors are undocumented (Fairlie and Woodruff 2010).

The "mixed embeddedness" school of thought offers an explanatory framework for the stunted development of informal economy workers, vendors, or quasi-legal small businesses.[3] Its proponents argue that in addition to market conditions, state policy and the extent of legal enforcement contribute to the opportunity structure that immigrants (and natives) navigate. The mixed embeddedness approach specifically argues that the legal-political and regulatory contexts that immigrants confront along with market conditions and access to ownership help to shape business development and, thus, the life chances of entrepreneurs.[4] Although there are fewer state regulations involved in opening small businesses in the US than there are in Europe, even the most hard-working and entrepreneurial people living in the US face significant obstacles if they are undocumented. Since unauthorized residency in the US is against the law, undocumented people do not have access to the official identification cards, social security numbers, or tax returns necessary for business. Not only do aspiring entrepreneurs find it challenging to make their business ideas viable without such official paperwork (which migrants refer to as "*papeles*"), but undocumented migrants attempt to evade deportation by living in the shadows. As a result, many ignore free municipal government programs, such as business workshops that assist prospective entrepreneurs with business plans, out of fear of exposing their immigration status.[5] Others forego many networking opportunities for the same reason.

Because being undocumented blocks access to important business opportunities and networks, Ramirez and Hondagneu-Sotelo (2009) liken obtaining legal status to something akin to acquiring "legal capital." As with all concepts relying on the notion of capital, legal capital signifies that when the state grants immigrants the right to live and work in the nation, that legal status designation, along with its attendant official identifications and other paperwork, create exchange values. Until very recently in California (2015),[6] for example, illegal status made it impossible to obtain driver's licenses, which, for their part, give access to economic opportunity (Ramirez and Hondagneu-Sotelo 2009). To illustrate further, many people require identification issued by a US government agency for the rental of storefronts or other commercial space. Crucially, legal status is still generally necessary in California for business loans because Social Security numbers make it possible to show the official tax returns usually required for such loans.[7] The undocumented, however, have historically not had access to these types of documents and, as of the early 2000s, most did not have *any* formal ties to financial institutions. Without access to bank loans for small business ventures,[8] rungs in the ladder of upward mobility have simply been missing for millions of people without the legal right to live and work in the US. As noted, even free local government programs aimed at supporting new, small business ventures are beyond the reach of those without legal status if they are required to file official tax returns.[9]

Our point, however, is not merely to restate the obvious fact that legal status gives access to some of the resources necessary for upward mobility, including business opportunity. Rather, we find the notion of legal capital interesting because, depending on when it is accumulated, legal entrepreneurs will have more or less time to make use of the resources not available to their undocumented counterparts. The idea of advantages accumulating over time builds on Kerstin Gentsch's and Douglas Massey's argument that "experience accumulated under legal auspices" matters for labor market outcomes (2011: 876). They argue that experiences accumulated over time while "in undocumented or temporary status might not carry the same benefits and returns as time accumulated in permanent resident status" (2011: 876). Gentsch and Massey clearly move beyond the "legal" versus "illegal" binary by conceptualizing variant returns to experiences accumulated over time under the auspices of various legal statuses. We build on their logic by suggesting that the proprietor's legal status is not the only factor that matters for good business outcomes. Nor is business longevity, or business duration, the only way to capture how time (or experience) itself contributes to business success. Our reasoning takes a third step beyond (i) access to resources (Ramirez and Hondagneu-Sotelo 2009) or (ii) time with resources (Gentsch and Massey 2011). The third point in our argument is that the sooner newly legal entrepreneurs utilize resources that undocumented people do not have, the more proficient they become at using them, and this efficiency ultimately yields better business outcomes.

We use the term legal capital, then, as shorthand to capture these three points. The concept does more than simply indicate whether someone has the legal right to work and live in the US. Building on Pierre Bourdieu's notion of cultural capital (discussed earlier), legal capital is a subtype of cultural knowledge. The concept of legal capital captures the fact that entrepreneurs who have invested more time in the formal business economy (with legal status) during the course of their working lives develop knowledge that helps them to succeed in this economy. Such knowledge might include insights about what formal banking institutions require for loans and about suppliers, business ordinances, and so on, and that new knowledge helps them develop better business practices.[10] The legal status and dominant language skills of small proprietors are not enough to allow them to understand the paperwork, the interests on their loans, and the extent of risk that they assume through bank loans. Operating earlier in the formal economy (i.e., with legal status) not only acquaints them with financial institutions but also gives them experience with business permits, the business inspection process, insurance companies, retail sites, real estate rules, etc. As importantly, legal status grants access to broader networks of people outside of family, as well as to people who are not co-ethnics. Broader networks with weaker ties, in turn, yield non-repetitive information about business opportunity.

The base of knowledge not only expands when operating with legal status, it potentially creates additional advantages because entrepreneurs regularly make business decisions. In other words, entrepreneurs can leverage their expanding knowledge about how institutions in the formal economy work at each decision-making juncture. They can also leverage their networks to seize new opportunities, including those created by local government. Legal capital, then, means that the knowledge and practices accumulated in the formal business economy under the auspices of legal status have an exchange value. As such, the earlier it is invested, the more it accumulates over time and the better the business outcomes.

Our analysis, in short, focuses on the proprietors' business trajectory *over time* in the formal economy. We suggest that immigrant entrepreneurs with more legal capital have a bigger payoff as measured by more earnings or better business performance than those who accumulate less time and experience in the formal business economy under the auspices of legal status. To offer an analogy, just as young immigrants have more time in the host country to earn higher wages over their working lifetimes than older immigrants do, the sooner immigrants open their businesses once they have legalized their immigration statuses, the more time they have to reap the benefits of legal capital, all else equal. Our prediction also parallels research showing that immigrants who naturalize have greater access to higher paying, public sector, white-collar, and union jobs that ensure higher wage growth *over time* relative to immigrants who do not naturalize (Bratsberg et al. 2002). In this specific example, the premium comes not with naturalization per se, but rather with how it manifests over time, as immigrants find their way into better jobs that accelerate wage growth.

If our propositions are correct, we should see better business outcomes among firms that opened shortly following the legalization of the proprietors' immigration status. This should be true even for those businesses in operation for ten or more years. To restate this formally, *we hypothesize that the sooner one operates a business with "legal capital" the better it is for business outcomes even in the poorest and most segregated Mexican residential neighborhoods of Los Angeles.*

Before testing this hypothesis with a regression analysis, we first describe how the immigrants in our study responded when their legal status changed from undocumented to "legal." To be clear, all analyses in this chapter are exploratory because our sample size is much smaller here as compared to previous chapters. This is due to the fact that some immigrants in our sample entered the US legally, with authorization, while others had not (yet) legalized their status at the time of the survey.[11] As not everyone in our sample transitioned from undocumented to LPR, our sample for the analyses in this chapter is ($N = 79$, see Table 6.1). When we run the regression to test our hypothesis, the sample drops to 73 cases because of missing data on some of the variables in the equation.

FINDINGS

Table 6.1 shows demographic and firm characteristics. As indicated, the majority of our respondents admitted that they entered the US without the government's authorization (72%) or that they overstayed a visa (5%). Men were more likely than were women to enter in an unauthorized capacity. As we noted earlier, the migrants in our study were young, on average only 18 or 19 years old, when they arrived in the US. At some point over the course of their lives, the vast majority legalized their US residency and became LPRs.[12] Indeed, fully 93% of them had already obtained their "green cards" at the time of the survey, and a little more

Table 6.1 Migrant characteristics and business history

Migrant characteristics	All entrepreneurs	Men	Women	N^a
Currently undocumented (%)	7%	6%	9%	110
Unauthorized entry	72%	81%	63%	108
Visa overstay	5%	4%	6%	108
Median age at entry	19	19	18	107
Median age at time of survey	44	45	43	108
Respondents now US citizens	55%	54%	55%	110
Median # of years to naturalize status	18	18	17	57
Median # years in the US at time of survey	26	29	24	110
Business history				
Opened business the year legalized or after	89%	85%	92%	79
Median # of years to open business once status legalized	8	4	12	79
Modal # of years to open business once status legalized	3	0	3	79

Source: Authors' survey of Mexican immigrant business owners in Los Angeles, 2007

Notes: [a]Our sample size varies slightly in some categories because a few respondents did not answer all questions. Our sample drops to 79 cases under the "Business history" heading because some of our respondents immigrated to the United States legally. Still others had not yet legalized their immigration status. As such, not everyone in our sample transitioned from undocumented to LPR status

than half (55%) eventually became US citizens. The women were slightly more likely than were men to remain undocumented (9% vs. 6%, respectively) and more than half of the women and men in our sample eventually naturalized their immigration status. The earliest year that one of our respondents became an LPR was 1974, and the latest year (in our sample) that someone legalized was 2008. Despite this 30-year range, fully three-quarters of our respondents who legalized their residency did so by 1988 (see Fig. 6.2). Only 7% of all of our respondents (or eight observations) were undocumented at the time of the survey, as shown in Table 6.1.

While many of the proprietors in our sample started their businesses shortly after legalizing their status, not all did. Table 6.1 indicates quite a bit of variation in the number of years to open a business upon legalizing immigration status, with a median number of eight years for all entrepreneurs but a modal response of three years for the same. The top third of

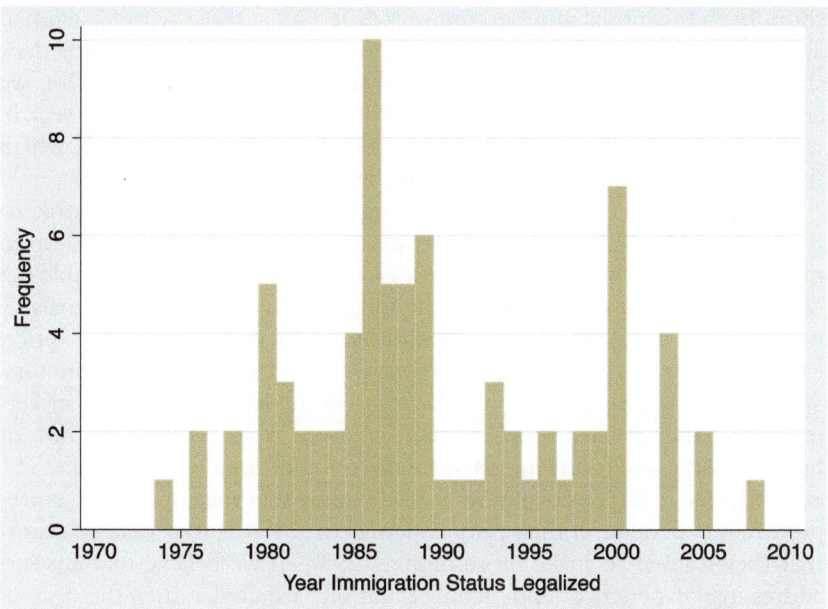

Fig. 6.2 Year in which legal permanent residency (LPR) green card acquired. Notes: mean = 1989.6, standard deviation = 7.964, N = 79. (Source: Authors' tabulations of their survey of Mexican immigrant business owners in Los Angeles, 2007)

all respondents said that they waited 12 or more years to start a business after having legalized their status and seven people even waited 20 or more years to open shop. Given this range, our data allow us to distinguish between entrepreneurs who are "early strikers" from those who are "late strikers." We define early strikers as immigrants who started their businesses during the process of legalizing their immigration status,[13] upon receiving green cards, or within the first five years of becoming "legal." This group comprised 43% of our sample of immigrants who legalized their status (so, 34/79 observations). The late strikers, in contrast, stayed in the labor market for six or more years after legalizing their immigration status but before starting their businesses.[14] They comprised a little more than half of the sample of entrepreneurs who legalized their immigration status (at 57%, or 45/79 observations).

Table 6.1 also shows that men and women differ in terms of how quickly they opened their businesses upon legalization. It is clear from the median numbers that women took three times as long as men to open shop. Even the modal numbers are very different, at three years for women and 0 years for men. In the case of the men, seven of them opened their shops the very year that they legalized their immigration status. So, we arrive at the "0" value of modal years for men by subtracting the year in which these seven men launched their businesses from the year in which they legalized their status (to illustrate, 1998–1998 = 0).

We first address the difference in timing between early versus late strikers. Recall from Chap. 2 that immigrants in our study tended to open shop to make more money or because they saw no other economic option. Table 6.2 offers a percentage distribution of the migrants according to their goals by whether they were early versus late strikers. Table 6.2 shows a clear difference in motivation between our early- and late-striking proprietors. Specifically, the early strikers were far more likely than were the late strikers to say that they opened shop because they were experienced in business or because they were following their family tradition in a specific trade. The early strikers, in fact, were almost as likely to say that they opted into entrepreneurship because of their prior experiences (24%) as they were to report that they wanted to make more money (29%). If we believe that answers addressing "experience" and "family tradition" are similar, then the story of the early strikers is telling: The vast majority went straight into business upon legalizing their status with a sense of confidence about their prospects based on their prior experiences. We might even say that they were "pulled" into business proprietorship.

Table 6.2   Percent distribution of reasons for going into business, by early or late strikers, 79 entrepreneurs

Early/ late striker	Make more money; better lifestyle; retire early	Be own boss; spend time with family; better working conditions	Lost job; no other option; needed steady job	Had experience; all respondent knows how to do	Family tradition	Give others job; help people	Total (%)	N
Early striker	29%	18%	18%	24%	9%	3%	101	34
Late striker	47%	24%	16%	7%	2%	4%	100	45
Total count	31	17	13	11	4	3	100	79
Pearson χ^2	7.67* (d.f. = 5)							

Source: Authors' survey of Mexican immigrant business owners in Los Angeles, 2007

Notes: *$p < 0.10$ (one-tailed test); *Early Strikers* go into business within the first five years of having a work permit or a green card. *Late Strikers* wait six or more years after receiving a green card before going into business. The "Inspired by Others" category in Table 2.4 is not listed in this table because no respondent (included in this table) reported that they started a business because they were inspired by others. The totals add up to more than 100% due to rounding error

Late strikers, in contrast, seem more likely to have been pushed out of the labor market. We know this because they were far less likely to report feeling experienced in the business (at only 7%) or having a family tradition of entrepreneurship (2%) relative to the early strikers. They were also more likely to report that they sought more money and better working conditions as compared to the early strikers (compare, e.g., 71% of the late strikers vs. 47% of the early strikers). The differences between the two groups are not accidental ($p = 0.09$, one-tailed tests). As such, the table strongly suggests that the late strikers felt constrained by the labor market and pursued small business to circumvent their blocked mobility.

Table 6.3 identifies the ways that the entrepreneurs procured their start-up capital. The findings in the table are consistent with our conclusion that the late strikers appear to have responded to labor market constraints rather than to have followed through on long-held business plans. We infer this from the fact that the late strikers had fewer personal savings or assets from which to start their businesses as compared to the early strikers (compare 51% vs. 76% in Table 6.3). Consequently, they were more likely

Table 6.3   Percent distribution of methods of obtaining start-up capital, 78 entrepreneurs[a]

Independent variable	Personal savings or assets	Loan from a relative or friend	Cundina, tanda, cooperativa	Credit card or from a financial institution	Other type of loan	Total (%)	N
Early striker	76%	6%	6%	6%	6%	100	33
Late striker	51%	11%	4%	16%	18%	100	45
Total count	48	7	4	9	10	100	78
Pearson χ^2	6.044*						
	(d.f. = 4)						

Source: Authors' tabulations of their survey of Mexican immigrant business owners in Los Angeles, 2007
Notes: *p < 0.10, **p < 0.05, ***p < 0.01 (two-tailed tests), ^p < 0.10 (one-tailed test)
[a]One early striker did not answer the question, so N drops to 33 from 34

to borrow from a relative or friend, a credit card, or indeed another type of loan as compared to the early strikers. These differences are statistically significant (p = 0.10, one-tailed test).

Because these two groups of entrepreneurs appear to have somewhat distinct motivations as well as unequal resources, we explore our theory that differences in legal capital explain variations in the long-term business outcomes of early strikers versus late strikers. Specifically, our regression controls for start-up capital, educational levels, prior experience with family business, marital status, as well as several other controls. Recall that we hypothesized that those entrepreneurs who open a business shortly following the legalization of their immigration status would have a longer period to utilize resources not available to undocumented entrepreneurs; and that this would sharpen their business knowledge by virtue of spending more of their working careers in the formal business economy. This theory, then, predicts that net of other differences, late strikers will also accumulate less legal capital. We suspect that they are disadvantaged as eventual entrepreneurs relative to the early strikers. We suspect that while late strikers hone skills in the labor market under the auspices of legal status, they improve blue-collar or manual labor skills. Such skills are less helpful to business performance over time. Put simply, we suspect that the late strikers accumulate less legal capital than do early strikers because they spend more time in the labor market under the auspices of legal status (see Fig. 6.1).

We begin to explore this second proposition with descriptive data from our survey question asking, "*What kinds of jobs have you had in the U.S. prior to opening your business?*" Respondents answered this open-ended question by listing the types of jobs they held just prior to opening their businesses, as described in Table 6.4. Sometimes, respondents were specific and said that they "sewed" or were in "tuxedo sales" before becoming shopkeepers. Other times, they simply said that they had worked in "a restaurant." As evidenced in Table 6.4, the most common job listed by both early and late strikers was "sales." While this is a relatively low-skill service job, we single it out in the table because it arguably prepares immigrants for the most important aspect of their role as small shopkeepers. As the table shows, the early strikers were more than two times as likely to be in sales as compared to the late strikers (compare 26% vs. 11%).

However, their apparent advantage is offset by the fact that the early strikers were far *less* likely than were the late strikers to have been in white-collar jobs prior to opening their businesses, as shown in the list of jobs that begins with the category "low-level manager." As the table shows, the white-collar jobs included low-level managers (e.g., of a McDonalds or of production), health aid workers, a loan officer, a computer teacher, someone who helped prepare taxes, and someone in social work (specific job description not identified). Fully 23% of the late strikers were in comparable white-collar jobs, as compared to only 6% of the early strikers. These occupational differences between early and late strikers in our sample were statistically significant (see the notes in Table 6.4). To put it mildly, the late strikers in our sample were not disadvantaged relative to the early strikers in terms of the kinds of jobs they had prior to opening their businesses. If anything, they may have been slightly more advantaged insofar as they were more than three times as likely to be in white-collar jobs prior to opening their shops. The evidence in Table 6.4 thus suggests that some of the white-collar workers in our sample may have struck significantly later in business because they sought to advance in other careers.

While it is not the case that the late strikers in our study were disadvantaged relative to the early strikers, the majority of the late strikers were blue-collar workers (29 people out of 45 later strikers = 64%). This means that they were neither in sales nor in white-collar occupations. Some non-exhaustive examples of the jobs engaged by female late strikers included hairdressers, domestics or hotel cleaners, restaurant workers, factory workers, sewers, and cashiers. A few men said that they were mechanics or

Table 6.4   Percent distribution of jobs held by early and late striking entrepreneurs, 79 Entrepreneurs

Jobs	Early strikers N	Early strikers (%)	Late strikers N	Late strikers (%)
None	1	3	0	0
Sales	9	26	5	11
Mechanic/appliance repair person	7	21	4	9
Hairdresser/barber/ cosmetologist	4	12	3	7
Factory worker	2	6	2	4
Sewing	2	6	4	9
Machine operator	0	0	3	7
Waitress	0	0	2	4
Chauffeur	2	6	0	0
Cook/other food service	2	6	2	4
Contractor	1	3	0	0
Supermarket clerk	1	3	1	2
Farmworker	0	0	1	2
Domestic service/hotel cleaning service	0	0	3	7
Miscellaneous blue collar	1	3	3	7
Owned trucking company	0	0	1	2
Low-level manager	0	0	3	7
Human resources	1	3	0	0
EMT/health aid worker	1	3	2	4
Countrywide country loans	0	0	1	2
Computer/or computer teacher	0	0	2	4
Accounting/preparing taxes	0	0	2	4
Social work	0	0	1	2
Total N	34	101	45	98

Source: Authors' survey of Mexican immigrant business owners in Los Angeles, 2007

Notes: Columns do not total to 100% because of rounding error. Among the early strikers, 26% are in sales, 6% in white collar jobs, and 66% in non-sales blue-collar jobs. Among the late strikers, 11% are in sales, 23% are in white-collar jobs, and 64% are in non-sales, blue-collar jobs. With these data, it is easy to re-create a table (not shown here) of the percent distribution of jobs held by the entrepreneurs in only four categories (sales, white collar, blue collar, or no jobs), by early- and late-striking entrepreneurs. This table would show a statistically significant Pearson χ^2 value of 6.6 (with three degrees of freedom). $p < 0.05$ (one-tailed test).

appliance repair people; some were factory workers, machine operators, a valet parking assistant, a welder, and a farm worker. These occupations are not the kinds of "strategic" jobs that build the skills necessary for the long-term viability of small business firms[15] and certainly do not give access to the broadest possible business networks. The evidence in the table is thus consistent with our theory that the late-striking entrepreneurs do not build the skills that they need to be the most successful shopkeepers by remaining in the labor market upon their legalization. Further, as the table shows, the early strikers were as likely as were the late strikers to be in working-class occupations before they launched their business shortly after legalizing their immigration status (compare 66% and 64%).

To more carefully explore our hypothesis that the *sooner* one operates a business in the formal economy with "legal capital," the better it is for business outcomes, we add the variable YRS2OPEN (years to open business once legalized) to our baseline regression model.[16] This continuous variable is the actual number of years it took our respondents to open their shops in the formal economy *once legalizing his/her immigration status.* Our legal capital variable "years to open" has the advantage over a dummy variable (legal/illegal) insofar as it allows us to see whether there is any long-term benefit to conducting business in the formal economy with legal status, as predicted by our "legal capital" theory. To reiterate, this measure is not the same as length of time in business. We include a business duration variable in our model as a control. Our model thus allows us to gauge whether there is a legal capital advantage even among those who have operated their businesses for 10 or more years. Recall that the baseline regression model also controls for the level of education, the amount of start-up capital, and parental business experience. So, these variables should control for any advantages by either the early or the late strikers. In addition, the baseline model controls for gender, marital status, years in the US, business sector, hours logged per week, whether the business was purchased from another entrepreneur or developed from the bottom up, support from co-ethnics, and the extent to which the neighborhoods in which their small firms are located are poor, segregated, and foreign-born.

As predicted, Table 6.5 shows that, indeed, the later a proprietor starts a business under the auspices of legal status, the worse the business outcomes, net of all control variables, including the amount of start-up capital and business duration longer than ten years. The negative coefficient means that the longer it takes an immigrant to start a business after

Table 6.5 The impact of legal capital on business outcomes (Poisson regression)

	All entrepreneurs	Men	Women
Gender (GENDER)	−0.147		
	(0.263)		
Married (MARR)	0.703***	1.139**	0.650^
	(0.253)	(0.512)	(0.403)
Years of schooling (EDUC)	−0.0039	0.027	−0.025
	(0.024)	(0.033)	(0.062)
Years in the US (YRSINUS)	0.066***	0.085***	0.044
	(0.019)	(0.032)	(0.036)
Retail sector (RETAIL)	−0.702^	12.45	−1.514**
	(0.484)	(1662.9)	(0.664)
Services sector (SERVICE)	−0.075	13.69	−0.629
	(0.474)	(1662.9)	(0.567)
Log hours worked per week (HRS)	0.761**	1.301**	0.511
	(0.368)	(0.558)	(1.092)
Business open more than 10 years (DUR)	−0.827**	−0.469	−0.584
	(0.328)	(0.608)	(0.517)
Log start-up capital (STARTUP)	0.129^	0.354**	−0.120
	(0.090)	(0.137)	(0.187)
Neighborhood's percent foreign-born (FB)	0.068***	0.087**	0.078^
	(0.025)	(0.039)	(0.053)
Parent business owner (PARBUS)	1.073***	0.326	1.310**
	(0.282)	(0.605)	(0.589)
Residential poverty > LA (POV)	−0.652**	−0.587^	−0.701^
	(0.265)	(0.373)	(0.465)
Mexican concentration (COETHNIC)	−0.010^	−0.006	−0.037*
	(0.007)	(0.009)	(0.021)
Primarily Spanish spoken to clients (SPAN)	0.694**	1.354***	−0.337
	(0.317)	(0.505)	(0.672)
Prior existing business (EXIST)	0.0119	0.328	0.644^
	(0.250)	(0.385)	(0.479)
Years to open once legalized (YRS2OPEN)	−0.032*	−0.084***	0.004
	(0.018)	(0.032)	(0.030)
N	73	40	33
Pseudo R-square	0.263	0.382	0.278

Source: Authors' survey of Mexican immigrant business owners in Los Angeles, 2007

Notes: $*p < 0.10$, $**p < 0.05$, $***p < 0.01$ (two-tailed tests), $^p < 0.10$ (one-tailed test), standard errors in parentheses. Dependent variable is the number of paid employees. GENDER (female = 1; male = 0). MARR (married = 1; not married = 0). EDUC represents the number of years of schooling. YRSINUS represents the number of years the immigrant has resided in the US. RETAIL is a dummy variable for operating in the retail sector, SERVICE is a dummy variable for operating in the services sector. The professional sector is the omitted group. The variable HRS is the log of weekly hours devoted to the business. DUR is a dummy variable that represents whether a respondent's business has been open for more than ten years. The variable STARTUP is the log of the amount of start-up capital reported by the subject. FB represents the percent foreign-born by neighborhood as reported in the 2000 Census. PARBUS controls for whether the respondents' parent(s) had business experience in Mexico (coded 1 for yes). POV is a dummy variable for whether poverty was greater than the poverty level for LA. COETHNIC is a measure of Mexican concentration in the area. SPAN is a dummy variable indicating whether the business owner spoke predominately Spanish to clients. EXIST is a dummy variable if the business owner purchased an existing business or not

legalizing her/his immigration status, the lower the business outcomes, all else equal. Immigrants who remain in the labor market with their new legal status essentially postpone entrepreneurship at a price: Even if they had been in business over ten years, they still end up hiring fewer workers over time than those who struck early in entrepreneurship as newly legalized (LPR) immigrants. Our evidence, thus, suggests that striking early in business under the auspices of legal status generates more legal capital and, thus, better business outcomes than striking later in business. Striking earlier in business appears to accumulate advantages that improve business outcomes and this was shown by the greater number of employees ultimately hired by the early strikers in our sample.

Table 6.5 also shows results by gender. When we restrict the sample by gender, the sample size reduces to 40 observations for men and 33 observations for women. Table 6.5 thus suggests that only men experience a negative effect of waiting longer to open their businesses after legalization. The effects for women become statistically insignificant because the coefficients are more sensitive to outliers when the sample is restricted to just 33 observations. Thus, even though the median number of years before opening a business after legalizing one's status was three times longer for women than for men, women do not appear to experience the same disadvantage as men. However, we are reluctant to conclude that our main findings are driven only by men given how small the samples become when we run separate regressions for men and women.[17]

The skeptical reader might reasonably argue that our finding could have to do with the personality of people who seize upon entrepreneurship on legalizing their immigration status. It could well be that the early strikers are simply more interested in entrepreneurship and, therefore, more successful at it. Even if this explanation accounts for an unmeasured portion of our findings, social science research has long identified other social factors that contribute to business outcomes. Although we did not control for "personality" differences, our model controlled for some key individual differences, as well as the extent of prior business experience, including with parents. We are thus confident that something more than personality drives their business performance. In other words, our regression results suggest something in addition to individual or even investment capital differences between the early business strikers as compared to the late strikers. We propose that early strikers perform better over time (all else equal) because legal status gives them access to the formal economy, which they learn to navigate earlier in their career span. While our late strikers also hone skills in jobs taken after legalizing their immigration status, we show that the majority (at least 64%) remained in low-skill or dead-end jobs (see Table 6.4). Low-skill work under the auspices of legal status is certainly a low-risk strategy, but it does not create the learning opportunities that yield significant advantages to business in the formal economy. These findings, then, suggest that how and when immigrants pursue economic opportunities with legal status shapes experiences in ways that can yield cumulative business advantages over time.

DISCUSSION AND CONCLUSION

To understand how legal status matters to small business owners, we began this chapter by reiterating the points from Chap. 2 that stressed that labor market conditions worsened in the context of increasingly puni-tive legislation aimed at the undocumented since 1996. Given their blocked mobility, aspiring entrepreneurs faced a crossroads upon legaliz-ing their status. They could pursue better-paying jobs or they could launch a small business. Those who stayed in the labor market upon legalization eventually also became business owners. Others retooled early and radi-cally by launching businesses shortly after legalizing their status.

We demonstrated that the timing of the business venture relative to the year undocumented migrants obtained legal status led to better or worse long-term business outcomes net of start-up capital, education, number of years in the US, gender, prior business experience, and other traditional variables. Therefore, those who establish storefronts upon legalizing their status do better as compared to the late strikers, people who linger in the labor market after legalizing their status. The difference between early and late strikers held even among proprietors who had been in business for ten or more years. The evidence presented in this chapter is consistent with our theory that operating small businesses in the formal economy earlier in one's career span allows for a longer period of time to utilize legal capi-tal as well as helps legal entrepreneurs build additional legal capital. The late strikers, in contrast, remained in low-skill or dead-end jobs longer in the course of their working careers; and these were not the "strategic occupations" that yield advantages to businesses over time.

The findings of this chapter have implications for contemporary theo-ries of social stratification in the context of regular and irregular migra-tion globally. A general lesson is that legal status is dynamic and is, indeed, a stratification variable. Another general lesson is that the economic experiences of previously undocumented people can vary dramatically under the auspices of legal status, with some experiences resulting in more long-term benefits than others. The concept of legal capital captures the accumulation of small advantages to immigrant proprietors who were once unauthorized. These advantages take the form of new knowledge about banks, municipal government ordinances, or simply opportunities, and about suppliers, retail sites, and the like. Experiences in the formal economy not only sharpen business acumen, but they grant access to broader networks in ways that have a financial exchange value. Legal capital, then, is a specific subtype of cultural capital, one that applies only to previously undocumented immigrant entrepreneurs whose sociolegal status once cut them off from the formal economy. Since the concept captures how experiences shape business "know how" under the auspices of legal status, it foregrounds how the law affects social mobility. As Cecilia Menjívar and Sarah M. Lakhani recently argued, state power clearly "exerts control over individuals through law" (2016: 1820).

Likewise, this chapter also sheds light on how social disadvantages accumulate over time. We observed that prospective entrepreneurs who launched businesses early did so with considerably more confidence about their prior experiences than the late strikers. As emphasized throughout, prior and direct business experience is good for business outcomes as compared to a lack of experience (Waldinger et al. 1990: 44). However, we also showed that some of the late strikers were in white-collar jobs and thus, theoretically, better positioned than their blue-collar counterparts to succeed in business. Yet, the white-collar workers were prudent. They remained in the labor market considerably longer than their more confident but more low-skill counterparts did and they paid a price for their delay. Remaining in the labor force after legalizing their immigration status yielded neither sufficient risk capital (see Table 6.3) nor the most helpful skills for the long-term viability of the small businesses that they eventually started.

Finally, our findings suggest that even if entrepreneurship generally creates an opportunity for upward mobility, moving into the ranks of the petite bourgeoisie is harder for those in the social and legal margins. In the context of much social hostility, previously illegal Mexican immigrants from underprivileged backgrounds have less to invest from the start, and their tiny firms generate small profit margins. Nevertheless, most still benefit from an entrepreneurship boost (see also Light and Roach 1996), though, clearly, some did better than others did. What explains these unequal outcomes? We found that slight differences among comparably underprivileged co-ethnics become small competitive advantages or disadvantages that matter to shops that always operate on the edge of failure. One small, but reliable, advantage for the long-term viability of small firms is for prospective entrepreneurs to make the most of their newly acquired legal status by investing in business earlier rather than later in their working careers. Doing so appears to generate more legal capital.

Notes

1. For a broad discussion of the transformative effects of legalizing one's immigration status, see Celia Menjívar and Sarah M. Lakhani (2016).
2. Estimates of the wage penalty for being unauthorized range between 14% and 24% (Kossoudji and Cobb-Clark 2002).
3. Other scholars have similarly established that legal status affects the lives of immigrants and their children in every possible way. See Takei et al. (2009), Abrego (2011), Donato and Armenta (2011), Fassin (2011), Quesada (2011), Dreby (2015).
4. See Waldinger et al. (1990) on the importance of both national and local government policies on leasing laws, loan programs, permits, incubator policy, and the like (p. 31).
5. One such program offered by Los Angeles' municipal government is called "Great Streets Great Businesses." This program seeks to offer easier access to loans and assistance with retail lease negotiation.
6. When a California law, Assembly Bill (AB) 60, went into effect in January of 2015, it made it possible for the Department of Motor Vehicles to issue California Driver's Licenses to undocumented drivers.
7. Although undocumented people find illegal ways to circumvent the problem of not having a valid Social Security number for work, they have fewer options for obtaining credit. A few years after the Patriot Act passed, some undocumented people were able to use the US government's Income Tax Identification Number (ITIN) to open bank accounts. The ITIN number is issued to people who do not have a Social Security Number but who can pay taxes. As of 2005, an increasing number of banks accepted ITIN numbers for bank accounts, and roughly 18 financial institutions accepted them for mortgage loans (see Bergsman 2005; Gallagher 2005: 3). While the extent to which ITIN numbers were used for the more high-risk business loans is unknown, we do know that the respondents in our sample tended not to borrow from financial institutions. Similarly, in the early 2000s, Bank of America, Citibank, Washington Mutual and Wells Fargo also accepted the *matrícular consular* identification card issued by the Mexican

government to open bank accounts (O'Neil 2003; Gallagher 2005). However, fewer than 40% of bank branches in California accepted the alternative identification cards issued by the Mexican government. As of 2005 in Los Angeles, there were only "2.3 banks that accept the Consular Cards as identification per 10,000 Mexican ancestry population" (Gallagher 2005: 4). To repeat, our respondents did not generally rely on formal banking institutions for their start-up capital.

8. According to Gallagher, as of 2005, the vast majority of undocumented Mexicans had no ties to formal financial institutions and only 25% of all Mexican immigrants (irrespective of legal status) had bank accounts.

9. For example, the "New Business Tax Holiday" exempts small businesses from paying taxes to the City of Los Angeles for the first two-years of operation. This program, however, requires showing the City of Los Angeles official tax returns.

10. To give one brief example about just how daunting banking institutions can appear to some people, a small study conducted in Scotland captured the intimidation that a shopkeeper from a working-class background felt about banking institutions in her native Scotland, where she was a citizen who functioned without any language barriers. The authors interviewed the shopkeeper, Sadie, who reported that she "had little idea about formal finances and this had prevented her from approaching the bank to borrow additional capital" (Anderson and Miller 2003: 26). If Sadie, who had operated more than one small shop and who had purchased eight Rolls Royces for her wedding service business, found it intimidating to approach a bank, we suggest that immigrants find it at least as hard.

11. We do not analyze the extent to which being undocumented is a disadvantage in business since we had too few cases ($n = 8$) in our sample of people who were still undocumented at the time of the survey. A preliminary percentage distribution shows that those who are undocumented hire fewer employees but our results were not statistically significant because there are too few observations of people with undocumented status at the time of the survey.

12. We did not ask our respondents about the specific legal criteria according to which they were able to legalize their immigration status. There are several pathways, but the two most common for Mexicans are through family reunification or through their employers (see Jasso 2011 for a summary). Some immigrants can obtain conditional green cards if they invest a large sum of money in the US economy or by starting a business. Given that the median capital invested by our respondents was much lower than the threshold required for what are called conditional green cards, we doubt that our respondents legalized through this mechanism.

13. Becoming an LPR is a lengthy process that starts at the submission of a green card application. The average processing time for men who seek to legalize (or adjust) their immigration status is just over seven years; for women it is just shy of six years (5.95) (Jasso 2011). According to Jasso (2011), lost documents extend the waiting period, and Mexicans are more likely than are most other immigrants to suffer the setbacks of documents lost by the INS/USCIS (or both the state and the INS/USCIS) (2011: 1305). Fortunately, immigrants waiting for the government's approval of their green card applications (to become an LPR) can legally work in the US for one year if they successfully apply for a "temporary work permit." The fact that these work permits are renewable could explain why some of our respondents said that they started their businesses shortly before obtaining their official green cards (and achieved LPR status).

14. Six years struck us as a long time to consider launching a business after legalization given that at least half of all new businesses go out of business within their first five years of operation. After the first five years, the survival rates of young businesses flatten out and do so irrespective of business sector. See https://www.sba.gov/sites/default/files/Business-Survival.pdf

15. On strategic occupations that build entrepreneurial skills, see Waldinger et al. (1990: 45).

16. We ran a Poisson regression for the reasons discussed in Chap. 3.

17. To state this differently, we suspect that the legal capital results for women would be statistically significant with a larger sample because the women in our sample were considerably more likely than men to be late strikers.

References

Abrego, Leisy J. 2011. Legal Consciousness of Undocumented Latinos: Fear and Stigma as Barriers to Claims Making for First and 1.5 Generation Immigrants. *Law and Society Review* 45 (2): 337–369.

Anderson, Alistair R., and Claire J. Miller. 2003. "Class Matters": Human and Social Capital in the Entrepreneurial Process. *Journal of Socio-Economics* 32: 17–36.

Argueta, Carla N. 2016. *Border Security: Immigration Enforcement Between Ports of Entry*. Congressional Research Service Report Prepared for Members and Committees of Congress 7-5700. www.crs.gov R42138.

Bergsman, Steve. 2005. Banks Are Quietly Wooing Undocumented Immigrants. *USBANKER*, June.

Bratsberg, Bernt, James F. Ragan Jr., and Zaffar M. Nasir. 2002. The Effect of Naturalization on Wage Growth: A Panel Study of Young Male Immigrants. *Journal of Labor Economics* 20 (3): 568–597.

Donato, Katharine M., and Amada Armenta. 2011. What We Know About Unauthorized Migration. *Annual Review of Sociology* 37: 529–543.

Donato, Katharine M., and Blake Sisk. 2012. Shifts in the Employment Outcomes Among Mexican Migrants to the United States, 1976–2009. *Research in Social Stratification and Mobility* 30 (1): 63–77.

Dreby, Joanna. 2015. *Everyday Illegal: When Policies Undermine Immigrant Families.* Oakland: University of California Press.

Fairlie, Robert, and Christopher Woodruff. 2010. Mexican American Entrepreneurship. *The B.E. Journal of Economic Analysis and Policy* 10 (1): 1–34.

Fassin, Didier. 2011. Policing Borders, Producing Boundaries: The Governmentality of Immigration in Dark Times. *Annual Review of Anthropology* 40: 213–226.

Flippen, Chenoa A. 2012. Laboring Underground: The Employment Patterns of Hispanic Immigrant Men in Durham, NC. *Social Problems* 59 (1): 21–42.

Gallagher, Mari. 2005. Alternative IDs, ITIN Mortgages, and Emerging Latino Markets. *Profitwise News and Views*, March.

Gentsch, Kerstin, and Douglas S. Massey. 2011. Labor Market Outcomes for Legal Mexican Immigrants Under the New Regime of Immigration Enforcement. *Social Science Quarterly* 92 (3): 875–893.

Hall, Matthew, Emily Greenman, and George Farkas. 2010. Legal Status and Wage Disparities for Mexican Immigrants. *Social Forces* 89 (2): 491–514.

Jasso, Guillermina. 2011. Migration and Stratification. *Social Science Research* 40 (5): 1292–1336.

Jasso, Guillermina, Douglas S. Massey, Mark R. Rosenzweig, and James P. Smith. 2008. From Illegal to Legal: Estimating Previous Illegal Experience Among New Legal Immigrants to the United States. *International Migration Review* 42 (4): 803–843.

Kossoudji, Sherrie A., and Deborah A. Cobb-Clark. 2002. Coming Out of the Shadows: Learning About Legal Status and Wages from the Legalized Population. *Journal of Labor Economics* 20 (3): 598–628.

Light, Ivan, and Elizabeth Roach. 1996. Self-Employment: Mobility Ladder or Economic Lifeboat? In *Ethnic Los Angeles*, ed. Roger Waldinger and Mehdi Bozorgmehr, 193–214. New York: Russell Sage Foundation.

Massey, Douglas S., and Julia Gelatt. 2010. What Happened to the Wages of Mexican Immigrants? Trends and Interpretations. *Latino Studies* 2 (8): 328–354.

Massey, Douglas S., Jorge Durand, and Nolan J. Malone. 2002. *Beyond Smoke and Mirrors: Mexican Immigration in an Era of Economic Integration.* New York: Russell Sage Foundation.

Menjívar, Cecilia, and Sarah M. Lakhani. 2016. Transformative Effects of Immigration Law: Immigrants' Personal and Social Metamorphoses Through Regularization. *American Journal of Sociology* 121 (6): 1818–1855.

O'Neil, Kevin. 2003. *Consular ID Cards: Mexico and Beyond.* Published by the Migration Policy Institute, April 1. http://www.migrationpolicy.org/article/consular-id-cards-mexico-and-beyond

Quesada, James. 2011. No Soy Welferero: Undocumented Latino Laborers in the Crosshairs of Legitimation Maneuvers. *Medical Anthropology* 30 (4): 386–408.

Ramirez, Hernan, and Pierrette Hondagneu-Sotelo. 2009. Mexican Immigrant Gardeners: Entrepreneurs or Exploited Workers? *Social Problems* 56 (1): 70–88.

Rivera-Batiz, Francisco L. 1999. Undocumented Workers in the Labor Market: An Analysis of the Earnings of Legal and Illegal Mexican Immigrants in the United States. *Journal of Population Economics* 12 (1): 91–116.

Takei, Isao, Rogelio Saenz, and Jing Li. 2009. Cost of Being a Mexican Immigrant and Being a Mexican Non-citizen in California and Texas. *Hispanic Journal of Behavioral Sciences* 31 (1): 73–95.

Tienda, Marta, and Audrey Singer. 1995. Wage Mobility of Undocumented Workers in the United States. *International Migration Review* 29 (1): 112–138.

Waldinger, Roger, Howard Aldrich, and Robin Ward. 1990. *Ethnic Entrepreneurs: Immigrant Business in Industrial Societies.* Newbury Park: Sage.

CHAPTER 7

Conclusion: Making It in Business from the Outside-In

The preceding chapters focused on the individual-level factors as well as the broader labor market, neighborhood, and social-legal and temporal circumstances that block people from moving up the rungs of the economic ladder despite their best efforts. The Mexican immigrants in our study took well-rehearsed steps toward upward mobility but because most of their LA businesses stagnated, they did not advance very far. Although some of our survey respondents performed better in business than others did, all of the firms in our study were small, and most appeared vulnerable to the consequences of economic downturns. Yet, despite their vulnerability, the proprietors in our study did experience a small boost from entrepreneurship, and their short-distance mobility reveals an underlying story of grit and determination given the many obstacles that our respondents overcame. Therefore, if our analysis is not an ethnic version of a Horatio Alger type of story, it is because we studied people with more than poverty to overcome.

To begin, because most of our survey respondents moved to the US without authorization, they lived under the threat of deportation for long stretches of time. Spanish language television, radio, and print media regularly report on the growing number of national, state, and local laws aimed at curbing unauthorized migration, and such reports make it painfully obvious both that undocumented people are unwelcome in the US and that the state's capacity to remove them is enhanced. Even if undocumented people live in predominantly Mexican communities within

© The Author(s) 2018
D. Trevizo, M. Lopez, *Neighborhood Poverty and Segregation in the (Re-)Production of Disadvantage*,
https://doi.org/10.1007/978-3-319-73715-7_7

the relative safety of Los Angeles, they face the consequences of the development of a harsher immigration enforcement regime, as well as the effects of industrial restructuring. Chapter 2 explains why the stricter enforcement of immigration policy resulted in a larger and more permanently settled unauthorized population in Los Angeles. The unintended caging effects that resulted from new immigration legislation not only led to an increase in the size of the undocumented population—which is now many times larger than it was in the late 1980s—but the constant negative political attention on Mexican immigrants contributed to the intensification of racist attitudes toward them and their descendants. They experience greater discrimination in the labor market and the effects of such discrimination combine with a large (and, until recently, growing) supply of immigrants to undercut wages. Irrespective of legal status, Mexican immigrants find themselves in intense competition for low-wage jobs, and their growing poverty has resulted in higher levels of neighborhood segregation in Los Angeles, as described in Chaps. 2, 3, and 4 of this book.

Yet, because our respondents were able to legalize their immigration status, they were more fortunate than the millions of others in similar circumstances. The legalization process is not only complex, time-consuming, and costly, but legalization is objectively harder to achieve in the twenty-first century given the ten-year bans imposed on millions of people since the passage of the Illegal Immigration Reform and Immigrant Responsibility Act (IIRIRA) in 1997. Therefore, when the state granted our respondents Legal Permanent Residence status, many leveraged their new rights by launching small business ventures. Their new legal permanent resident (LPR) status offered them the opportunity to circumvent their blocked mobility in the labor market. Put another way, achieving LPR status proved to be a pivotal moment for our respondents, one that gave them license to pursue the dreams of their youth, the ones that inspired their migration journeys. We hold that the benefits of legalization are greater in the twenty-first century than previously because of the increased odds of deportation and because the low-skill labor market offers fewer prospects for upward mobility than it did in the past. Our data in Chap. 2 specifically show the sharpest increase in business start-ups among our survey respondents happened after immigration enforcement grew more stringent at the start of the twenty-first century. Further, a higher percentage of our survey respondents who started their businesses after 2000, as compared to those who opened their shops before 2000, reported that they did so because they felt that they had no other option.

Chapter 2 thus offers both objective and subjective evidence of blocked labor market mobility that we argue is due to tougher immigration laws as well as industrial restructuring.

Although most proprietors in our study pursued business to improve their circumstances, only a few did very well, while others struggled to stay afloat. Which of their firms stagnated and which ones showed signs of promise and why? Chapter 6 presented evidence suggesting that the entrepreneurs who lingered in the labor market after legalizing their immigration status found it harder to do well in the businesses that they would eventually open. The jobs that they held after achieving legal status were not the kinds of strategic occupations that would help them to develop the skills necessary for business. To put it boldly, grueling work does not develop the administrative, marketing, banking, or other skills necessary to small business development. As such, an unrewarding labor market would continue to cost them time and earnings capacity even after they legalized their status.

In addition, the entrepreneurs whose shops were located in the poorest and most segregated neighborhoods of Los Angeles operated within weak markets comprised of people with little buying power. Further, Mexican immigrants may easily purchase authentic Mexican products from a large number of co-ethnic entrepreneurs in Los Angeles. Therefore, while there are many socially adaptive benefits to the spatial concentration of co-ethnic immigrants, our analyses of the demographic profiles of the neighborhoods as well as the broader geographic areas of Los Angeles suggests that too much social homophily saturates markets quickly. As demonstrated in Chap. 4, high levels of segregation of the racialized poor is not good for business performance. The data in Chaps. 3 and 4 clearly indicate that Mexican immigrant storefront owners concentrated in high poverty neighborhoods with large concentrations of co-ethnics perform worse than do their counterparts whose firms are located in more diverse neighborhoods with lower levels of poverty. The results in Chap. 4 clearly show that disadvantaged neighborhoods that spatially concentrate poor co-ethnics put downward pressure on the mobility trajectories of small business owners, the very people who have invested capital and long hours to move out of poverty. In undermining the developmental capacity of their small firms, disadvantaged neighborhoods also undercut employment opportunities for unemployed locals from the area. The downward pressure experienced by Mexican immigrant entrepreneurs in the neighborhoods in which they managed their small businesses sheds light on how the spatial concentration of disadvantage reinforces social inequality.

In addition to the spatial dimension of neighborhood inequality, our results also point to temporal dynamics—for example, as manifested in the intergenerational transmission of class inequality or, as noted, in the specific timing of business ventures—as well as to some gendered patterns about them. We found, for example, that migrants whose parents were not entrepreneurs did worse than people who, as children in Mexico, acquired the cultural capital of their business-owning parents. This was especially the case for immigrant women who, over time, accumulate fewer and less diverse labor market experiences within the US as compared to their male counterparts. As Chap. 5 showed, their pre-migration microclass experiences mattered more for Mexican women in the US context than it did for men, and variation in their experiences with entrepreneurial parents helps to explain why some women did worse in business as compared to other women of the same ethnic group.

Our results point to other gendered patterns, such as the fact that the women in our study had less experience in business than men did, and the performance of their firms proved more sensitive to the industry type as compared to those owned by men. Somewhat surprisingly, non-married women fared worse than did their married female counterparts, though married men benefited the most from the marriage boost to business. We suspect that unmarried women were disadvantaged as business owners because they do not have a spouse with whom to pool economic resources or with whom to share labor responsibilities in the firm itself. Our results, in short, clearly indicate that gender matters to entrepreneurial outcomes, but that it does so in complicated and in class-specific ways.

If moving into the ranks of the petite bourgeoisie is so hard for people on the economic, spatial, social, and legal margins, how does short-distance social mobility happen? How do unwelcome immigrants in tough economies create narrow pathways for even a small degree of upward mobility? We found that while all of the shopkeepers in our study took risks, the gamble proved less risky and more beneficial for some migrants as compared to others. Those who by virtue of having business-owning parents acquired a cultural disposition toward entrepreneurship in their youth had a small competitive advantage. Importantly, small returns on cultural capital matter to shops that operate near the edge of failure, and surviving in the context of a harsh labor market is already a boost. To refer again to women's experiences, those whose parents were business owners in Mexico performed better than the women whose parents were not entrepreneurs, all else equal. In addition, women who purchased an already existing firm did better than women who started their businesses from the bottom up and, as noted, they benefitted further from the marriage boost. We conclude that the cultural capital of some women, as well as the more conservative business strategy of other women, mitigated some of the extra challenges that they confronted as immigrant women in Los Angeles.

Importantly, the more successful proprietors exited the labor market more quickly than others did upon the legalization of their immigration status and, in doing so, managed their firms in the formal economy earlier in their working lives. As such, they had more time to develop and then make the best use of what we called legal capital. In other words, the prospective entrepreneurs who immediately made the most of their newly acquired legal status gave their firms a greater chance of developing. They generated more legal capital just by investing earlier in business rather than losing more time from their working careers in an unrewarding labor market. Our findings thus suggest that while legal status is an important stratification variable, it is more than a binary variable. Not only can legal status change over time but also how and when people make use of their LPR status varies. If it is generally true that how LPR status affects social mobility depends on where people are in the life course, we add a nuance in showing that *when* in their working careers immigrants acquire LPR status as well as *how* they leverage it during their work lives also affects their social trajectory.

In addition to the timing of their start-up ventures as well as other individual-level differences, place concentration clearly matters for the success of small shops. Chapters 3 and 4 demonstrate that neighborhoods are crucial to business performance, reminding us of the real-estate maxim "location, location, location!" Concretely, less poor and less segregated neighborhoods gave Mexican immigrant shopkeepers a competitive advantage because such communities had more buying power. In addition, the more multiethnic neighborhoods created incentives for shopkeepers to expand their products, services, and possibly even their practices in response to multiethnic customers. What is clear from our regression results in Chap. 4 is that when small business proprietors sell to multiethnics, they are slightly more competitive, and these findings held for both men and women.

Our analysis of the reproduction of inequality at the neighborhood level focuses on the effects of the spatial concentration of racially and economically disadvantaged immigrants and thus takes its cues from the theory of concentrated disadvantage. We also suggest that this theory could account for some of the contradictory findings presented by ethnic enclave and mixed economy scholars. After describing the debate between scholars from these two schools of thought in Chap. 4, we reported that though some of our own findings are consistent with both theories, they lend more support to the mixed economy thesis. Yet, we argue that the theory of concentrated disadvantage does the best job of explaining at least some of the mixed results from our study because it makes no claims about cultural solidarity. To restate this differently, the theory of concentrated disadvantage can take for granted various forms of cultural solidarity on the assumption that how cultural solidarity matters economically is conditional on the educational, economic, and social advantages or disadvantages of the people clustered together in a neighborhood. Concretely, the theory specifically maintains that because neighborhoods concentrate people who are economically, educationally, and socially (under)-privileged, their spatial concentration may result in either positive or negative business outcomes, depending on the group's combined resources as well as the degree to which they are racially stigmatized. As we have emphasized throughout, not all immigrants—not even those from the same sending country—have comparable class or educational backgrounds, and thus the very poor among them would be unable to pool sufficient financial resources to create business opportunities for their co-ethnics despite caring deeply about and investing in various forms of cultural solidarity. Further, different groups face different degrees and kinds of racialization. It thus makes sense that business outcomes not only vary by immigrant group but even within group, as well as by gender and even the broader geographic regions of the country in which their firms operate (see also Logan et al. 2003).

In addition to a spatial analysis of neighborhood (dis)-advantage, a Bourdieusian perspective sheds light on some temporal dynamics in the reproduction of class inequality. We not only offered evidence of an intergenerational transmission of microclass cultural capital, but we demonstrated that the entrepreneurial disposition could register as a small competitive advantage in another country, if in gender-specific ways. Our analysis of an entrepreneurial disposition as a subtype of cultural capital is different from the other types of benefits that accrue to second-generation entrepreneurs. We maintain that our respondents leveraged cultural capital, and this is a different type of advantage than what previous scholars have described, given that our respondents reported that they did not work in their parents' firms. Indeed, many were in their late teenage years when they set off on their US journeys. Further, their parents' business networks in Mexico would not be especially helpful to them in Los Angeles. Although the migrants in our study reported relying on their personal finances or borrowing from friends and family to start their small firms, we controlled for financial start-up as well as human capital in all of our regression analyses. Our research thus highlights the role of a tacit cultural disposition as an entrepreneurial advantage in a host country. Finally, if only by analogy, the Bourdieusian perspective provided a theoretical framework that allowed us to understand how the timing of entrepreneurship vis-à-vis the timing of the legalization of immigration status develops what we referred to as legal capital.

As useful as the concentrated disadvantage and cultural capital theories are for explaining some spatial and temporal dimensions in the reproduction of inequalities, the intersectional analytic strategy that we deployed in Chap. 5 also proved helpful. It specifically illuminated how variously positioned migrants within Mexican neighborhoods fared in business, depending on their class, gender, and marital status standing within their ethnic community. Somewhat surprisingly, Chap. 5 made it clear that women did not experience a larger negative impact associated with neighborhood poverty and ethnic concentration as compared to men, as we might have expected from prior research on women's business performance. Rather, their microclass advantage, their small business boost from marriage, and the fact so many were strategically cautious about purchasing existing businesses helped some of the Mexican immigrant women in our study. We conclude that because all three perspectives seek to explain social inequalities—whether by focusing on class reproduction over time through intergenerational dynamics, the spatial segregation of people in neighborhoods, or on gender position within communities and families—each framework sheds light on important factors in the reproduction of social class and inequality.

POLICY IMPLICATIONS

While our small case study of Mexicans in Los Angeles suggests that poor and under-skilled immigrants are more effective in business under certain conditions as compared to others, additional comparative research is necessary to determine the robustness of our results. Yet, even if our findings about the buoyancy of small shops are specific to Mexicans in Los Angeles, there are still some policy implications from our research that might very well help small businesses create jobs elsewhere. One implication of our work is that the site selection of small shops is crucial to their long-term business performance. Policymakers could, thus, help immigrant shopkeepers find the optimal locations for the goods and services that they sell. Such policy might help small businesses to stay afloat and perhaps even expand enough to create jobs, even if in small numbers. In addition, our findings are consistent with other research pointing to the benefits of simplifying current immigration policies so that undocumented people may achieve legal status more easily. Having legal status clearly makes it possible for immigrants to pursue higher education, better-paying jobs, and, as we demonstrated here, even undertake entrepreneurial ventures. What is clear 20 years into the enactment of the more punitive immigration laws of the late 1990s is that they have not worked. The ten-year bans from legalization do not force unauthorized people out of the US for many reasons, and one among them is that their lives in the shadows in the US tend to be, on average, better than what they would be in Mexico, where unemployment has historically been high and where violent crime has, in the twenty-first century, developed into a humanitarian crisis.

Briefly, a crisis has been developing in Mexico since 2006, when the government escalated its war against drug cartels, and the criminals who lead them, in turn, have escalated inter-cartel violence. Thus far, about 100,000 people have died as a result, and criminal violence has internally displaced one-quarter of a million people, with 10,000–30,000 people who are unaccounted for and are defined by non-governmental organizations (NGOs) as missing (on the internal displacement of people, see Rios Contreras 2014). Instead of forcing people out of the US to return to a country where they would almost certainly face greater poverty and violence, immigration policy has trapped the unauthorized in a status that only destroys their ability to create better futures for themselves and their children. When millions of people have been deprived of hope, society, in general, is affected and not just in the short term. US-born children raised in segregated and economically disadvantaged neighborhoods will themselves have many challenges to overcome, as the research on concentrated disadvantage shows. Therefore, reforming immigration laws to make the pathways to legality easier would help to unleash the creative and productive capacity of the people trapped in the undocumented status.

Because the economic integration of migrants is important for improving what Georg Simmel once referred to as "stranger" relations, our analysis could be relevant to policymakers and scholars who seek ways to help other disadvantaged migrants or refugees settle in their host societies. As civil conflict, criminal violence, poverty, and natural disasters displace millions of people all over the world on a yearly basis, migrants and refugees find themselves settling in what are frequently unwelcoming societies. At least one of the major global challenges of our time involves finding the optimal ways of integrating migrants and refugees who, according to a myriad of journalistic reports, are vulnerable to the scapegoating rhetoric of the nativists who want to expel them. Therefore, understanding the conditions under which small business proprietorship is most likely to help migrants and refugees achieve some measure of economic self-determination could help mitigate certain social tensions by reducing poverty and, with it, the conditions that help to generate both racism and crime. Given that only a small portion of the population is willing to assume the risks associated with shopkeeping, policy that supports entrepreneurs would, of course, be only one instrument in a much bigger toolkit of other poverty-reducing policies. Yet, such policy would be an important tool for poverty reduction because when entrepreneurship creates jobs, it directly contributes to the economic vibrancy of immigrant neighborhoods.

REFERENCES

Logan, John R., Richard D. Alba, and Brian J. Stults. 2003. Enclaves and Entrepreneurs: Assessing the Payoff for Immigrants and Minorities. *International Migration Review* 37 (2): 344–388.

Rios, Viridiana Contreras. 2014. The Role of Drug-Related Violence and Extortion in Promoting Mexican Migration: Unexpected Consequences of a Drug War. *Latin American Research Review* 49 (3): 199–217.

APPENDIX A: CHARACTERISTICS OF ENTREPRENEURS, A COMPARISON

	Hispanic immigrant entrepreneurs in California	Mexican immigrant entrepreneurs in Los Angeles
Characteristic of owner		
Female	29.2	37.4
Select age categories		
25–34	9.9	18.4
35–44	29.6	34.7
45–54	34.2	27.7
Less than high school	36.8	59.9
High school or more	62.0	40.1
Hours a week spent on business		
Less than 40	35.4	36.9
40–59	46.3	55.5
60 or more	17.5	7.6
Previously self-employed	29.9	No data
Founded the business	79.5	No data
Characteristics of business		
Year established business		
Before 1990	18.8	No data
1990–1999	23.5	No data
2000–2007	49.7	No data
Sources of start-up capital		
Savings	62.5	No data

(*continued*)

© The Author(s) 2018   177
D. Trevizo, M. Lopez, *Neighborhood Poverty and Segregation in the (Re-)Production of Disadvantage*,
https://Doi.org/10.1007/978-3-319-73715-7

(continued)

	Hispanic immigrant entrepreneurs in California	Mexican immigrant entrepreneurs in Los Angeles
Credit cards	10.7	No data
Loan from relative or friend	2.5	No data
Bank	5.1	No data
Conducted transactions in Spanish	65.9	No data
Mean workers hired	7.5	. No data
Workers hired quartiles		
No employees	72.8	No data
1–2 employees	6.7	No data
3–4 employees	5.4	No data
5 or more employees	15.2	No data
Amount of start-up capital		
$0–$5K	28.7	No data
$6K–$49K	28.9	No data
$50K–$100K	5.9	No data
More than $100K	14.5	No data
Mean receipts	$1,353.63	No data
Median receipts	$50.00	No data
N	5751	1182

Source: Data for Hispanic entrepreneurs comes from the US Census 2007 Survey of Business Owners, public use file. Data for Mexican entrepreneurs come from the 2007 American Community Survey

Notes: The ACS does not provide data on business characteristics

APPENDIX B: STATE OF ORIGIN OF LA ENTREPRENEURS

State in Mexico	N	Percent
Aguascalientes	0	0
Baja California	3	2.8
Baja California Sur	0	0
Campeche	0	0
Chiapas	1	0.9
Chihuahua	4	3.7
Coahuila	2	1.8
Colima	1	0.9
Distrito Federal	16	14.7
Durango	6	5.5
Guanajuato	3	2.8
Guerrero	5	4.6
Hidalgo	1	0.9
Jalisco	22	20.2
Estado. De México	3	2.8
Michoacán	13	11.9
Morelos	1	0.9
Nayarit	8	7.3
Nuevo León	0	0
Oaxaca	1	0.9
Puebla	2	1.8
Querétaro	0	0
Quintana Roo	0	0
San Luis Potosí	0	0

(*continued*)

© The Author(s) 2018
D. Trevizo, M. Lopez, *Neighborhood Poverty and Segregation in the (Re-)Production of Disadvantage*,
https://doi.org/10.1007/978-3-319-73715-7

(continued)

State in Mexico	N	Percent
Sinaloa	3	2.8
Sonora	2	1.8
Tabasco	0	0
Tamaulipas	1	0.9
Tlaxcala	1	0.9
Veracruz	3	2.8
Yucatán	0	0
Zacatecas	7	6.4
Total N	109	100

Source: Authors' survey of Mexican immigrant business owners in Los Angeles, 2007

APPENDIX C: HISTORICAL HIGHLIGHTS OF THE ECONOMIC AND ETHNIC LANDSCAPE OF LOS ANGELES' LATINO CONCENTRATED AREAS

© The Author(s) 2018
D. Trevizo, M. Lopez, *Neighborhood Poverty and Segregation*
in the (Re-)Production of Disadvantage,
https://doi.org/10.1007/978-3-319-73715-7

181

Area of Los Angeles Count	Labor market/economy	Ethnic/immigrant composition
Central Los Angeles	**1980s:** Thirty percent of the Latino population in Pico Union have incomes below the poverty level. Manufacturing jobs replaced by low wage service sector jobs. **1990s:** Growth in Central American immigrant-owned firms (grocery stores, restaurants, banks, etc.). In 1997, Pico Union had the highest rate of new business formation in LA County. The Guatemala Trade and Investment Office was established in 1992 to promote trade between Guatemala and LA.	**1970s:** Movement of European immigrants out of Pico Union and a large movement of Mexican immigrants into Pico Union. **1980s:** Large influx of Central American immigrants fleeing war and political persecution. Sixty-five percent of population in Pico Union was foreign born. **1990s:** Pico Union/Westlake is a majority Latino neighborhood while other areas in Central Los Angeles, such as Hollywood, are more heterogeneous.
East Los Angeles	**1920s:** LA industries had a strong relationship with the local Mexican labor force and many Mexicans easily found jobs in unskilled and semiskilled low-wage, low-mobility jobs. **1940s:** Lack of industrial sector that was burgeoning in other outer parts of Los Angeles, forcing Mexicans to take jobs in low-end manufacturing.	**1910:** Movement of European immigrants to West LA, leaving East LA as the center of Mexican American life, indeed home to a significant number of Mexican American political organizations. Most Mexicans were unable to relocate to the west side of LA due to restrictive covenants. **1980:** Over 50 percent of the population in East Los Angeles was foreign born.
Northeast Los Angeles	**1940s:** Arroyo Seco Parkway completed, which resulted in a decline in the rail line and real estate market in Highland Park. **1970s:** Increase in poverty.	**1950s:** Decline in rents in Highland Park led to an increase in Mexicans seeking an affordable place to live. **1960s and 1970s:** Hub for the LA Chicano political and cultural movement. **1980s:** Hispanic/Latino population at 52 percent.

San Gabriel Valley	1920s: Mexicans employed in low-wage, labor-intensive jobs in La Puente, such as in agriculture (walnut, citrus, and avocado). 1940s and 1950s: Agricultural sector diminished and the number of housing developments, tract homes, and freeways increased, creating a suburbanized community. 1990s: Combination of low-wage immigrant labor and poor working conditions for immigrants (garment factories and service industries) and highly skilled technicians and engineers in research centers.	Long-established presence of Mexicans in Southeast LA cities, such as La Puente, since the 1920s due to the growing agricultural sector. 1950s: Influxes of Mexican Americans from the East side of LA, Japanese Americans from the East and West sides of LA, and Chinese Americans from Chinatown, due to the affordable housing developments. 1970s: Population change from Anglo American dominant to increasingly Mexican in areas such as La Puente and El Monte. Glendora, La Verne, and Pasadena remained predominantly white. Large influx of immigrants from China. 1980s: Rising immigrant population. 1990s: Latino population comprised 75 percent of the population in La Puente.
San Fernando Valley	1950s: High concentrations of aerospace and high-technology industries. 1970s: Movement of high-tech sector out of the San Fernando Valley toward Ventura. 1990s: Economic decline as a result of the aerospace crisis and rise in service industries.	1950s: Anglo Americans comprised 90 percent of the population. 1970s: Influx of immigrant communities in Canoga Park, Panorama City, and Van Nuys 1980s: Large increase in the Latino population. From 1990 to 2000, the Hispanic population increased 86 percent in Panorama City. 2000: Latino population was 42.6 percent.
Southeast Los Angeles	1930s: Mid-level paying, unionized, stable, durable manufacturing (auto, steel, and rubber) jobs for Anglo Americans and a hub for labor and community organizing. Small Latino workforce employed in low-wage, low-mobility, durable manufacturing jobs. 1980s: Transition to low-wage, low-mobility, non-unionized, light manufacturing jobs (garment, food, and plastic).	1920s: Movement of Anglo Americans to the west side of LA. Restrictive zoning laws prevented Mexicans from moving to the west side of LA. 1970s: Population change from Anglo American dominant to a large Mexican population. 1970s: Increase in immigrant population (predominantly Mexican immigrant and smaller percentages of Central American and Cuban immigrants). 1990s: Latino population comprised more than 92 percent of the population in Southeast Los Angeles.

Sources: Donahoe (2005), Ochoa (2004), Cheng (2013), Bedolla (2005), Peterson (2017), Kotkin and Ozuna (2002), Pastor and Ortiz (2009), Wasilco et al. (2013), Romo (1983), and Pastor (2001)

APPENDIX D: MEXICAN SENDING STATES AND LOS ANGELES NEIGHBORHOODS, REGIONS, AND SELECT VARIABLES

© The Author(s) 2018   185
D. Trevizo, M. Lopez, *Neighborhood Poverty and Segregation
in the (Re-)Production of Disadvantage,*
https://doi.org/10.1007/978-3-319-73715-7

		Los Angeles neighborhood	Geographic area in Los Angeles	Mexico's sending state	Urban/rural origins in Mexico	Number of years living in the U.S.	Spouse present at time of interview
Los Angeles neighborhood	Pearson correlation	1					
	p-value						
	N	111					
Geographic area in Los Angeles	Pearson correlation	−0.282***	1				
	p-value	0.001					
	N	111	111				
Mexico's sending state	Pearson correlation	−0.003	0.135	1			
	p-value	0.488	0.081*				
	N	109	109	109			
Urban/rural origins in Mexico	Pearson correlation	−0.146*	−0.110	−0.355***	1		
	p-value	0.065	0.128	0.000			
	N	109	109	107	109		
Number of years living in the U.S.	Pearson correlation	0.002	0.060	−0.030	−0.011	1	
	p-value	0.491	0.267	0.380	0.454		
	N	110	110	108	108	110	
Spouse present at time of interview	Pearson correlation	0.056	−0.022	0.076	−0.096	−0.030	1
	p-value	0.280	0.410	0.219	0.163	0.380	
	N	110	110	108	108	109	110

Source: Authors' survey of Mexican immigrant business owners in Los Angeles, 2007

Notes: *$p < 0.10$, **$p < 0.05$, ***$p < 0.01$ (one-tailed tests)

REFERENCES

Abrego, Leisy J. 2011. Legal Consciousness of Undocumented Latinos: Fear and Stigma as Barriers to Claims Making for First and 1.5 Generation Immigrants. *Law and Society Review* 45 (2): 337–369.

Aguilera, Michael Bernabé. 2009. Ethnic Enclaves and the Earnings of Self-employed Latinos. *Small Business Economics* 33: 413–425.

Alarcón, Rafael. 2011. U.S. Immigration Policy and the Mobility of Mexicans (1882–2005). *Migraciones Internaciones* 6 (1): 185–218.

Alarcon, Rafael, Luis Escala, and Olga Odgers. 2016. *Making Los Angeles Home: The Integration of Mexican Immigrants in the United States.* Oakland: University of California Press.

Aldrich, Howard, and Albert Reiss. 1976. Continuities in the Study of Ecological Succession: Changes in the Race Composition of Neighborhoods and Their Businesses. *American Journal of Sociology* 81: 846–866.

Aldrich, H., J. Cater, T. Jones, D. McEvoy, and P. Velleman. 1985. Ethnic Residential Concentration and the Protected Market Hypothesis. *Social Forces* 63 (4): 996–1009.

Allison, Paul D. 2009. Missing Data. In *The SAGE Handbook of Quantitative Methods in Psychology*, ed. Roger E. Millsap and Alberto Maydeu-Olivares, 72–89. Thousand Oaks: Sage.

Amuedo-Dorantes, Catalina, and Cynthia Bansak. 2012. The Labor Market Impact of Mandated Employment. *American Economic Review: Papers & Proceedings* 102 (3): 543–548.

———. 2014. Employment Verification Mandates and the Labor Market of Likely Unauthorized and Native Workers. *Contemporary Economic Policy* 32 (3): 671–680.

© The Author(s) 2018   187
D. Trevizo, M. Lopez, *Neighborhood Poverty and Segregation in the (Re-)Production of Disadvantage,*
https://doi.org/10.1007/978-3-319-73715-7

Amuedo-Dorantes, Catalina, Cynthia Bansak, and Steven Raphael. 2007. Gender Differences in the Labor Market: Impact of IRCA's Amnesty Provisions. *American Economic Review* 97 (2): 412–416.

Amuedo-Dorantes, Catalina, Thitima Puttitanun, and Ana P. Martinez-Donate. 2013. How Do Tougher Immigration Measures Affect Unauthorized Immigrants? *Demography* 50: 1067–1091.

Anderson, Alistair R., and Claire J. Miller. 2003. "Class Matters": Human and Social Capital in the Entrepreneurial Process. *Journal of Socio-Economics* 32: 17–36.

Andreas, Peter. 2000. *Border Games: Policing the US–Mexico Divide*. Ithaca: Cornell University Press.

Argueta, Carla N. 2016. *Border Security: Immigration Enforcement Between Ports of Entry*. Congressional Research Service Report Prepared for Members and Committees of Congress 7-5700. www.crs.gov R42138.

Bachmeier, James D. 2013. Cumulative Causation, Coethnic Settlement Maturity and Mexican Immigration to the U.S. Metropolitan Areas, 1995–2000. *Social Forces* 91 (4): 1293–1317.

Bader, Michael. 2016. L.A. Is Resegregating and Whites Are a Major Reason Why. *Los Angeles Times*, Op-Ed, April 1.

Bader, Michael D.M., and Siri Warkentien. 2016. The Fragmented Evolution of Racial Integration Since the Civil Rights Movement. *Sociological Science* 3: 135–166.

Bansak, Cynthia, and Steven Raphael. 2001. Immigration Reform and the Earnings of Latino Worker: Do Employer Sanctions Cause Discrimination? *Industrial and Labor Relations Review* 54 (2): 275–295.

Bansak, Cynthia, Nicole Simpson, and Madeline Zavodny. 2015. *The Economics of Immigration*. New York: Routledge.

Bates, Timothy. 1990. Entrepreneur Human Capital Inputs and Small Business Longevity. *The Review of Economics and Statistics* 72 (4): 551–559.

———. 1994. Social Resources Generated by Group Support Networks May Not Be Beneficial to Asian Immigrant-Owned Small Business. *Social Forces* 72 (3): 671–689.

———. 1997. *Race, Self-Employment and Upward Mobility: An Illusive American Dream*. Washington, DC: Woodrow Wilson Center Press.

Bean, Frank D., and Lindsay Lowell. 2003. Immigrant Employment and Mobility Opportunities in California. *The State of California Labor* 3: 87–116.

Bean, Frank D., and Gillian Stevens. 2003. *America's Newcomers and the Dynamics of Diversity*. New York: Russell Sage.

Bean, Frank D., and Marta Tienda. 1987. *The Hispanic Population of the United States*. New York: Russell Sage Foundation.

Bean, Frank D., Barry Edmonston, and Jeffrey S. Passel, eds. 1990. *Undocumented Migration to the United States: IRCA and the Experience of the 1980s.* New York: Urban Institute Press.

Bean, Frank D., Mark Leach, and B. Lindsay Lowell. 2004. Immigrant Job Quality and Mobility in the United States. *Work and Occupations* 31 (4): 499–518.

Becker, Gary S. 1993. *Human Capital: A Theoretical and Empirical Analysis, with Special Reference to Education.* 3rd ed. Chicago: The University of Chicago Press.

Bedolla, Lisa. 2005. *Fluid Borders: Latino Power, Identity, and Politics in Los Angeles,* 44–52. Berkeley: University of California Press.

Benson, Rodney. 1999. Field Theory in Comparative Context: A New Paradigm for Media Studies. *Theory and Society* 28 (3): 463–498.

Bergsman, Steve. 2005. Banks Are Quietly Wooing Undocumented Immigrants. *USBANKER,* June.

Blank, Rebecca. 2010. *Women-Owned Businesses in the 21st Century.* US Department of Commerce, Economics and Statistics Administration.

Bohn, Sarah, and Magnus Lofstrom. 2013. Employment Effects of State Legislation. In *Immigration, Poverty, and Socioeconomic Inequality,* ed. David Card and Steven Raphael, 282–314. New York: Russell Sage.

Bonacich, Edna. 1987. "Making It" in America: A Social Evaluation of the Ethics of Immigrant Entrepreneurship. *Sociological Perspectives* 30 (4): 446–466.

Bonacich, Edna, and John Modell. 1980. *The Economic Basis of Ethnic Solidarity: Small Business in the Japanese American Community.* Berkeley: University of California Press.

Borjas, George J. 1999. The Economic Analysis of Immigration. In *Handbook of Labor Economics,* ed. Orley Ashenfelter and David Card, vol. 3A, 1697–1760. Amsterdam: North-Holland.

———. 2006. Making It in America: Social Mobility in the Immigrant Population. *Future of Children* 16 (2): 55–71. http://files.eric.ed.gov/fulltext/EJ1042192.pdf

Bourdieu, Pierre. 1984 [1979]. *Distinction: A Social Critique of the Judgement of Taste.* Cambridge, MA: Harvard University Press.

———. 2001. *Masculine Domination.* Cambridge: Polity Press.

———. 2002. Nouvelles réflexions sur la domination masculine. *Cahiers du Genre* 33 (2): 225–233. https://doi.org/10.3917/cdge.033.0225.

Bourdieu, Pierre, and Loïc J.D. Wacquant. 1992. *An Invitation to Reflexive Sociology.* Chicago: University of Chicago Press.

Boyd, Monica. 1989. Family and Personal Networks in International Migration: Recent Developments and New Agendas. *International Migration Review* 23: 638–680.

Bratsberg, Bernt, James F. Ragan Jr., and Zaffar M. Nasir. 2002. The Effect of Naturalization on Wage Growth: A Panel Study of Young Male Immigrants. *Journal of Labor Economics* 20 (3): 568–597.

Braymen, Charles B., and Florence Neymotin. 2014. Enclaves and Entrepreneurial Success. *Journal of Entrepreneurship and Public Policy* 3 (2): 197–221.

Brewer, Rose, Cecilia Conrad, and Mary King. 2002. The Complexities and Potential of Theorizing Gender, Caste, Race and Class. *Feminist Economics* 8 (2): 3–18.

Browne, Irene, and Joya Misra. 2003. The Intersection of Gender and Race in the Labor Market. *Annual Review of Sociology* 29: 487–513.

Brubaker, Rogers. 1985. Rethinking Classical Theory: The Sociological Vision of Pierre Bourdieu. *Theory and Society* 14 (6): 745–775.

Butler, John Sibley. 1991. *Entrepreneurship and Self-Help Among Black Americans: A Reconsideration of Race and Economics*. Albany: State University of New York Press.

Butler, John Sibley, and George Kozmetsky. 2004. *Immigrant and Minority Entrepreneurship: The Continuous Rebirth of American Communities*. Westport: Praeger Publishers.

Butler, John Sibley, Alfonso Morales, and David L. Torres. 2009. *An American Story: Mexican American Entrepreneurship & Wealth Creation*. West Lafayette: Purdue University Press.

Campos, Raymundo, Gerardo Esquivel, and Nora Lustig. 2012. *The Rise and Fall of Income Inequality in Mexico: 1989–2010*. WIDER Working Paper, No. 2012/10. ISBN 978-929-230-473-7

Chang, Cindy, and Kate Mather. 2016. LAPD Will Not Help Deport Immigrants Under Trump Chief Says. *Los Angeles Times*, November 14.

Chavez, Leo R. 2001. *Covering Immigration: Population Images and the Politics of the Nation*. Berkeley: University of California Press.

———. 2013. *The Latino Threat: Constructing Immigrants, Citizens, and the Nation*. 2nd ed. Stanford: Stanford University Press.

Cheng, Wendy. 2013. The Changs Next Door to the Diazes: Suburban Racial Formation in Los Angeles's San Gabriel Valley. *Journal of Urban History* 39 (1): 15–35.

Chiswick, Barry, and Paul Miller. 2005. Do Enclaves Matter in Immigrant Adjustment? *City and Community* 4 (1): 5–35.

Collins, Patricia Hill. 2015. Intersectionality's Definitional Dilemmas. *Annual Review of Sociology*. 41: 1–20.

Cornelius, Wayne A. 1992. From Sojourners to Settlers: The Changing Profile of Mexican Immigration to the United States. In *U.S.-Mexico Relations: Labor Market Interdependence*, ed. J.A. Bustamante, C.W. Reynolds, and R.A. Hinojosa Ojeda, 155–195. Stanford: Stanford University Press.

————. 2001. Death at the Border: Efficacy and Unintended Consequences of U.S. Immigration Control Policy. *Population and Development Review* 27: 661–1399.

Cornelius, Wayne A., David Scott FitzGerald, and Pedro Lewin Fischer. 2007. *Mayan Journeys: The New Migration from Yucatán to the United States.* Boulder: Lynne Rienner Publishers.

Craig, Richard B. 1971. *The Bracero Program: Interest Groups and Foreign Policy.* Austin: University of Texas Press.

Crenshaw, Kimberle. 1991. Mapping the Margins: Intersectionality, Identity Politics, and Violence Against Women of Color. *Stanford Law Review* 43: 1241–1299.

Daly, Mary, and Fred Furlong. 2002. Profile of a Recession: The U.S. and California. *Federal Reserve Bank of San Francisco Economic Letter,* Number 2002-04, February 22. http://www.frbsf.org/economic-research/files/el2002-04.pdf

Dávila, Alberto, and Marie T. Mora. 2009. English Proficiency and Entrepreneurial Income Among Mexican Immigrant Men in the United States, 1990, 2000, and 2005. In *An American Story: Mexican American Entrepreneurship and Wealth Creation,* ed. John Sibley Butler, Alfonso Morales, and David L. Torres. West Lafayette: Purdue University Press.

Davis, Susan E.M., and Dinah D. Long. 1999. Women Entrepreneurs: What Do They Need? *Business and Economic Review* 45 (4): 25–26.

De Genova, Nicholas. 2005. *Working the Boundaries: Race, Space and "Illegality" in Mexican Chicago.* Durham/London: Duke University Press.

De Leon, Arnoldo. 1993. *Mexican Americans in Texas: A Brief History.* Wheeling: Harlan Davidson.

Devine, Theresa. 1994. Characteristics of Self-Employed Women in the U.S. *Monthly Labor Review* 117 (3): 20–34.

Diaz McConnell, Eileen, and Enrico A. Marcelli. 2007. Buying into the American Dream? Mexican Immigrants, Legal Status, and Homeownership in Los Angeles County. *Social Science Quarterly* 88 (1): 199–221.

Doms, Mark, Ethan Lewis, and Alicia Robb. 2010. Local Labor Force Education, New Business Characteristics, and Firm Performance. *Journal of Urban Economics* 67: 61–77.

Donahoe, Myrna Cherkoss. 2005. Economic Restructuring and Labor Organizing in Southeast Los Angeles, 1935–2001. In *Latino LA: Transformations, Communities, and Activism,* ed. Enrique C. Ochoa and Gilda L. Ochoa, 83–107. Tucson: University of Arizona Press.

Donato, Katharine M., and Amada Armenta. 2011. What We Know About Unauthorized Migration. *Annual Review of Sociology* 37: 529–543.

Donato, Katharine M., and Douglas S. Massey. 1993. Effects of the Immigration Reform and Control Act on the Wages of Mexican Migrants. *Social Science Quarterly* 74 (3): 523–541.

Donato, Katharine M., and Blake Sisk. 2012. Shifts in the Employment Outcomes Among Mexican Migrants to the United States, 1976–2009. *Research in Social Stratification and Mobility* 30 (1): 63–77.

Donato, Katharine M., Brandon Wagner, and Evelyn Patterson. 2008a. The Cat and Mouse Game at the Mexico-U.S. Border: Gendered Patterns and Recent Shifts. *The International Migration Review* 42 (2): 330–359.

Donato, Katharine M., Chizuko Wakabayashi, Shirin Hakimzadeh, and Amada Armenta. 2008b. Shifts in the Employment Conditions of Mexican Migrant Men and Women: The Effect of U.S. Immigration Policy. *Work and Occupations* 35 (4): 462–495.

Dreby, Joanna. 2015. *Everyday Illegal: When Policies Undermine Immigrant Families*. Oakland: University of California Press.

Dunn, Timothy J. 1996. *The Militarization of the U.S.–Mexico Border, 1978–1992: Low-Intensity Conflict Doctrine Comes Home*. Austin: Center for Mexican American Studies, University of Texas at Austin.

Dunn, Thomas, and Douglas Holtz-Eakin. 2000. Financial Capital, Human Capital, and the Transition to Self-Employment: Evidence from Intergenerational Links. *Journal of Labor Economics* 18 (2): 282–305.

Durand, Jorge, and Douglas S. Massey. 2003. The Costs of Contradiction: U.S. Border Policy 1986–2000. *Latino Studies* 1 (2): 233–252.

Ellingwood, Ken. 2004. *Hard Line: Life and Death on the U.S.-Mexico Border*. New York: Pantheon Books.

Elliott, James R., and Mario Sims. 2001. Ghettos and Barrios: The Impact of Neighborhood Poverty and Race on Job Matching Among Blacks and Latinos. *Social Problems* 48 (3): 341–361.

Enchautegui, María E. 1998. Low-Skilled Immigrants and the Changing American Labor Market. *Population Development Review* 24 (4): 811–824.

Eschbach, Karl, Glenn V. Ostir, Kushang V. Patel, Kyriakos S. Markides, and James S. Goodwin. 2004. Neighborhood Context and Mortality Among Older Mexican Americans: Is There a Barrio Advantage? *American Journal of Public Health* 94 (10): 1807–1812.

Fairchild, Gregory B. 2008. Residential Segregation Influences on the Likelihood of Black and White Self-Employment. *Journal of Business Venturing* 23 (1): 46–74.

Fairlie, Robert, and Magnus Lofstrom. 2014. Immigration and Entrepreneurship. In *The Handbook on the Economics of International Migration*, ed. B. Chiswick and P. Miller. Amsterdam: Elsevier.

Fairlie, Robert, and Alicia Robb. 2007. Families, Human Capital, and Small Business: Evidence From the Characteristics of Business Owners Survey. *Industrial and Labor Relations Review* 60 (2): 225–245.

———. 2009a. Gender Differences in Business Performance: Evidence from the Characteristics of Business Owners Survey. *Small Business Economics* 33: 375–395.

————. 2009b. *Entrepreneurship, Self-Employment and Business Data: An Introduction to Several Large, Nationally-Representative Datasets.* IZA Discussion Paper 4052.

————. 2010. *Race and Entrepreneurial Success: Black, Asian, and White-Owned Businesses in the United States.* Cambridge, MA: MIT Press.

Fairlie, Robert, and Christopher Woodruff. 2007. Mexican Entrepreneurship: A Comparison of Self-Employment in Mexico and the United States. In *Mexican Immigration to the United States*, ed. George Borjas, 123–158. Chicago: University of Chicago Press.

————. 2010. Mexican American Entrepreneurship. *The B.E. Journal of Economic Analysis and Policy* 10 (1): 1–34.

Fassin, Didier. 2011. Policing Borders, Producing Boundaries: The Governmentality of Immigration in Dark Times. *Annual Review of Anthropology* 40: 213–226.

Feldmeyer, Ben. 2010. The Effects of Racial/Ethnic Segregation on Latino and Black Homicide. *The Sociological Quarterly* 51 (4): 600–623.

Fiscal Policy Institute. 2012. *Immigrant Small Business Owners: A Significant and Growing Part of the Economy.* Report from the Immigration Research Initiative.

Fischer, Mary J., and Douglas S. Massey. 2000. Residential Segregation and Ethnic Enterprise in U.S. Metropolitan Areas. *Social Problems* 47 (3): 408–424.

Fligstein, Neil, and Doug McAdam. 2011. Toward a General Theory of Strategic Action Fields. *Sociological Theory* 29 (1): 1–26.

Flippen, Chenoa A. 2012. Laboring Underground: The Employment Patterns of Hispanic Immigrant Men in Durham, NC. *Social Problems* 59 (1): 21–42.

Forman, Robert E. 1971. *Black Ghettos, White Ghettos, and Slums.* Englewood Cliffs: Prentice Hall.

Friedmann Marquardt, Marie, Timothy J. Steigenga, Philip J. Williams, and Manuel A. Vásquez. 2011. *Living 'Illegal': The Human Face of Unauthorized Migration.* New York: New Press.

Galarza, Ernesto. 1978 (1964). *Merchants of Labor: The Mexican Bracero Story.* Santa Barbara: McNally and Loftin, West.

Gallagher, Mari. 2005. Alternative IDs, ITIN Mortgages, and Emerging Latino Markets. *Profitwise News and Views*, March.

García, Juan Ramon. 1980. *Operation Wetback: The Mass Deportation of Mexican Undocumented Workers in 1954.* Westport: Greenwood Press.

Gentsch, Kerstin, and Douglas S. Massey. 2011. Labor Market Outcomes for Legal Mexican Immigrants Under the New Regime of Immigration Enforcement. *Social Science Quarterly* 92 (3): 875–893.

Gibbs, Jewelle Taylor, and Teiahsha Bankhead. 2001. *Preserving Privilege: California Politics, Propositions, and People of Color.* Westport: Praeger.

Gold, Steve. 1994. Patterns of Economic Cooperation Among Israeli Immigrants in Los Angeles. *International Migration Review* 28: 114–135.

Gold, Steven J., and Ivan Light. 2000. Ethnic Economies and Social Policy. *Research in Social Movements, Conflicts and Change* 22: 165–191.

Gonzales, Robert G. 2016. *Lives in Limbo: Undocumented and Coming of Age in America*. Oakland: University of California Press.

Gonzalez, Saul. 2015. Inside an LA Bakery That Crosses Bicultural Borders. *PRI's The World and Globalpost*, November 24. https://www.pri.org/stories/2015-11-24/inside-la-bakery-crosses-bicultural-borders

Gonzalez-Barrera, Ana, and Jens Manuel Krogstad. 2017. *What We Know About Illegal Immigration from Mexico*. Pew Hispanic Research Center. http://www.pewresearch.org/fact-tank/2017/03/02/what-we-know-about-illegal-immigration-from-mexico/

Granberry, Phillip J., and Enrico A. Marcelli. 2011. Social Capital Is Associated with Earnings Among Foreign-Born Mexican Men but Not Women in Los Angeles County. *International Migration* 49 (6): 113–128.

Granovetter, Mark S. 1973. The Strength of Weak Ties. *American Journal of Sociology* 78 (6): 1360–1380.

Grebler, Leo, Joan W. Moore, and Ralph C. Guzman. 1970. *The Mexican American People: The Nation's Second Largest Minority*. London: Free Press/Macmillan.

Greene, William H. 2000. *Econometric Analysis*. 4th ed. Upper Saddle River: Prentice Hall.

Greene, Patricia G., and Candida S. Brush. 2004. Women Entrepreneurs: An Explanatory Framework of Capital Types. In *Immigrant and Minority Entrepreneurship*, ed. J.S. Butler and G. Kozmetsky. Westport: Praeger.

Gurak, Douglas T., and Fe Caces. 1992. Migration Networks and the Shaping of Migration Systems. In *International Migration Systems: A Global Approach*, ed. Mary M. Kritz, Lin Lean Lim, and Hania Zlotnick. Oxford/New York: Clarendon Press/Oxford University Press.

Gurley-Calvez, Tami, Katherine Harper, and Amelia Biehl. 2009. *Self-Employed Women and Time Use*. Small Business Administration Office of Advocacy, SBAHQ-07-M-0409.

Gutierrez, David G. 1995. *Walls and Mirrors: Mexican Americans, Mexican Immigrants, and the Politics of Ethnicity*. Berkeley: University of California Press.

Hagan, Jacqueline. 1994. *Deciding to Be Legal. A Maya Community in Houston*. Philadelphia: Temple University Press.

———. 1998. Social Networks, Gender and Immigrant Settlement: Resource and Constraint. *American Sociological Review* 63 (1): 55–67.

Hagan, Jacqueline, Nichola Lowe, and Christian Quingla. 2011. Skills on the Move: Rethinking the Relationship Between Human Capital and Immigrant Economic Mobility. *Work and Occupations* 38 (2): 149–178.

Hagan, Jacqueline, Jean Luc Demonsant, and Sergio Chávez. 2014. Identifying and Measuring the Lifelong Human Capital of 'Unskilled' Migrants in the Mexico-US Migratory Circuit. *Journal of Migration and Human Security* 2 (2): 76–100.

Haldane, Andrew G. 2017. *Work, Wages and Monetary Policy.* Speech Given by Bank of England Chief Economist at the National Science and Media Museum, Bradford. https://www.bis.org/review/r170630f.pdf

Hall, Matthew, Emily Greenman, and George Farkas. 2010. Legal Status and Wage Disparities for Mexican Immigrants. *Social Forces* 89 (2): 491–514.

Hanson, Gordon. 2009. *The Economics and Policy of Illegal Immigration in the United States.* Migration Policy Institute Report. http://www.migrationpolicy. org/research/economics-and-policy-illegal-immigration-united-states

Harding, David J. 2009. Collateral Consequences of Violence in Disadvantaged Neighborhoods. *Social Forces* 88: 757–784.

———. 2010. *Living the Drama: Community, Conflict, and Culture Among Inner-City Boys.* Chicago: University of Chicago Press.

Haynes, Chris, Jennifer Merolla, and S. Karthick Ramakrishnan. 2016. *Framing Immigrants: News Coverage, Public Opinion, and Policy.* New York: Russell Sage Foundation.

Hernández-León, Rubén. 2004. Restructuring at the Source: High-Skilled Industrial Migration from Mexico to the United States. *Work and Occupations* 31 (4): 424–452.

———. 2008. *Metropolitan Migrants: The Migration of Urban Mexicans to the Unites States.* Berkeley: University of California Press.

Hipp, John R. 2007. Income Inequality, Race and Place: Does the Distribution of Race and Class Within Neighborhoods Affect Crime Rates? *Criminology* 45 (3): 665–697.

———. 2010. A Dynamic View of Neighborhoods: The Reciprocal Relationship Between Crime and Neighborhood Structural Characteristics. *Social Problems* 57 (2): 205–230.

Hipp, John R., George E. Tita, and Robert T. Greenbaum. 2009. Drive-Bys and Trade-Ups: Examining the Directionality of the Crime and Residential Instability Relationship. *Social Forces* 87 (4): 1777–1812.

Hoffman, Anders, Martin Junge, and Nikolaj Malchow-Moller. 2015. Running in the Family: Parental Role Models in Entrepreneurship. *Small Business Economics* 44: 79–104.

Hopkins, Daniel J. 2010. Politicized Places: Explaining Where and When Immigrants Provoke Local Opposition. *American Political Science Review* 104: 40–60.

Horton, Hayward Derrick. 2004. Black Entrepreneurs, 1970–1990: A Demographic Perspective. In *Immigrant and Minority Entrepreneurship: The Continuous Rebirth of American Communities,* ed. John Sibley Butler and George Kozmetsky. Westport: Praeger Publishers.

Hundley, Greg. 2000. Male/Female Earnings Differences in Self-Employment: The Effects of Marriage, Children, and the Household Division of Labor. *Industrial and Labor Relations Review* 54 (1): 95–114.

Huntington, Samuel P. 2004. *Who Are We? The Challenges to America's National Identity*. New York: Simon and Schuster.

Jacobson, Robin Dale. 2008. *The New Nativism: Proposition 187 and the Debate Over Immigration*. Minneapolis: University of Minessota Press.

Jargowsky, Paul A. 2009. Immigrants and Neighborhoods of Concentrated Poverty: Assimilation or Stagnation? *Journal of Ethnic and Migration Studies* 35: 1129–1151.

Jasso, Guillermina. 2011. Migration and Stratification. *Social Science Research* 40 (5): 1292–1336.

Jasso, Guillermina, Douglas S. Massey, Mark R. Rosenzweig, and James P. Smith. 2008. From Illegal to Legal: Estimating Previous Illegal Experience Among New Legal Immigrants to the United States. *International Migration Review* 42 (4): 803–843.

Jiménez, Tomás R., and David Fitzgerald. 2007. Mexican Assimilation: A Temporal and Spatial Reorientation. *DuBois Review* 4 (2): 337–354.

Joassart-Marcelli, Pascale. 2009. The Spatial Determinants of Wage Inequality: Evidence from Recent Latina Immigrants in Southern California. *Feminist Economics* 15 (2): 33–72.

Johnson, Phyllis. 1988. The Impact of Ethnic Communities on the Employment of Southeast Asian Refugees. *Amerasia Journal* 14 (1): 1–22.

Jones, Michael P. 1996. Indicator and Stratification Methods for Missing Explanatory Variables in Multiple Linear Regression. *Journal of the American Statistical Association* 91: 222–230.

Jonsson, Jan O., David B. Grusky, Matthew Di Carlo, Reinhard Pollak, and Mary C. Brinton. 2009. Microclass Mobility: Social Reproduction in Four Countries. *American Journal of Sociology* 114 (4): 977–1036.

Kallick, David D. 2015. *Bringing Vitality to Main Street: How Immigrant and Businesses Help Local Economies Grow*. New York: Americas Society and Council of the Americas.

Kanas, Agnieszka, Frank van Tubergen, and Tanja van der Lippe. 2009. Immigrant Self-Employment: Testing Hypotheses About the Role of Origin- and Host-Country Human Capital and Bonding and Bridging Social Capital. *Work and Occupations* 36 (3): 181–208.

Keister, Lisa A., Jody A. Vallejo, and E.P. Borelli. 2015. Mexican American Mobility: Early Life Processes and Adult Wealth Ownership. *Social Forces* 93 (3): 1015.

Kilgore, James. 2015. *Understanding Mass Incarceration: A People's Guide to the Key Civil Rights Struggle of Our Time*. New York: The New Press.

Kim, Dae Young. 1999. Beyond Co-ethnic Solidarity: Mexican and Ecuadorean Employment in Korean-Owned Businesses in New York City. *Ethnic and Racial Studies* 22 (3): 581–605.

Kim, Marlene. 2009. Race and Gender Differences in the Earnings of Black Workers. *Industrial Relations* 48 (3): 466–488.

Kitroeff, Natalie, and Victoria Kim. 2017. Behind a $13 Shirt, a $6-an-Hour Worker: How Forever 21 and Other Retailers Avoid Liability for Factories that Underpay Workers to Sew Their Clothes. *Los Angeles Times*, August 31.

Knight, Frank H. 1921. *Risk, Uncertainty, and Profit*. New York: Houghton Mifflin Company.

Knight, Melanie. 2016. Race-ing, Classing and Gendering Racialized Women's Participation in Entrepreneurship. *Gender, Work, and Organization* 23 (3): 310–327.

Kossoudji, Sherrie A., and Deborah A. Cobb-Clark. 2002. Coming Out of the Shadows: Learning About Legal Status and Wages from the Legalized Population. *Journal of Labor Economics* 20 (3): 598–628.

Kotkin, Joel, and Erika Ozuna. 2002. *The Changing Face of the San Fernando Valley*. Pepperdine University, School of Public Policy. https://publicpolicy. pepperdine.edu/davenport-institute/content/reports/changing-face.pdf

Krogstad, Jens Manuel. 2016. *10 Facts for National Hispanic Heritage Month*. Pew Hispanic Research Center. http://www.pewresearch.org/fact-tank/2016/09/15/facts-for-national-hispanic-heritage-month/

Krozer, Alice, and Juan Carlos Moreno-Brid. 2014. Inequality in Mexico. *World Economics Association Newsletter* 4 (5). ISSN 2049-3274. http://www. worldeconomicsassociation.org/files/newsletter/Issue-4-5.pdf

Kuratko, Donald F. 2014. *Entrepreneurship: Theory, Process, and Practice*. 9th ed. Boston: Cengage.

Lee, Jennifer, and Min Zhou. 2014. From Unassimilable to Exceptional: The Rise of Asian Americans and 'Stereotype Promise'. *New Diversities* 16 (1): 7–22.

———. 2015. *The Asian American Achievement Paradox*. New York: Russell Sage Foundation.

Li, Peter S. 2001. Immigrants' Propensity to Self-Employment: Evidence from Canada. *The International Migration Review* 35 (4): 1106–1128.

Light, Ivan. 1972. *Ethnic Enterprise in America: Business and Welfare Among Chinese, Japanese, and Blacks*. Berkeley: University of California Press.

Light, Ivan, and Steven J. Gold. 2000. *Ethnic Economies*. San Diego: Academic Press.

Light, Ivan, and Elizabeth Roach. 1996. Self-Employment: Mobility Ladder or Economic Lifeboat? In *Ethnic Los Angeles*, ed. Roger Waldinger and Mehdi Bozorgmehr, 193–214. New York: Russell Sage Foundation.

Light, Ivan, and Carolyn Rosenstein. 1995. *Race, Ethnicity, and Entrepreneurship in Urban America*. New York: Aldine De Gruyter.

Linthicum, Kate. 2016. *Los Angeles Times*, May 16.

Livingston, Gretchen. 2006. Gender, Job Searching, and Employment Outcomes Among Mexican Immigrants. *Population Research and Policy Review* 25: 43–66.

Lofstrom, Magnus, and Timothy Bates. 2009. How Successful are Female Hispanic Entrepreneurs? In *An American Story: Mexican American Entrepreneurship & Wealth Creation*, ed. John Sibley Butler, Alfonso Morales, and David Torres, 79–98. West Lafayette: Purdue University Press.

Lofstrom, Magnus, and Chunbei Wang. 2007. Mexican-Hispanic Self-Employment Entry: The Role of Business Start-Up Constraints. *Annals of the American Academy of Political and Social Science* 613 (1): 32–46.

Logan, John R., Richard D. Alba, and Thomas L. McNulty. 1994. Ethnic Economies in Metropolitan Regions: Miami and Beyond. *Social Forces* 72 (3): 691–724.

Logan, John R., Wenquan Zhang, and Richard D. Alba. 2002. Immigrant Enclaves and Ethnic Communities in New York and Los Angeles. *American Sociological Review* 67: 299–322.

Logan, John R., Richard D. Alba, and Brian J. Stults. 2003. Enclaves and Entrepreneurs: Assessing the Payoff for Immigrants and Minorities. *International Migration Review* 37 (2): 344–388.

Lopez, David E. 1996. Language: Diversity and Assimilation. In *Ethnic Los Angeles*, ed. Roger Waldinger and Mehdi Bozorghmehr, 139–164. New York: Russell Sage Foundation.

Lopez, Mary, and Dolores Trevizo. 2009. Mexican Immigrant Entrepreneurship in Los Angeles: An Analysis of the Determinants of Entrepreneurial Outcomes. In *An American Story: Mexican American Entrepreneurship and Wealth Creation*, ed. John Sibley Butler, Alfonso Morales, and David L. Torres, 127–149. West Lafayette: Purdue University Press.

Los Angeles Times. 2016. Large Crowd of Demonstrators Scatters After Night of Protest Outside Trump Rally. April 29. http://www.latimes.com/politics/la-na-trailguide-04282016-crowd-gathers-ahead-of-trump-rally-chants-build-1461888244-htmlstory.html. Accessed 12 May 2016.

Loscocco, Karyn, Joyce Robinson, Richard Hall, and John K. Allen. 1991. Gender and Small Business Success: An Inquiry into Women's Relative Disadvantage. *Social Forces* 70 (1): 65–85.

Lowell, B. Lindsay, Jay D. Teachman, and Zhongren Jing. 1995. Unintended Consequences of Immigration Reform: Discrimination and Hispanic Employment. *Demography* 32 (4): 617–628.

Lowrey, Ying. 2005. *Business Density, Entrepreneurship and Economic Well-Being*. Annual Conference Papers, American Economic Association Meeting, Philadelphia, January 7–9.

Malpica, Melero Daniel. 2005. Indigenous Mexican Migrants in a Modern Metropolis: The Reconstruction of Zapotec Communities in Los Angeles. In *Latino Los Angeles: Transformations, Communities, and Activism*, ed. Enrique C. Ochoa and Gilda L. Ochoa, 2005. Tucson: University of Arizona Press.

Marcelli, Enrico A. 2004. The Institution of Unauthorized Residency Status, Neighborhood Context, and Mexican Immigrant Earnings in Los Angeles County. In *The Institutionalist Tradition in Labor Economics*, ed. Dell P. Champlin and Janet T. Knoedler. Armonk: M.E. Sharpe.

Marcelli, Enrico A., and Wayne A. Cornelius. 2001. The Changing Profile of Mexican Migrants to the United States: New Evidence from California and Mexico. *Latin American Research Review* 36 (3): 105–131.

Martos, Sofia D. 2010. Coded Codes: Discriminatory Intent, Modern Political Mobilization, and Local Immigration Ordinances. *New York University Law Reivew* 85: 2099–2137.

Massey, Douglas S. 2001. Segregation and Violent Crime in Urban America. In *Problem of the Century*, ed. E. Anderson and D.S. Massey, 314–344. New York: Russell Sage.

———. 2007. *Categorically Unequal. The American Stratification System*. New York: Russell Sage Foundation.

———. 2009. Racial Formation in Theory and Practice: The Case of Mexicans in the United States. *Race Social Problems* 1: 12–26.

Massey, Douglas S., and Stefanie Brodmann. 2014. *Spheres of Influence: The Social Ecology of Racial and Class Inequality*. New York: Russell Sage Foundation.

Massey, Douglas S., and Julia Gelatt. 2010. What Happened to the Wages of Mexican Immigrants? Trends and Interpretations. *Latino Studies* 2 (8): 328–354.

Massey, Douglas S., and Karen A. Pren. 2012. Unintended Consequences of U.S. Immigration Policy: Explaining the Post-1965 Surge from Latin America. *Population Development Review* 38 (1): 1–29.

Massey, Douglas S., and Ilana Redstone. 2006. Immigrant Intentions and Mobility in a Global Economy: The Attitudes and Behavior of Recently Arrived U.S. Immigrants. *Social Science Quarterly* 87 (5): 954–971.

Massey, Douglas S., Rafael Alarcón, Jorge Durand, and Humberto González. 1987. *Return to Aztlan: The Social Process of International Migration from Western Mexico*. Berkeley: University of California Press.

Massey, Douglas S., Andrew Gross, and Mitchell Eggers. 1991. Segregation, the Concentration of Poverty, and the Life Chances of Individuals. *Social Science Research* 20: 397–420.

Massey, Douglas, Luin Goldring, and Jorge Durand. 1994. Continuities in Transnational Migration: An Analysis of Nineteen Mexican Communities. *American Journal of Sociology* 99 (6): 1492–1533.

Massey, Douglas S., Jorge Durand, and Nolan J. Malone. 2002. *Beyond Smoke and Mirrors: Mexican Immigration in an Era of Economic Integration*. New York: Russell Sage Foundation.

Matsunaga, Michael. 2008. *Concentrated Poverty in Los Angeles*. Economic Roundtable Research Report, February. https://economicrt.org/wp-content/uploads/2008/02/Concentrated_Poverty_Los_Angeles_2008.pdf

Mazon, Mauricio. 1984. *The Zoot-Suit Riots: The Psychology of Symbolic Annihilation*. Austin: Austin University Press.

Mejia, Brittny. 2016. Market No Longer Feels the Love, Looks to Evolve: El Mercado Manager Aims to Draw a More Diverse Crowd. *Los Angeles Times*, July 14.

Menjívar, Cecilia, and Sarah M. Lakhani. 2016. Transformative Effects of Immigration Law: Immigrants' Personal and Social Metamorphoses Through Regularization. *American Journal of Sociology* 121 (6): 1818–1855.

Mijid, Naranchimeg. 2015. Why Are Female Small Business Owners in the United States Less Likely to Apply for Bank Loans Than Their Male Counterparts? *Journal of Small Business and Entrepreneurship* 27 (2): 229–249.

Mirchandani, Kiran. 1999. Feminist Insight on Gendered Work: New Directions in Research on Women and Entrepreneurship. *Gender, Work, and Organization* 6 (4): 224–235.

Moi, Toril. 1991. Appropriating Bourdieu: Feminist Theory and Pierre Bourdieu's Sociology of Culture Author(s). *New Literary History* 22 (4). Papers from the Commonwealth Center for Literary and Cultural Change (Autumn, 1991), pp. 1017–1049.

Molina, Natalia. 2014. *How Race Is Made in America: Immigration, Citizenship, and the Historical Power of Racial Scripts*. Berkeley: University of California Press.

Mora, Marie T., and Alberto Dávila. 2006. Mexican Immigrant Self-Employment Along the U.S. Mexico Border: An Analysis of 2000 Census Data. *Social Science Quarterly* 87: 91–109.

Mora, Marie T., and Alberto Davila. 2014. Gender and Business Outcomes of Black and Hispanic New Entrepreneurs in the United States. *American Economic Review* 104 (5): 245–249.

Morales, Alfonso. 2009. A Woman's Place Is on the Street: Purposes and Problems of Mexican American Women Entrepreneurs. In *An American Story: Mexican American Entrepreneurship and Wealth Creation*, ed. John S. Butler, Alfonso Morales, and David L. Torres, 99–126. West Lafayette: Purdue University Press.

Morando, Sarah J. 2013. Paths to Mobility: The Mexican Second Generation at Work in a New Destination. *The Sociological Quarterly* 54 (3): 367–398.

Ndofor, Hermann Achidi, and Richard L. Priem. 2011. Immigrant Entrepreneurs, the Ethnic Enclave Strategy, and Venture Performance. *Journal of Management* 37 (3): 790–818.

Nee, Victor, Jimmy M. Sanders, and Scott Sernau. 1994. Job Transitions in an Immigrant Metropolis: Ethnic Boundaries and the Mixed Economy. *American Sociological Review* 59: 849–872.

Newman, Katherine S., and Rebekah Peeples Massengill. 2006. The Texture of Hardship: Qualitative Sociology of Poverty, 1995–2005. *Annual Review of Sociology* 32: 423–446.

Nguyen, Mai, and Hannah Gill. 2015. Interior Immigration Enforcement: The Impacts of Expanding Local Law Enforcement Authority. *Urban Studies*: 1–22. https://doi.org/10.1177/0042098014563029.

O'Neil, Kevin. 2003. *Consular ID Cards: Mexico and Beyond*. Published by the Migration Policy Institute, April 1. http://www.migrationpolicy.org/article/consular-id-cards-mexico-and-beyond

Ochoa, Gilda. 2004. *Becoming Neighbors in a Mexican American Community: Power, Conflict, and Solidarity*, 45–69. Austin: University of Texas Press.

Ochoa, Enrique C., and Gilda L. Ochoa, eds. 2005. *Latino LA: Transformation, Communities, and Activism*. Tucson: The University of Arizona Press.

Orrenius, Pia M. 2001. Illegal Immigration and Enforcement Along the U.S.-Mexico Border: An Overview. *Federal Reserve Bank of Dallas Economic and Financial Review*, Qtr. 1.

Orrenius, Pia M., and Madeline Zavodny. 2009. The Effects of Tougher Enforcement on the Job Prospects of Recent Latin American Immigrants. *Journal of Policy Analysis and Management* 28 (20): 239–257.

Ortiz, Vilma. 1996. The Mexican-Origin Population: Permanent Working Class or Emerging Middle Class? In *Ethnic Los Angeles*, ed. Roger Waldinger and Mehdi Bozorghmehr, 247–278. New York: Russell Sage Foundation.

Park, Haeyoun, and Alicia Parlapiano. 2016 Supreme Court's Decision on Immigration Case Affects Millions of Unauthorized Immigrants. *New York Times*, June 23.

Passel, Jeffrey S., and D'Vera Cohn. 2009. *A Portrait of Unauthorized Immigrants in the United States*. Washington, DC: Pew Hispanic Center, Research Report. http://assets.pewresearch.org/wp-content/uploads/sites/7/reports/107.pdf

Pastor, Manuel. 2001. Economics and Ethnicity: Poverty, Race, and Immigration in Los Angeles County. In *Asian and Latino Immigrants in a Restructuring Economy: The Metamorphosis of Southern California*, ed. Marta Lopez Garza and David Diaz, 102–139. Stanford: Stanford University Press.

Pastor, Manuel, and Rhonda Ortiz. 2009. *Immigrant Integration in Los Angeles: Strategic Directions for Funders*. Program for Environmental and Regional Equity, and Center for the Study of Immigrant Integration. Los Angeles: University of Southern California (USC). Report found at https://dornsife.usc.edu/assets/sites/731/docs/immigrant_integration.pdf

Pastor, Manuel, Rhonda Ortiz, Vanessa Carter, Justin Scoggins, and Anthony Perez. 2012. *California Immigrant Integration Scorecard*. Center for the Study of Immigrant Integration.

Pearce, Susan C. 2005. Today's Immigrant Woman Entrepreneur. *Immigration Policy In Focus* 4:1. Washington, DC: Immigration Policy Center.

Pécoud, Antoine. 2002. Weltoffenheit Schafft Jobs': Turkish Entrepreneurship and Multiculturalism in Berlin. *International Journal of Urban and Regional Research* 26 (3): 494–507.

———. 2010. What Is Ethnic in an Ethnic Economy. *International Review of Sociology* 20 (1): 59–76.

Peterson, Robert. 2017. How a Neighborhood Disappears: The Life and Death of Pico Heights. *Lost LA, KCET*, January 10. https://www.kcet.org/shows/lost-la/how-a-neighborhood-disappears-the-life-and-death-of-pico-heights

Piacenti, David. 2012. Yucatec-Mayan Im/Migration to the Mission and Edison Neighborhoods: A Comparison of Social Conditions and Im/migrant Satisfaction. *Mexican Studies/Estudios Mexicanos* 28 (1): 95–132.

PolicyLink and The Program for Environmental and Regional Equity. 2017. An Equity Profile of the Los Angeles Region. http://dornsife.usc.edu/pere/equity-profile-los-angeles-region/

Portes, Alejandro. 1981. Modes of Structural Incorporation and Present Theories of Labor Immigration. In *Global Trends in Migration*, ed. Mary Kritz, Charles B. Keeley, and Silvano Tomasi, 279–297. New York: Center for Migration Studies.

———. 1995. Economic Sociology and the Sociology of Immigration: A Conceptual Overview. In *The Economic Sociology of Immigration: Essays on Networks, Ethnicity, and Entrepreneurship*, ed. A. Portes. New York: Russell Sage Foundation.

Portes, Alejandro, and Robert L. Bach. 1985. *Latin Journey: Cuban and Mexican Immigrants in the United States*. Berkeley/Los Angeles: University of California Press.

Portes, Alejandro, and Lief Jenson. 1992. Disproving the Enclave Hypothesis: Reply. *American Sociological Review* 57 (3): 418–420.

Portes, Alejandro, and Robert D. Manning. 1991. The Immigrant Enclave: Theory and Empirical Examples. In *Majority and Minority*, ed. Norman R. Yetman, 319–332. Boston: Allyn and Bacon.

Portes, Alejandro, and Rúben G. Rumbaut. 2001. *Legacies: The Story of the Immigrant Second Generation*. Berkeley: University of California Press.

Portes, Alejandro, and Julia Sensenbrenner. 1993. Embeddedness and Immigration: Notes on the Social Determinants of Economic Action. *American Journal of Sociology* 98: 1320–1350.

Portes, Alejandro, and Min Zhou. 1993. The New Second Generation: Segmented Assimilation and Its Variants Among Post-1965 Immigrant Youth. *Annals of the American Academy of Political and Social Science* 530: 74–96.

———. 1999. Entrepreneurship and Economic Progress in the 1990s: A Comparative Analysis of Immigrants and African Americans. In *Immigration and Opportunity: Race, Ethnicity, and Employment in the United States*, ed. F.D. Bean and S. Bell-Rose, 143–171. New York: Russel Sage Foundation.

Provine, Doris Marie, and Monica W. Varsanyi. 2012. Scaled Down: Perspectives on State and Local Creation and Enforcement of Immigration Law: Introduction to Special Issue of Law and Policy. *Law and Policy* 34 (2): 105–112.

Quesada, James. 2011. No Soy Welferero: Undocumented Latino Laborers in the Crosshairs of Legitimation Maneuvers. *Medical Anthropology* 30 (4): 386–408.

Quillian, Lincoln. 2012. Segregation and Poverty Concentration: The Role of Three Segregations. *American Sociological Review* 77 (3): 354–379.

Raijman, Rebeca, and Marta Tienda. 2003. Ethnic Foundations of Economic Transactions: Mexican and Korean Immigrant Entrepreneurs in Chicago. *Ethnic and Racial Studies* 26 (5): 783–801.

Ramirez, Hernan, and Pierrette Hondagneu-Sotelo. 2009. Mexican Immigrant Gardeners: Entrepreneurs or Exploited Workers? *Social Problems* 56 (1): 70–88.

Rios, Viridiana Contreras. 2014. The Role of Drug-Related Violence and Extortion in Promoting Mexican Migration: Unexpected Consequences of a Drug War. *Latin American Research Review* 49 (3): 199–217.

Riosmena, Fernando, and Douglas S. Massey. 2012. Pathways to El Norte: Origins, Destinations, and Characteristics of Mexican Migrants to the United States. *International Migration Review* 46 (1): 3–36.

Rivera-Batiz, Francisco L. 1999. Undocumented Workers in the Labor Market: An Analysis of the Earnings of Legal and Illegal Mexican Immigrants in the United States. *Journal of Population Economics* 12 (1): 91–116.

Rivera-Salgado, Gaspar. 2016. From Hometown Clubs to Transnational Social Movement: The Evolution of Oaxacan Migrant Associations in California. *Social Justice* 42 (3/4): 118–136.

Robb, Alicia, and Susan Coleman. 2009. A Comparison of New Firm Financing by Gender: Evidence from the Kauffman Firm Survey Data. *Small Business Economics* 33 (4): 397–411.

Robb, Alicia, and Robert Fairlie. 2007. Access to Financial Capital Among U.S. Businesses: The Case of African-American Firms. *The Annals of the American Academy of Political and Social Science* 613: 47–72.

———. 2009. Determinants of Business Success: An Examination of Asian-Owned Businesses in the USA. *Journal of Population Economics* 22: 827–858.

Robinson, Jeffrey, Laquita Blockson, and Sammie Robinson. 2007. Exploring Stratification and Entrepreneurship: African American Women Entrepreneurs Redefine Success in Growth Ventures. *The Annals of the American Academy of Political Science* 613 (1): 131–154.

Roche, Kristen. 2014. Female Self-Employment in the United States: An Update to 2012. *Monthly Labor Review, U.S. Bureau of Labor Statistics*, October. https://www.bls.gov/opub/mlr/2014/article/female-self-employment-in-the-united-states-an-update-to-2012.htm

Romero, Mary. 2008. Crossing the Immigration and Race Border: A Critical Race Theory Approach to Immigration Studies. *Contemporary Justice Review* 11 (1): 23–37.

Romero, Mary, and Zulema Valdez. 2016. Introduction to the Special Issue: Intersectionality and Entrepreneurship. *Ethnic and Racial Studies* 39 (9): 1553–1565.

Romo, Ricardo. 1983. *East Los Angeles: History of a Barrio*. Austin: University of Texas Press.

Rugh, Jacob S., and Douglas S. Massey. 2014. Segregation in Post-Civil Rights America: Stalled Integration or End of the Segregated Century. *DuBois Review: Social Science Research on Race* 11 (2): 205–232.

Rugh, Jacob S., Len Albright, and Douglas S. Massey. 2015. Race, Space, and Cumulative Disadvantage: A Case Study of the Subprime Lending Collapse. *Social Problems* 62: 186–218.

Sáenz, Rogelio, and Karen Manges Douglas. 2015. A Call for the Racialization of Immigration Studies: On the Transition of Ethnic Immigrants to Racialized Immigrants. *Sociology of Race and Ethnicity* 1 (1): 166–180.

Salcido, Olivia, and Cecilia Menjívar. 2012. Gendered Paths to Legal Citizenship: The Case of Latin-American Immigrants in Phoenix, Arizona. *Law & Society Review* 46 (2): 335–365.

Sampson, Robert. 2008. Moving to Inequality: Neighborhood Effects and Experiments Meet Social Structure. *American Journal of Sociology* 114 (1): 189–231.

Sampson, Robert J. 2012. *Great American City: Chicago and the Enduring Neighborhood Effect*. Chicago: University of Chicago Press.

Sampson, Robert J., Jeffrey D. Morenoff, and Thomas Gannon-Rowley. 2002. Assessing 'Neighborhood Effects': Social Processes and New Directions in Research. *Annual Review of Sociology*. 28: 443–478.

Sanchez, George J. 1995. *Becoming Mexican American: Ethnicity, Culture, and Identity in Chicano Los Angeles, 1900–1945*. New York: Oxford University Press.

Sanders, Jimy M., and Victor Nee. 1987. Limits of Ethnic Solidarity in the Enclave Economy. *American Sociological Review* 52 (6): 745–773.

———. 1996. Immigrant Self-Employment: The Family as Social Capital and the Value of Human Capital. *American Sociological Review* 61 (2): 231–249.

Santos, Maria Josefa. 2009. Knowledge and Networks: Mexican-American Entrepreneurship in Southwestern Michigan. In *An American Story: Mexican American Entrepreneurship and Wealth Creation*, ed. John S. Butler, Alfonso

Morales, and David L. Torres, 151–174. West Lafayette: Purdue University Press.

Schneider, Jack. 2008. Escape from Los Angeles: White Flight from Los Angeles and Its Schools, 1960–1980. *Journal of Urban History* 34 (6): 995–1012.

Schulz, Amy J., Srimathi Kannan, J. Timothy Dvonch, Barbara A. Israel, Alex Allen III, Sherman A. James, James S. House, and James Lepkowski. 2005. Social and Physical Environments and Disparities in Risk for Cardiovascular Disease: The Healthy Environments Partnership Conceptual Model. *Environmental Health Perspectives* 113: 1817–1825.

Shapira, Harel. 2013. *Waiting for Jose: The Minutemen's Pursuit of America*. Princeton: Princeton University Press.

Silva, Valentina. 2015. After Almost a Decade, La Monarca Bakery Is Still Stepping Up L.A.'s Pan Dulce Game. *Los Angeles Magazine*, September 10. http://www.lamag.com/digestblog/after-almost-a-decade-la-monarca-bakery-is-still-stepping-up-l-a-s-pan-dulce-game/

Simmel, Georg. 1971 [1908]. The Stranger. In *Georg Simmel: On Individuality and Social Forms*, ed. Donald Levine, 143–150. Chicago: University of Chicago Press. (The Title of the Original 1908 Version is *Soziologie. Untersuchungen über die Formen der Vergesellschaftung*. Berlin: Duncker & Humblot).

Smith, James P., and Barry Edmonston. 1997. *The New Americans: Economic, Demographic, and Fiscal Effects of Immigration*. Washington, DC: National Academies Press.

Spener, David, and Frank D. Bean. 1999. Self-Employment Concentration and Earnings Among Mexican Immigrants in the U.S. *Social Forces* 77 (3): 1021–1047.

Stevenson, Lois A. 1986. Against All Odds: The Entreprenurship of Women. *Journal of Small Business Management* 24 (4): 30–36.

———. 1990. Some Methodological Problems Associated with Researching Women Entrepreneurs. *Journal of Business Ethics* 9: 439–446.

Stumpf, Juliet. 2006. The Crimmigration Crisis: Immigrants, Crime, and Sovereign Power. *American University Law Review* 56 (2): 367–419.

Takei, Isao, Rogelio Saenz, and Jing Li. 2009. Cost of Being a Mexican Immigrant and Being a Mexican Non-citizen in California and Texas. *Hispanic Journal of Behavioral Sciences* 31 (1): 73–95.

Thomas, William, and Florian Znaniecki. 1974 [1927]. *The Polish Peasant in Europe and America*. New York: Octagon. Reprint.

Tienda, Marta, and Norma Fuentes. 2014. Hispanics in Metropolitan American: New Realities and Old Debates. *Annual Review of Sociology* 40: 499–520.

Tienda, Marta, and Audrey Singer. 1995. Wage Mobility of Undocumented Workers in the United States. *International Migration Review* 29 (1): 112–138.

Torres, David. 2009. The Mexican American Self-Employed Population. In *An American Story: Mexican American Entrepreneurship and Wealth Creation*, ed.

John S. Butler, Alfonso Morales, and David L. Torres, 9–42. West Lafayette: Purdue University Press.

Treichel, Monica Zimmerman, and Jonathan A. Scott. 2006. Women-Owned Businesses and Access to Bank Credit: Evidence from Three Surveys Since 1987. *Venture Capital* 8 (1): 51–67.

Trevizo, Dolores. 1990. *Latina Baby-'Watchers' and the Commodification of Care*. M.A. Thesis, University of California Los Angeles.

———. 2011. *Rural Protest and the Making of Democracy in Mexico, 1968–2000*. University Park: The Pennsylvania State University Press.

Trevizo, Dolores, and Mary Lopez. 2016. Neighborhood Segregation and Business Outcomes: Mexican Immigrant Entrepreneurs in Los Angeles County. *Sociological Perspectives* 59 (3): 668–693.

Valdez, Zulema. 2011. *The New Entrepreneurs: How Race, Class, and Gender Shape American Enterprise*. Stanford: Stanford University Press.

———. 2016. Intersectionality, the Household Economy, and Ethnic Entrepreneurship. *Ethnic and Racial Studies* 39 (9): 1618–1636.

Varsanyi, Monica W. 2008. Immigration Policing Through the Backdoor: City Ordinances, the 'Right to the City,' and the Exclusion of Undocumented Day Laborers. *Urban Geography* 29 (1): 29–52.

Villarreal, Mary Ann. 2009. Life on the 'Hill': Entrepreneurial Strategies in 1940s Corpus Christi. In *An American Story: Mexican American Entreprneurship and Wealth Creation*, ed. John Sibley Butler, Alfonso Morales, and David L. Torres. West Lafayette: Purdue University Press.

Vinogradov, Evgueni, and Lars Kolvereid. 2007. Cultural Background, Human Capital and Self-Employment Rates Among Immigrants in Norway. *Entrepreneurship and Regional Development* 19 (4): 359–376.

Volery, Thierry. 2007. Ethnic Entrepreneurship: A Theoretical Framework. In *Handbook of Research on Ethnic Minority Entrepreneurship*, ed. Leo-Paul Dana, 30–41. Cheltenham: Edward Elgar Publishing Limited.

Waldinger, Roger. 1986. *Through the Eye of the Needle: Immigrants and Enterprise in New York's Garment Trades*. New York: New York University Press.

———. 1999. Not the Promised City: Los Angeles and Its Immigrants. *Pacific Historical Review* 68 (2): 253–272.

Waldinger, Roger, and Mehdi Bozorgmehr. 1996. *Ethnic Los Angeles*. New York: Russell Sage Foundation Press.

Waldinger, Roger, and Michael I. Lichter. 2003. *How the Other Half Works: Immigration and the Social Organization of Labor*. Berkeley: University of California Press.

Waldinger, Roger, Howard Aldrich, and Robin Ward. 1990. *Ethnic Entrepreneurs: Immigrant Business in Industrial Societies*. Newbury Park: Sage.

Warman, Arturo. 2001. Los Indios de Mexico. *NEXOS* 23, No. 280, April.

Wasilco, Jadie, Kate Lefkowitz, and Steven Katigbak. 2013. The State of Highland Park. *UCLA Luskin School of Public Affairs.* http://www.highlandparknc.com/pdf/The_State_of_Highland_Park.pdf

Weber, Max. 1930. *The Protestant Ethic and the Spirit of Capitalism.* Trans. Talcott Parsons. London: Unwin Hyman Ltd.

———. 1946. Class, Status, Party. In *From Max Weber: Essays in Sociology,* ed. H.H. Gerth and C. Wright Mills. New York: Oxford University Press.

Wilkes, Rima, and John Iceland. 2004. Hypersegregation in the Twenty-First Century: An Update and Analysis. *Demography* 4: 23–36.

Wilson, William Julius. 1987. *The Truly Disadvantaged: The Inner City, the Underclass, and Public Policy.* Chicago: University of Chicago Press.

Wilson, Kenneth L., and Alejandro Portes. 1980. Immigrant Enclaves: An Analysis of the Labor Market Experiences of Cubans in Miami. *American Journal of Sociology* 86 (2): 295–319.

Wodtke, Geoffrey T., David J. Harding, and Felix Elwert. 2011. Neighborhood Effects in Temporal Perspective: The Impact of Long-Term Exposure to Concentrated Disadvantage on High School Graduation. *American Sociological Review* 76 (5): 713–736.

Wong, Tom K. 2012. 287(g) and the Politics of Interior Immigration Control in the United States: Explaining Local Cooperation with Federal Immigration Authorities. *Journal of Ethnic and Migration Studies* 38 (5): 737–756.

Wyrwich, Michael. 2015. Entrepreneurship and the Intergenerational Transmission of Values. *Small Business Economics* 45: 191–213.

Xie, Yu, and Margaret Gough. 2011. Ethnic Enclaves and the Earnings of Immigrants. *Demography* 48: 1293–1315.

Zamora, Emilio. 1993. *The World of the Mexican Worker in Texas.* College Station: Texas A&M University Press.

Zentgraf, Kristine. 2001. Through Economic Restructuring, Recession, and Rebound: The Continuing Importance of Latina Immigrant Labor in the Los Angeles Economy. In *Asian and Latino Immigrants in a Restructuring Economy,* ed. Marta López-Garza and David R. Diaz, 46–74. Stanford: Stanford University Press.

Zhou, Min. 2004. The Role of the Enclave Economy in Immigrant Adaptation and Community Building: The Case of New York's Chinatown. In *Immigrant and Minority Entrepreneurship: The Continuous Rebirth of American Communities,* ed. J.S. Butler and G. Kozmetsky, 37–60. Westport: Praeger Publishers.

Zhou, Min, Jennifer Lee, Jody A. Vallejo, Rosaura Tafoya-Estrada, and Yang S. Xiong. 2008. Success Attained, Deterred, and Denied: Divergent Pathways to Social Mobility in Los Angeles's New Second Generation. *The Annals of the American Academy of Political and Social Science* 620: 37–61.

Index[1]

[1] Note: Page numbers followed by 'n' refer to notes.

© The Author(s) 2018
D. Trevizo, M. Lopez, *Neighborhood Poverty and Segregation
in the (Re-)Production of Disadvantage,*
https://doi.org/10.1007/978-3-319-73715-7